CORNU

OF IDEAS

A GLOBAL IDEAS BANK COMPENDIUM

EDITED BY
NICHOLAS ALBERY
NICK TEMPLE
STEPHANIE WIENRICH
& RETTA BOWEN

Published September 1st 2001 by

The Institute for Social Inventions
20 Heber Road
London NW2 6AA, UK
tel 020 8208 2853
fax 020 8452 6434
e-mail: rhino@dial.pipex.com
web: www.globalideasbank.org

Further copies of this book are available from
the Institute for £15 incl. p&p.

This compendium is an experimental susbstitute for
Social Inventions journal (Numbers 52-54), ISSN 0954-206X

The Institute for Social Inventions, founded in 1985, is part of an
educational charity, and its aim is to help improve the quality of life by
encouraging the development of imaginative and socially innovatory
ideas and projects

The Social Inventions Awards, with £1,000 in total award money, are
judged each year by the directors of the Institute for Social Inventions.
Members of the public can submit their own ideas and projects (with a
deadline of June 1st each year). The Institute also monitors the media for
good schemes and has a network of correspondents worldwide and sister
Institutes in several other countries. The Assistant Editor in the States is
Roger Knights

British Library Cataloguing-in-Publication Data. A catalogue record for
this book is available from the British Library
ISBN 0 948826 58 4
Printed by Antony Rowe Ltd., Chippenham, Wiltshire

This book is dedicated to Nicholas Albery, the
founder of the Institute for Social Inventions,
who died on June 3rd 2001.

CONTENTS

Institute for Social Inventions, £15 subs, £17 from abroad by credit card, tel London 020 8208 2853

WORK & EMPLOYMENT

ECONOMICS AND BUSINESS

WELFARE

CRIME & THE LAW

HEALTH & THERAPY

20 Heber Road, London NW2 6AA, UK (rhino@dial.pipex.com), 2001, 300pp, ISBN 0 948826 58 4

20 Heber Road, London NW2 6AA, UK (rhino@dial.pipex.com), 2001, 300pp, ISBN 0 948826 58 4

20 Heber Road, London NW2 6AA, UK (rhino@dial.pipex.com), 2001, 300pp, ISBN 0 948826 58 4

Future making

Brian Eno

Brian Eno, musician, producer, artist and author, is a patron of the Institute for Social Inventions.

Nicholas Albery was one of the really bright spots in British life. We have a lot of well-paid professional cynics, but I used to cite him as an example of whatever is the opposite of a cynic – a shameless enthusiast, I suppose. He was a shameless enthusiast for ideas, especially ideas that would liberate people and make the world a better place. As far as I can tell, he did this out of sheer goodness of heart – that and a very clear understanding that humans do one thing better than anyone else. They imagine how things could otherwise be.

To imagine a Britain without him in it is a bit of a bleak prospect. He seems to me irreplaceable. Nick inspired me, made me think that it was worth carrying on talking ideas, and made me believe – by his own example – that anyone could make a difference. He knew that whatever we have to do, we have to do it ourselves and not wait until the political world slowly grinds into action. We all say that to each other, but Nick really lived it.

He asked me to write a foreword for 'Cornucopia of Ideas'. I wrote this just before he died:

Someone once said: "If you want to change the world, start with the details". As I become more and more disappointed with the grandly idealistic (and often ideological) attempts to plan our futures, I look towards the more modest ideas that turn out to make a big difference. Sometimes such ideas are astonishingly mundane at first sight, but far-reaching in effect. For example the Nigerian potter who invented a pot that could keep food fresh for several days longer than normal probably didn't suspect that the effect of his invention was to liberate village girls from the daily shopping trip and thus enable them to go to school, thereby radically changing the dynamics and possibilities of his society.

'The little seeds that grow into big forests'

'Cornucopia of Ideas' is a compendium of new ideas, new ideas that could

Institute for Social Inventions, £15 subs, £17 from abroad by credit card, tel London 020 8208 2853

make a big difference. You have to realise that you're at the coal-face here, that some of these ideas might never materialise, but some of them might be the little seeds that grow into big forests. If you have a taste for seeing the beginnings of things, then this volume is for you.

We live in highly agendized times. By that I mean that there is a self-feeding conspiracy (in which we all participate) about what is important and what is not – what is on the agenda. The media, reflecting our tastes, consolidate a few accidental interests until they start to seem like the only important things (eg the dot.com phenomenon). Meanwhile, the rest of the world gets on with its business, creating and inventing, while no-one pays much attention.

I like 'Cornucopia of Ideas' because it does pay attention. It acknowledges that big changes start with people thinking, "How might this be done better?" – even if 'this' is 'simply' making a pot. It isn't necessarily the kind of thing making it to the Six O'Clock News or the colour supplements – but it is the kind of thing that will make our futures.

Nicholas Albery and the Global Ideas Bank

Retta Bowen, Nick Temple and Stephanie Wienrich

Co-editors of the Global Ideas Bank.

Nicholas Albery, the founder of the Institute for Social Inventions (in 1985) and main editor of the Global Ideas Bank, died in a car accident on June 3rd this year. He was working on this book in the weeks preceding his death, selecting and editing social innovations with his customary intensity.

Behind all his work and projects lay the understanding that information is the key to empowerment; and that information freely supplied denies the possibility of some people holding an advantage over others. In that sense, the internet was the perfect medium for him, with the social innovations on the Global Ideas Bank now being available to millions. And, in return, more and more ideas are submitted to the bank as knowledge of its existence spreads. The resource of thousands of ideas that the Global Ideas Bank has become is just one of his many legacies.

It has been a privilege to work with Nicholas, and to have been involved at the very heart of the Institute's projects. The three of us are committed to driving the Institute for Social Inventions forward, to continue to spread the word about ideas that can improve society and, as Nicholas did so well, to help make some of those ideas a reality. More than ever, we will need the help of our subscribers in this effort: please do send in your own ideas, articles that you

20 Heber Road, London NW2 6AA, UK (rhino@dial.pipex.com), 2001, 300pp, ISBN 0 948826 58 4

think may be of interest and genuinely innovative projects taking place around the world.

Nicholas' death has left a void that is impossible to fill, but with the collective efforts of friends, colleagues and readers, we hope to make the Global Ideas Bank and other projects a living, breathing memorial to him.

SOCIAL INNOVATIONS AWARDS 2001

The first awards of the new millennium

The Institute for Social Inventions hereby announces its awards for social innovations for 2001. As we enter the new millennium, there is as great a need for ideas to improve society as there has ever been. The ideas and projects that follow are living proof that imaginative and innovative minds continue to address the problems of the world in all its many and varied aspects.

Institute for Social Inventions, 20 Heber Road, London NW2 6AA, UK (tel Int.+44 [0]20 8208 2853; fax Int.+44 [0]20 8452 6434; e-mail: rhino@dial.pipex.com; web: www.globalideasbank.org).

Community administration of Brazilian prisons to break the cycle of criminality

The £1,000 Social Innovations Award for 2001 goes to Roberto da Silva, founder of the Brazilian project which puts communities in charge of their local prison to change the way criminals are treated. The idea is based on community-based associations running their local prisons and taking responsibility for each prisoners rehabilitation and care.

'The locals are responsible for the running of the prison including the provision of healthcare, education, work and food'

Each local association has signed an agreement with the government, under which the locals are responsible for the administration of the prison, with the government providing the budget for each prisoner. The community association is then fully responsible for running the prison, with everything that involves. See page 58 for further details.

DIPEx – a database of patients' experiences of medical treatment

The Medical Social Innovations Award 2001 goes to a specialist medical team in Oxford, which is collating a database of patients' experiences (DIPEx) to be accessible via the Internet or by CD ROM.

'Patients will get an indication of the feelings of others who have experienced similar procedures'

Their aim is to improve understanding of people's experience of illness and promote a more balanced encounter between patient and health professional. Patients will be able to use the database as a resource which will provide them with some indication of the feelings of others who have experienced similar procedures. Health professionals, on the other hand, will get an indication of patients' priorities and of details of many procedures of which they may not be as experienced. See page 96 for further details.

Transform the Korean demilitarized zone into a wildlife sanctuary

The International Social Innovations Award 2001 goes to a Korean-born entomologist, Ke Chung Kim, who has proposed the creation of a peace park

20 Heber Road, London NW2 6AA, UK (rhino@dial.pipex.com), 2001, ISBN 0 948826 58 4

and wildlife preserve to transform the huge demilitarized zone between North and South Korea.

'It has become a sanctuary for rare birds, mammals, fish and plants'

In the 47 years since the end of the Korean war, it has become a sanctuary for birds, mammals, fish and plants that have been wiped out elsewhere. Ke Chung Kim also sees the idea as an opportunity to cement the better relationship between the two Koreas. See page 218 for further details.

Brazilian city where neighbourhood groups allocate the budget

The Neighbourhood Social Innovations Award 2001 goes to Porto Alegre Council for their radical participative budget. For the past decade, the people of the city have decided how the budget for public works should be allocated; and the scheme has been extremely successful.

'The new budget scheme has increased democratic participation substantially'

This method of budget allocation has had the triple effect of avoiding corruption and mishandling of funds, improving concrete matters on the ground, and increasing democratic participation in the city substantially. See page 130 for further details.

A restaurant in complete darkness to educate about blindness

The Education Social Innovations Award 2001 goes to Jorge Spielmann, who set up the Blind Cow restaurant in Zurich. The restaurant is staffed by blind waiters and everybody eats in complete darkness, in order to provide work for blind people and to give sighted people a brief 'blind' experience.

As Adrian Schaffner, the restaurant's (sighted) manager, explains, "We hope to make people more sensitive to the problems of the blind. It's a new experience for diners: you take one sense away, so you have to use all the others much more." See page 197 for further details.

People with learning disabilities running their own workshop

The Work and Employment Social Innovations Award 2001 goes to Dave Kirsopp, a student at the School for Social Entrepreneurs, whose new project Thumbprint, will enable people with learning disabilities to set up and run projects which they themselves control.

'Practical support systems to enable people with learning difficulties to make their ideas a reality'

Thumbprint aims to develop a support system to enable people to run their own working lives; not to be a provider so much as a catalyst for change. This will involve working alongside people on ideas they may have, as well as identifying opportunities for possible projects to bring to fruition. See page 46 for further details.

Making Media Labs from trash

The Computing/IT Social Innovations Award 2001 goes to a group of artists from Sheffield, called the Redundant Technology Initiative, who have created a media lab with scavenged computers and open source software.

'Their drop-in lab in Sheffield allows local people access to creative technology'

They've managed to create web pages, process images, publicise creative projects, set up networks and much more, relying particularly on Linux as their free operating system. They are currently running an exhibition with a cost-free video wall, and they run a drop-in lab in Sheffield which allows access to creative technology for people in the area. See page 157 for further details.

20 Heber Road, London NW2 6AA, UK (rhino@dial.pipex.com), 2001, ISBN 0 948826 58 4

A night without men to cut down on crime and abuse

The **Relationships Social Innovations Award 2001** goes to Antanas Mockus, mayor of Bogota, who initiated the city's 'Night Without Men' to encourage women to come out for the night to have a good time and to leave the men at home with the kids. Street crime and domestic abuse are usually both prevalent in the city, but serious crime fell by a quarter on the night.

One local spoke for most of Bogota's women when she said, "It was great. You had a large group of people dancing and having fun in the streets, and there was no violence like there would have been with men around." See page 30 for further details.

Community orchards for nutrition, education and relaxation

The **Environmental Social Innovations Award 2001** goes to the Common Ground charity, who seek to promote community orchards as educational and recreational havens for a society increasingly divorced from nature.

'Orchards generate interest in horticulture, ensuring skills and knowledge are passed between generations'

While providing fruit for sale or consumption, these orchards can act as wildlife havens, places to play and relax, or as a sort of outdoor village hall for local festivities. They also help to generate interest in horticulture, ensuring skills and knowledge are passed between generations. See page 143 for further details.

Fax your MP for free, and be directly involved in democracy

The **Politics Social Innovations Award 2001** goes to the group of individuals behind the website Fax Your MP.com, which uses a customised 'web to fax gateway' to enable you to fax your questions or concerns direct to your own MP. The process is a simple one: type in your postcode to discover the name of your MP, put in your own details and write your letter, and then simply click to send the fax.

'Constituents can make direct contact with the MP that represents them'

The website is run by a not-for-profit group of individuals, whose aim is simply to allow constituents to make direct contact with the MP who is duty bound to represent them. See page 249 for further details.

Let bureaucrats know how it feels with a form of your own

The Wild Card Social Innovations Award 2001 goes to Claire Wolfe and Charles Curley whose 'Bureaucracy Encounter Form' is a response to bureaucrats' intrusive requests for personal information and is intended to give them a taste of their own paperwork. Their forms request certain information for personal records, demand that the form be filled out in triplicate and request that the bureaucrat in question should fill out a separate form for each request that they themselves have made. See page 190 for further details.

Young at Heart – political theatre from the over 65s

The Old Age Social Innovations Award 2001 goes to the Young@Heart theatre group for their use of theatre as a means of community building and communication between generations. Their performances have helped build bridges across a divided community and also provide immense benefits to the people involved.

'Their appeal is certainly not limited to their own generation'

They continue to perform to schools, and their appeal is certainly not limited to their own generation, with their present tour involving direct interaction with students. See page 257 for more details.

20 Heber Road, London NW2 6AA, UK (rhino@dial.pipex.com), 2001, ISBN 0 948826 58 4

SOCIALLY INNOVATIVE VISIONS & SCHEMES

CHILDREN & EDUCATION

List names at school in reverse alphabetical order

Mayer Hillman

From a submission to the Global Ideas Bank.

I suggest that from next year schools and other comparable institutions, whose administrative practices operate with this unfair outcome for people at the lower end of the alphabet, list names in reverse alphabetical order (from Z to A), and that each year the order is reversed. In this way, people with surnames later in the alphabet will not feel disadvantaged at always coming last.

The disadvantage applies as much to joint authors of an article as to a list of sportsmen or a school register. I would hazard a guess that, for this reason, the success of some academics has been somewhat furthered by the fact that their names are recorded before that of their colleagues. Furthermore, where there are several names, it is commonplace to use the first surname followed by the phrase et al, not only implying a lesser role for these 'others' but even resulting in their being overlooked. In the case of school activities, possibly limited by the availability of time or the exigencies of the weather, individuals whose surname is closer to the earlier part of the alphabet have a greater chance of involvement or practice. 14 years of coming at the end of a list could also have a subconsciously demoralising effect, with the expectation of coming last being constantly reaffirmed. A simple reversal of the list could change all that.

I should add that with a surname towards the middle of the batting order, I have, to mix metaphors, no particular axe to grind.

• *Mayer Hillman, The Coach House, 7a Netherhall Gardens, London NW3 5RN, UK (tel/fax Int.+44 [0]20 7794 9661).*

Institute for Social Inventions, £15 subs, £17 from abroad by credit card, tel London 020 8208 2853

Walking club 'discussion salons' for schools

Valerie Yule

From a submission to the Global Ideas Bank.

A brilliant teacher at my school led a 'Walking Club', which went on walks, rather than hikes, out in the countryside and both staff and older students would join in together. About 15-30 of us would all go out by train, and we would straggle along some tracks through the countryside and stop for a leisurely picnic lunch somewhere.

We had a marvellous non-ageist time and the discussions did far more for my (I should say 'our') education than what we did in classes.

All schools could have these informal walking outings for *real* education. Nobody has to join the club – they just have to turn up, and start talking and walking.

• *Valerie Yule, 57 Waimarie Drive, Mount Waverly, Victoria, Australia 3149 (tel Int.+61 [0]3 807 4315; e-mail: vyule@labyrinth.net.au). Valerie Yule also runs the Australian Ideas Bank on the web (at www.vicnet.au/~ozideas).*

Kids get school credit for tutoring each other

Aaron Campbell

Adapted from a submission to the Global Ideas Bank.

Kids who know a lot are rarely put to much use, and rarely get much from their knowledge aside from high grades. A great way to validate a child's learning (and teaching) skills would be to give them the opportunity to use those skills in helping their peers learn. Children would be helping each other, and coming to realise that education is not just about grades and competing but about a cooperative process of learning.

For an hour after school (or in the afternoon to keep kids occupied if their parents are still at work) the kids could meet and do homework with the help of tutors in their own grade level. The tutors would earn an occupational credit or a life-skill credit or something similar, although the satisfaction of helping their peers may provide a more lasting reward.

• *Aaron Campbell (aaroncampbell@netscape.net).*

20 Heber Road, London NW2 6AA, UK (rhino@dial.pipex.com), 2001, 300pp, ISBN 0 948826 58 4

40 per cent off tuition fees for taking part in extra-curricular activities

Summarised from an article by Stephanie Simon, entitled 'Fun for profit? Small Missouri college is offering tuition breaks', in the Seattle Times (page A9, March 24th 2000), monitored for the Global Ideas Bank by Roger Knights.

A small college in Missouri has started a scheme in which tuition fees will be reduced by 40 per cent for students who take part in a set number of extra-curricular activities. William Woods University will slash its $13,200 tuition by $5,000 next year for incoming students who pledge to participate in a specified number of activities outside their academic studies.

'Each activity will be assigned a point value
and every freshman who earns 45 points will
receive the discount'

Each activity will be assigned a point value, so playing intra-mural volleyball might merit one point while serving on student government might be worth four. Every freshman who earns 45 points will receive the discount. Although some students may well attend events rather grudgingly at first for the sake of that $5,000, the dean of the college, Larry Kramer, predicts that most will develop a genuine enthusiasm for campus life.

Kramer also expects students to carry on this habit after graduation. As he puts it, "Once they get that job as a computer specialist, we still want them to go to the symphony, to the theatre, support the local zoo." While some might question whether students should be bribed into being well-rounded individuals, the ends may, in this case, justify the means.

Parents text messaged to reduce childrens' truancy

Summarised from an article in Yahoo! News, entitled 'School trounces truancy with phone messaging' (April 3rd 2001).

A school in Singapore has come up with a novel approach to tackling the problem of truancy – automatically text messaging the parents and so alerting them to the child's absence.

Yishun Town secondary school has installed a Short Message Service (SMS) broadcast system which is connected to an electronic database used by teachers for registration in the mornings. As soon as the teacher marks the child as absent from class, a message is automatically sent to the parents. The parents can then choose one of four different stock replies, in which they either explain the child's absence or state they are unaware of the child's whereabouts.

'The system provides each teacher with a summary of the day's attendance, complete with parental replies to text messages'

At the end of the day, the system provides each teacher with a summary of the day's attendance, complete with parental replies to earlier text messages. Tan Teck Hock, the headmaster of the school, hopes that it will reduce the amount of administrative work for teachers and improve school-home communication. Initially, it is being tested on 400 13-year-old students, but will then be widened out to include the whole school; and with 70 per cent of parents having mobile phones (a number which is increasing all the time), the majority of any truant children will be pinpointed very rapidly.

Using video games to treat attention deficit disorder

Summarised from an article by Michael Menduno, entitled 'Adventures in Mind Control', in Wired magazine (January 2001 issue) monitored for the Global Ideas Bank by Roger Knights. Additional information from the East3 website (www.east3.com) and from an article by Karen Wright, entitled 'Winning Brain Waves', in Discover magazine (March 2001), also monitored for the Global Ideas Bank by Roger Knights.

For children who suffer from attention deficit disorder (ADD), playing video games might help treatment of the disorder and improve attention spans. In a recent study, researchers used specially adapted Sony Playstations to help train the children to modify their brain waves. Research has shown that by learning to increase waves to about 12 Hz, patients are much more able to relax and concentrate on the matter in hand; this is normally done by showing brain wave data on a computer screen.

'As the child's brain waves approached an optimal pattern, the controller becomes more responsive'

20 Heber Road, London NW2 6AA, UK (rhino@dial.pipex.com), 2001, 300pp, ISBN 0 948826 58 4

Rather than trying to get hyperactive children to sit and observe their fluctuating brain waves on a computer, though, the researchers decided to use Playstations. Sensors attached to each child's scalp measured his or her brain waves, and these signals were then transmitted through a processing unit to the Playstation controllers. As the child's brain waves approached an 'optimal pattern', the controller would become more responsive, thus encouraging the child to produce those brainwave patterns to succeed at the game.

The researchers who conducted the study worked in tandem with NASA's Langley Research Center in Virginia which had patented similar technology to measure pilot's responses in flight simulators. With NASA's help, the special game-playing consoles helped the children with ADD achieve improvements in half the normal time. As the lead researcher Olafur Palsson says, "Their brains were lured into changing their behaviour in a healthy way." Although a drug like Ritalin may be quicker and cheaper in producing effects, this research aims to find a long term solution instead of a quick fix. As Lydia Thompson, a director of the Attention Deficit Disorder Center in Toronto, puts it, "It's so powerful for a child to learn how to self-regulate, to learn what it feels like to concentrate – that's where the real change happens."

NASA are now looking into producing a consumer version of the machine. And one company, East 3, released a video game-based attention trainer in 2001. Their attention trainer reveals brain wave activity to the player in real time, and thus teaches the person over time to control their brain waves, although the supervision of a doctor is still recommended in the early stages of use. East 3's website describes such attention training as "a painless and noninvasive technique best described as a learning exercise that trains people to control their attention."

• *Further information on the East 3 trainer can be found at www.east3.com/ attention_faq.html and at www.attention.com. The website for the Attention Deficit Disorder Centre is www.add-toronto.org, and that of the National Attention Deficit Disorder Association is www.add.org*

A computer game to highlight the dangers of web predators

Summarised from an article by Marci McDonald, entitled 'New kids' video game spotlights web predators', in US News and World Report (February 5th 2001), monitored for the Global Ideas Bank by Roger Knights.

A new computer game called *Missing* aims to teach children the dangers of online predators. The number of cases of online enticement have been rising rapidly as the Internet's growth continues, and policing the web for paedophiles and their ilk is an increasingly complex business. So some groups in North America are taking a different approach: 'streetproofing' the children before they go off naively surfing into chat rooms.

The *Missing* game is based on the true story of a Canadian boy who almost absconded with a convicted paedophile. It is part video thriller and part detective puzzle, with the children having to solve clues to unlock each chapter of the mystery. And as they enjoy the game, they are also learning of the web's dangers.

The game was devised by Colin Savage and Drew Ann Wake at the behest of the Royal Canadian Mounted Police, and it is being tested in 20 separate programs before getting a national release. One organisation testing the game was the YMCA's Youth Centre in San Diego, and their computer chief Anne Neville was pleased with the way it seemed to work:

"There's nothing out there that teaches Internet safety without being a lecture. One of the things that impressed me about this game is that it didn't talk down to kids."

'Many children don't tell their parents about such incidents for fear of losing their computer privileges'

That could be a key point for getting the message across to children who refuse to listen to their parents, and who may not even tell them of any incidents on the Web for fear of their computer privileges being taken away. *Missing* could change that attitude and increase children's awareness without making them feel as if they are being admonished. As one girl at the San Diego trial put it, "I guess it's teaching us a lesson, but in a fun way".

• *For more information on the game* Missing, *see www.livewwwires.com*

Reducing kids' TV time reduces aggressive behaviour

Summarised from an article by Ben Macintyre, entitled 'Switching off TV cuts childhood aggression', in the London Times (January 16th 2001).

Allowing children to watch less television could make them less aggressive. This is the finding of a new study by professors at Stanford University, who compared children aged eight and nine in two different schools. The children in one school were given no instructions at all, while pupils at the other stopped watching television and videos for ten days, and then limited themselves to seven hours a week. By the end of the study, the latter group's

20 Heber Road, London NW2 6AA, UK (rhino@dial.pipex.com), 2001, 300pp, ISBN 0 948826 58 4

aggressive and violent behaviour had fallen by 25 per cent, while the former's had remained the same. The behaviour was assessed by parents, teachers, professional observers and by the kids themselves, and a definite reduction in aggression was noted in the group whose viewing time was limited.

'Aggressive behaviour resulting from television and video watching could be reversible'

This could mean that aggressive behaviour resulting from television and video watching is reversible. As the typical American child is estimated to have witnessed 200,000 acts of violence on TV by the time they reach 18, this finding could be of no small import. On average, American children spend over five hours a day either watching television and videos or playing video games. Cutting this amount down could also cut down the amount of violent behaviour occurring amongst children. Dr Thomas Robinson, who led the study, suggests that parents start by making sure children do not have a television in their bedroom and then by negotiating some sort of weekly TV allowance or budget with their kids.

Television and video cannot solely be blamed for the problem of violence and aggression amongst children, with unresponsive over-sized schools, economic inequalities, availability of guns, and inadequate support systems also being contributory factors. But reducing the amount of violence seen by children on TV could certainly be a step in the right direction, especially if it occurs in tandem with them being educated about the media – both will ultimately reduce the impact of television, or at least mediate the effect it has.

The Poetry Challenge North America and International Poetry Challenge Day

Summarised from information on the Poetry Challenge website (www.poetrychallenge.org.uk)

Inspired by the UK's Poetry Week and with Andrew Motion, the UK Poet Laureate, as its patron, International Poetry Challenge Day is held on the first Sunday of October each year (eg Sunday October 7th 2001). People of all ages are urged to learn a poem by heart to recite on this day to at least one other person, and preferably to a larger audience; and to get sponsored by relatives and friends for a chosen favourite non-profit cause (sending any money you raise directly to the charity).

Institute for Social Inventions, £15 subs, £17 from abroad by credit card, tel London 020 8208 2853

Schools are also urged to take part, but for schools the Poetry Challenge is for anytime during the autumn or spring term. Teachers and pupils should send in a report to Poetry Challenge, 20 Heber Road, London NW2 6AA, UK (tel 00 44 (0)20 8208 2853, e-mail: rhino@dial.pipex.com). There will be awards and small money prizes for the best entries.

To provoke you to organise similar events in your locality see for instance the details of the Poetry Challenge being organised for London, UK, on International Poetry Challenge Day. You can post up your own participatory events on www.DoBe.org for many of the major cities.

Learn a poem and raise money for your school's charity

The Poetry Challenge issues this challenge to young people at school and to their teachers, parents and friends: Learn a poem by heart during the Autumn Term 2001 or Spring Term 2002 – and by doing so, support a non-profit cause of your school's choice. Robert Pinsky, the United States Poet Laureate, and Andrew Motion, the UK Poet Laureate, both support the Poetry Challenge – "it's a wonderful project" says Pinsky.

'Learning a poem exercises the brain and elevates the spirit. Over 150,000 poems a year are being learnt by heart in schools'

Learning a poem exercises the brain and elevates the spirit. The programme has worked well in the UK, where it has led to over 150,000 poems a year being learnt by heart in schools. As the UK's Chief Inspector of Schools has said: "The poetry we learn as children stays with us for ever – a resource upon which to draw throughout our lives."

A school's participation is free. The guidelines for the challenge are simple:

• Agree as a school whichever non-profit cause you want to raise money for.

• Get as many people as possible to take part – pupils, teachers, parents, friends.

• Get them all to agree to learn a poem by heart, one they have never learnt before, and to recite it out loud to at least one person. (The poem can be any poem, old or new, or even one they have written themselves.)

• Each person reciting tries to get sponsored for the school's chosen charity, raising at least five dollars from one or more friends.

• During the Autumn or Spring Term, you each recite your poems. Shy people can recite their poem to just one person, braver folk can recite to an audience such as the whole class, and the bravest of the brave can recite to the whole school assembly.

20 Heber Road, London NW2 6AA, UK (rhino@dial.pipex.com), 2001, 300pp, ISBN 0 948826 58 4

• Afterwards, your school sends the money raised direct to the chosen cause. And either the teacher or one or more of the pupils please e-mail a brief report to rhino@dial.pipex.com saying how your school got on. The Poetry Challenge will send a free copy of the booklet *Auction of Promises – How a school can raise $25,000 in one evening* to the first 50 schools to send in a report (please also send any press cuttings if there are any). The deadline for sending in reports for these prizes is December 10th 2001 but whenever you end up doing your challenge DO PLEASE SEND A REPORT. It helps keep the event funded if feedback is received.

'It's amazing how every word you've remembered disappears from your memory as soon as you get up to recite'

So, get training and exercise those brain cells. There is big money to be raised for your school. Do practise your poem on an audience of friends beforehand. It's amazing how every word you've remembered disappears from your memory as soon as you get up to recite.

School raises $3,500 pounds for charity by reciting poems!

Elizabeth Howard writes: Inspired by your brilliant idea of a Poetry Challenge, our school decided to have a 'Poetry Happening'. Every child in the school from age three to 13 (240 children) chose and recited a poem. We devoted a whole week to this project.

One class recited a poem all together. A group of teachers recited and mimed 'Albert the Lion'.

The children recited their poems to other classes and, at our final assembly of the term, one child from each class recited their poem to the whole school – stage, lights, the works – a great success.

'Parents and children all loved the project...and actually found it fun to learn a poem by heart'

Parents and children all loved the whole project, said they enjoyed looking through poetry books, selecting their poem and actually found it fun and a pleasure to learn a poem by heart. Some children amazed us by the length of their poems. The teachers all participated with enthusiasm. We had a display of poetry books in the school entrance. Many of the children wrote out and illustrated their poems, which were also on display around the school. The older children organised the whole event, including collecting and counting the money! We raised the staggering sum of $3,500.

We intend to make this an annual event. We would like to include a reading by a poet and maybe have an evening to which the parents could be invited. The money will be divided between four good causes which we, as a school, support.

We also gave each child a certificate saying they had recited their poem successfully. We all thank you for this wonderful idea which was a total success in every way.

• *For more information on the Poetry Challenge, see www.poetrychallenge.org where there is a sample sponsorship form, a performance certificate and teachers' tips on how to run a successful Poetry Challenge event.*

• *The Poetry Challenge is part-sponsored by the excellent 486-page poetry anthology* A Poem A Day, *containing 366 poems, old and new, worth learning by heart. This can be ordered for $18 (plus $4 USA shipping and handling – $1 each additional copy) from your neighbourhood bookstore or online bookstore or direct from the publishers, Steerforth Press, by check or (9:00 to 5:00 EST) by Mastercard or Visa at their toll-free number Int.+1 800 639 7140, their fax Int.+1 802 763 2818 or from their address: PO Box 70, S. Royalton, VT 05068., USA. The anthology was reviewed in the School Librarian magazine as "Yes, fitting for bedside and classroom".*

How would you make the world a better place?

Gail Rappaport

From a submission to the Global Ideas Bank.

Most of us, during the course of growing up, were asked the question, "What do you want to be when you grow up?" – in one form or another, at one time or another.

'Wouldn't it be wonderful if the question we asked our children was more collective in outlook?'

Wouldn't it be wonderful if the question asked of our children was more like "What gifts of yours would you like to share with the world?" or "How would you like to contribute to making the world a better place?".

Remember: language is powerful.

• *Gail Rappaport (e-mail: mediate@silcom.com).*

20 Heber Road, London NW2 6AA, UK (rhino@dial.pipex.com), 2001, 300pp, ISBN 0 948826 58 4

The Memory Project to bring war experiences alive for Canada's youth

Summarised from information on the Memory Project website, and from an advert in the Toronto Star. This item was monitored for the Global Ideas Bank by Tim Albery.

The Memory Project aims to help Canadian war veterans share their experiences with students across the country. By giving the veterans the chance to tell their stories and communicate their reflections with young Canadians, it is hoped that their efforts will be remembered and that their tales of wartime will pass from generation to generation. Though not as involved in World War II as other countries, Canada nevertheless lost 42,000 men and women in the war, and this project aims to ensure that their sacrifice, and those of Canadians in other wars, will not be forgotten in the years to come.

'A database of veterans' stories provides students with the opportunity to become digital historians'

To achieve these goals, the Memory Project has a website with a number of features for students to look at. There is a database of stories shared by veterans, students, families and friends, an archive that helps students and veterans alike to become what the website calls 'digital historians', preserving Canada's military history for future generations. For teachers, the website provides lesson plans, timeline charts, and support materials. There is also a service which can connect veterans wishing to speak in schools with a school in an area near them.

'The effort of the war veterans will not be forgotten or underestimated'

With such a scheme, it seems assured that the effort of Canada's war veterans will not be forgotten or underestimated by present or future generations. Other countries could take note and undertake a similar project of their own, one simultaneously combining the maintaining of traditions and history with the opportunities provided by today's technology.

• *The website of the Memory Project is www.thememoryproject.com*

Institute for Social Inventions, £15 subs, £17 from abroad by credit card, tel London 020 8208 2853

School report cards on the internet reduce forgery and paperwork

Summarised from an article by Greg Toppo, entitled 'Schools Using Internet Report Cards', in Yahoo News and Associated Press (June 21st 2001).

Some schools in America have started putting their pupils' report cards on the internet to allow parents to track their progress better, and to eliminate any possibility of bad grades being doctored or hidden away. Other information uploaded includes test scores, class schedules, attendance records and even homework assignments. Parents are assigned particular passwords in order to be able to access the information whenever and wherever they want. Some assiduous parents even take the opportunity of asking for weekly progress reports and e-mailing their child's teacher about any issues concerning them.

Those using the system say it has revolutionized parent-teacher relationships, with parents' evenings being taken up with discussions of how the child can progress in the future because they already know their grades and marks. Similarly, teachers have been able to check on pupils' results and attendance in other classes, allowing them a broader view of each child's situation. The systems are as secure as those used for internet banking, with the main possibility of hacking coming from teachers leaving their computers on without logging off (the electronic equivalent of leaving their grade book open on a desk). Those parents without internet access are encouraged to use public library computers, while some can use touch-tone phones for access to records and information.

'Final report cards have been far less of a shock to parents at the school'

Students, understandably, have mixed reactions to the computerized system. Those with stricter parents have felt a greater pressure of expectation, but others have started logging on themselves to keep track of their work. And while those who have underachieved in certain subjects can no longer hide the fact, the computerized tracking has meant that final report cards have been far less of a shock to their parents.

- *Companies who install such systems include Powerschool (www.powerschool.com), K12 Planet (www.k12planet.com) and LetterGrade (www.lettergrade.com).*

20 Heber Road, London NW2 6AA, UK (rhino@dial.pipex.com), 2001, 300pp, ISBN 0 948826 58 4

RELATIONSHIPS

A night without men to cut down on crime and abuse

Summarised from an article by Will Weissert, entitled 'Women find splendor in gender', in the Seattle Times (March 11th 2001), monitored for the Global Ideas Bank by Roger Knights.

In Colombia's capital Bogota, the city had a 'Night Without Men' in March of this year, after the mayor encouraged women to come out for the night to have a good time and to leave the men at home with the kids. Street crime and domestic abuse are usually both prevalent in the city, but serious crime fell by a quarter on the night.

One local spoke for most of Bogota's women when she said, "It was great. You had a large group of people dancing and having fun in the streets, and there was no violence like there would have been with men around."

'Policemen had the night off, as solely female officers patrolled the streets'

Policemen had the night off, as solely female officers patrolled the streets and the fire brigade was also a completely non-male institution for the evening. The police chief even resigned for the night to allow his female understudy to take over. Mayor Antanas Mockus himself, who is renowned for his offbeat ideas, stayed in to read to his daughter.

But his plans do not stop at the 'Night Without Men': also scheduled is an 'Evening of Rediscovery' designed to further improve gender relations in the city by encouraging couples to go out together.

Pubs better than cafés for stimulating social interaction

Summarised from an article by Adam Sage, entitled 'Parisians find l'amour down the local', in the London Times (Summer 2000).

French anthropologists have recently conducted research which suggests that Anglo-Saxon pubs are ideal for social interaction and romance, more so than the traditional French cafés.

The reasons for this are twofold, according to the research:

Firstly, British-style pubs have an image of freedom and flirtation (to Parisians at least), while normal cafés are viewed as boring and conventional by Parisian youths.

Secondly, people meet while ordering drinks in a pub, unlike in Gallic establishments where customers await the garçon at their own table. The way a pub functions therefore actually increases the likelihood of meeting new people and interacting with them.

'The anthropologists believe that social barriers crumble at the bar'

The anthropologists believe that it is at the bar where social barriers crumble. As they put it, "A conversation seems to flow naturally from this situation of proximity." Men feel free to talk to women, and women do not feel harassed as they might if someone walked over to their café table. In this way, the pub allows a fusion of gender, race, and culture which is impossible in a French café.

Speed dating – seven minutes to converse before the next

Summarised from an article by Janet I. Tu, entitled 'Hurry Up and Date', in the Seattle Times (28th September 2000), monitored for the Global Ideas Bank by Roger Knights.

Speed dating, a meeting and choosing system, could help promote Jewish marriage whilst also providing a way of meeting people for those too busy to date and mingle. The speed-dating system works by giving men and women seven minutes to converse across individual tables before their time is up. Then, the man has to move to another table.

After each conversation, those taking part write down if they would like to see that person again. If both a man and a woman decide they want to see each other again, then each is given the other's phone number, with the man encouraged to call the woman first.

The system is promoted and run by Jewish organizations who are keen to foster links between Jewish people wherever possible, especially as one-faith communities are rapidly disappearing. Speed dating, as one of its organisers Danny Moskkowitz says, "gives them an interesting way to meet people who happen to be Jewish, which is in the back of their minds for most Jewish kids, if not their mothers."

20 Heber Road, London NW2 6AA, UK (rhino@dial.pipex.com), 2001, 300pp, ISBN 0 948826 58 4

'The organisers ring a bell and shout "Get ready! Get set! Date!" '

Each participant pays about £15 to take part, and the events are organised in ten year age groups (such as 22-32 or 30-40). Most of those involved seem enthusiastic with the way the idea works, despite the slightly frenetic atmosphere generated by the organisers ringing a bell and shouting "Get ready! Get set! Date!" at the beginning of the evening. There is time made for a brief halftime snippet of wisdom from the organising rabbi, but the dating soon begins again in earnest. One of the men taking part at an event in Seattle admitted that he was a bit tired by the end of it all, but that he found it better than "competing with the rest of all that chatter at a party." One of the women he'd been talking to also said that the experience was more of a marathon than a sprint, but found it a simple, fun way to meet like-minded people.

If one thinks of the system not so much as speed dating, perhaps, but as a focused dating agency with less pitfalls and no blind dates, the attraction becomes more apparent. That thousands of people have now tried it in cities all over America and in five other countries, including England and Australia, certainly seems to support that view. And it may not be long before the idea spreads beyond the Jewish community, providing a new option for single people everywhere.

• *For more information, see http://aish.com/speeddating/default.asp and also the similar ten minute dating at: http://www.meetinggame.com*

A mathematical formula for sharing out property in divorce cases

Summarised from an article by Larissa MacFarquhar, entitled 'Department of Human Nature', in the New Yorker (August 16th 1999), monitored for the Global Ideas Bank by Roger Knights. Additional information from an article by Robert Uhlig, entitled 'Divorce, by numbers', on the Canadian National Post website (www.fact.on.ca).

A new algorithm devised by two American professors divides up the goods of divorcing couples automatically. The 'Adjusted Winner' algorithm, devised by Steven Brams (a political scientist at New York University) and Alan Taylor (a maths professor at Union College), guarantees a stress-free process of sharing things out, according to its creators.

They came up with the formula after working out how to divide a cake up into three parts, with no one person being envious of another, because of, for instance, extra icing or decorations. Their algorithm therefore takes emotion and sentiment into account in its very process.

It works as follows:

'She allots 65 points to the house, 25 to the car and 10 to the machine'

Imagine that a couple called Britney and Justin are getting divorced. They own a house, a car and a karaoke machine. Britney never liked the karaoke, but desperately wants the house, so she allots 65 points to the house, 25 to the car and 10 to the machine. Justin, on the other hand, is in love with their car and little else, so he allots 60 points to the car, 25 to the house, and 15 to the machine. Each item then goes to whoever gave them the most points, so Britney gets the house, while Justin gets the car and the karaoke machine. This is obviously unfair, though, because Justin has received 75 of his 100 points, while poor Britney has only obtained 65 points of hers.

'The item rated most closely by both Britney and Justin is taken from Justin and sold off'

This, then, is where the adjustment comes in. The item rated most closely by both Britney and Justin is taken from Justin. Thus, the karaoke is taken from him, and his points total drops to 60 out of 100. The karaoke machine is then sold off, with Justin keeping three-fifths of the selling price, and Britney receiving the other two-fifths. This brings Justin's total up to 69 (three fifths of 15 = 9, added to his other 60) and Britney's also to 69 (two fifths of 10 = 4, added to her 65). Everything is thus fairly divided, with both getting the bulk of what they wanted in an envy-free fashion.

'Britney could award the car 70 or 80 points just to annoy Justin and take it away from him'

Clearly the method is not flawless. It only guarantees that a sincere person receives half of the goods as they value them. The two parties may well end up with packages of significantly different monetary worth. While this could be because of one person's emotional attachment to something, it could also be due to another's strategically dishonest ratings. In divorce cases, the issue of spite can also not be underestimated. In the example above, for instance, Britney could award the car 70 or 80 points just to annoy Justin and take it away from him.

Divorce lawyers might not be out of a job just yet then, but the system clearly has its merits. One conflict-resolution specialist in Montana has used

20 Heber Road, London NW2 6AA, UK (rhino@dial.pipex.com), 2001, 300pp, ISBN 0 948826 58 4

the formula to mediate in about 45 divorce cases, adapting the abstract theory to his own ends. Norman G. Lavery said the process was to be lauded, and could provide a useful framework for sharing out goods. It even helped alert him to certain issues which needed to be resolved: if someone has an irrational attachment to something ostensibly worthless, there is probably something behind that.

The inventors also believe that the algorithm could be applied in other situations where assets need to be divided up: corporate mergers, family feuds over estates, even peace negotiations in the Middle East or Northern Ireland. Whether anyone would be willing to trust such issues to a computer's decision is another matter. That may be taking the formula a step too far. For goods-sharing amongst separating parties, though, its usefulness is obvious. Any method that makes divorce less stressful would have to be welcomed.

Your personal e-mail code on the outside of rucksacks

Summarised from an article by Bridget Harrison, entitled 'You have e-male', in the London Times (July 21st 2000).

A designers' co-operative in Zurich have come up with an idea that they think could be the most effective route to love in the hectic dot-com world.

They manufacture items such as rucksacks which are branded with a large number on the exterior that doubles as a free personal e-mail address on their website.

The idea is that if someone sees you in the street or at a party but is too embarrassed or shy to say anything, then they can e-mail you instead. Skim.com, the website involved, describe it as a "new way for like-minded people to get in touch."

'Each piece of Skim clothing or accessory has a serial number linked to an e-mail account'

Each piece of Skim clothing or accessory has a serial number. Once you have set up your e-mail account on the website, it is simply a case of linking your serial number to that account. In this way, anyone could have any number of similarly branded clothes, wearing them how and with whatever they wanted, and all e-mails would still come to the same inbox. The account is private and as anonymous as you wish it to be.

While some might think this is an invitation to stalkers, it is no more so than a personal ad in a paper, and there is no requirement to respond to any e-mails you receive. The system of contact also makes it likely that similar-minded people will buy the items and respond to them. In Zurich and Berlin, the word is spreading, and several Skim wearers have made cyberfriends or met up with other people who understood the code. Numbered clothes could soon be more than the local prison population's preserve.

Touch for Health – the promotion of touching in social encounters

Nicholas Albery

Background: A report on 'Touch for Health Month' 1982

Prepared by Nicholas Albery, Natalie Rees, Caroline Holden, Kelly Petch and Tony Ogun, November 1982, whilst students at the School for Independent Study, North East London Polytechnic, London E15, UK.

Part One, Introduction

For the first two Fridays of groupwork in the autumn term of 1982, we discussed what to do for the term's work. In the local café we started talking about what we would study if we could study anything we wanted under the sun, forgetting for a moment the college criteria about being of relevance to the local community and involving serious research work.

One of our group of five said that the previous term's groupwork had made him very intrigued about the subject of Touch. There had been two women in his street theatre group who had improved the atmosphere of the work a great deal by going around arm in arm with other participants, or lying in the park during rehearsal time with heads in laps and so on. He had noticed that they were really the only two 'natural touchers' in the School for Independent Study (S. I. S.) and that they had a dramatic effect wherever they went – although touch was barely mentioned as a factor in college discussions and texts about 'improving group dynamics'.

Others agreed that this would make a possible lively subject. One of us thought the emphasis should be on Health, telling of his own interest in Tai Chi and other integrative and holistic health approaches.

Given that we had only seven Fridays left in which to work before the group product had to be ready, we decided to focus down on a very narrow concept. We agreed that research had already demonstrated that touch was valuable for infants and adults (though intensive reading was to make us aware just how

20 Heber Road, London NW2 6AA, UK (rhino@dial.pipex.com), 2001, 300pp, ISBN 0 948826 58 4

valuable), and that there was not much point in duplicating such research. The next stage was obviously to try to raise public consciousness and to help persuade people to do what the research had shown to be valuable, i.e. to touch each other more.

'A physical chain letter, whereby each person would touch three men and three women and to then get them to enrol six others in turn'

We decided to adopt the powerful idea of the chain letter, to start a physical chain letter, whereby each person would touch three men and three women whom they would not normally touch, and to then get them to enrol six others in turn.

Immediately we had decided this in our East London canteen, on October 15th 1982, we went off to find six people each to touch and enrol. Half an hour later we met again. Most of us had 'enrolled' six people with no difficulty; although, interestingly, the only natural toucher amongst us (thanks, she believes, to having a French mother) had had the most problems, suddenly becoming self-conscious about something that was second nature to her. (By the end of the month she had conquered this self-consciousness and was reporting possibly coincidental improvements in her own physical health).

Already the people we had touched were going off in search of others to touch, and it was indeed a touching sight to see one of the oldest grey-haired 'mature' students approaching and touching others with tact (from the Latin 'tactus' = touch).

'It seemed clear that the project might do a great deal to electrify the atmosphere in college, whatever the effects further afield'

It seemed clear now that the project might do a great deal to electrify the atmosphere in college, whatever the effects further afield.

On the next Friday, October 22nd 1982, the group considered a draft press release announcing November as Touch for Health month, and agreed to send an amended version to all the media except the popular tabloids, where the risk of distortion was greatest. It was also decided to try to get Time Out (the London listings magazine) to sponsor the month. In the event Time Out agreed to cover the idea but they were not prepared to sponsor it. The following press release was sent to 60 UK papers, and radio and TV programmes:

Press Release October 28th 1982

Touch for Health Month November 1982

"Touch someone today!", say a group of students at the North East London Polytechnic's School for Independent Study who are launching a 'Touch for Health Month' for November.

People are invited (1) to touch three males and three females during November, people they would not normally touch; (2) afterwards, to invite those touched in turn to touch six others, repeating the stage (1) and (2) procedures in full.

If people follow these guidelines faithfully, touching will increase at a geometric rate, and there will be very few people left untouched by this project in the whole of Britain, in theory anyway.

People are also invited to send in their stories of incidents, feelings or discussions provoked by touching others in this way – some accounts may be published and a small prize is offered for the most interesting.

'We are advocating social not sexual touching, in the belief that a touch expresses a lot more warmth than a volume of words'

"A friendly touch on the shoulder is the sort of touch we mean", says Caroline Holden, age 33, one of the five NELP students responsible for this project. "We are advocating social not sexual touching, in the belief that a touch often expresses a lot more warmth in a conversation than a volume of words.

"This project is part of our student group work for this term, which we take seriously, as one of the requirements is a scientific approach to a project of wider community benefit. We feel this project could make quite a difference to a lot of people.

"People aren't open enough in England", adds Natalie Rees, age 20, another of the students involved. "My mother is French and touching comes naturally to me. People suffer from second-hand intimacy – they read romantic novels or go to porn cinemas as an escape from real intimacy."

A third student, Nicholas Albery, age 34, outlines the research by Desmond Morris, Ashley Montague, Nancy Henley and others that supports touching as healthy: "Babies can die if they are not touched and handled enough, and it's been demonstrated that adults too can suffer from touch deprivation. One piece of research also showed that a librarian who touched customers when handing back books tended to make the female customers feel more positive about the library as a whole.

"We believe it's time that touch came out of the encounter group ghetto

20 Heber Road, London NW2 6AA, UK (rhino@dial.pipex.com), 2001, 300pp, ISBN 0 948826 58 4

and more into daily life. Unfortunately, where social touching does occur at present, it is often used in a patronising way, with bosses touching workers, adults touching children and men touching women more freely than vice versa. We hope this project will help restore innocence to touching and that people will touch with respect, and not only touch those they perceive as having less power or status than themselves. Personally, I'm very inhibited about touching, as are English people in general. It's been observed that in a cafe in Paris, 110 incidents of touching occurred per hour. In Britain the tally was zero. We hope this Touch for Health Month may help people feel they have more permission to risk a touch, and that gradually touching will become second nature to them."

'Individuals can develop a greater self-awareness and more understanding of others through touch'

Student Kelly Petch, age 33, is organising a Touch workshop at Plaistow NELP as part of the month's activities. "It will be a chance", he says, "for individuals to begin to develop, through touch, a greater self-awareness, more confidence and more understanding of others, and to take more responsibility for their health and well-being."

Also available is a campaign badge saying 'Touch for Health Month'. A small prize is offered for the best suggestions for future badge slogans. Suggestions so far, none especially inspired, include: "Keep in touch", "Touch me", "Are you above touch?", "Have you touched someone today?", "A friendly touch", "I'm not untouchable", and, for people wanting nothing to do with this project, a badge to say "Untouchable".

- *The non-profit website for participatory events in every city in the world, www.DoBe.org, is relaunching Touch for Health Month for May each year, starting with May 2001. For details see the website in the 'Social' category. Or for press releases, etc contact the Institute for Social Inventions at rhino@dial.pipex.com*

Shame – from an evolutionary perspective

Shame – Interpersonal behaviour, psychopathology and culture, *edited by Paul Gilbert and Bernice Andrews (published by Oxford University Press Inc, USA, ISBN 0 19 511480 9, 288 pages, £26.50; or $35 from www.amazon.com). Reviewed by Nicholas Albery.*

Shame is often regarded as pathological. Shame has been linked with symptoms of paranoid ideation, psychoticism, borderline personality disorders, alcoholism, drug abuse, domestic violence – and many problematic behaviours that are all seen as drastic, avoidant defences against chronic feelings of shame.

This book examines such states and the effect of shame on social behaviour, social values and mental states. But it also takes an interesting evolutionary perspective and sees how shame provides adaptive signals that warn the person of potential, but usually avoidable, negative consequences for successful reproduction and psychological well-being.

'The capacity to experience shame is hardwired in the human brain'

The capacity to experience shame is hardwired in the human brain. Shame helps match individuals' behaviours with the values of their group – without it, the protection of the group and access to mates might be lost. Shame can be more effective than feelings of guilt in restraining a person's behaviour – for instance, a man can be shamed into supporting his wife and children even though his internal conscience would not have led him to do so; or people will give to charity when asked to do so in a public place, who would not have done so in private.

Shame facilitates restorative behaviour – such as when the person shamed by losing a match seeks a rematch; or the individual who has been insulted demands an apology.

The wish to avoid the shame of low status can lead to such activities as intense efforts for weight control, or a desirable body shape and dressing fashionably, thereby increasing one's chance to acquire a desirable mate.

Shame signals – head down, gaze avoidance and hiding – are submissive and appeasement displays, which enable the de-escalation of conflicts.

'For the social inventor, a certain degree of shamelessness may be required'

The conclusion to be drawn from this book is that shame is a very powerful means of social control, even in supposedly individualistic societies. But for the social inventor, a certain degree of shamelessness may be required: to resist pressures towards conformity and to engage in risk-taking thinking and doing. As one chapter in the book puts it:

"Those relatively unconcerned with 'conformity shame' have more freedom to follow their own dictates. As a result, they can be more spontaneous and creative and may, on a personal level, feel more at ease and comfortable with themselves. At the social level, they might make significant contributions out of patterns of perception, thought and behaviour that are innovatively

20 Heber Road, London NW2 6AA, UK (rhino@dial.pipex.com), 2001, 300pp, ISBN 0 948826 58 4

different from the norm. ... The person who creates changes may at first be regarded as foolish, eccentric or a threat, but – if the new trend becomes standard – then the originator can reap fame, status and entitlements, all of which serve to enhance fitness."

It's quite a big "if" though.

A movement against verbal cruelty

Summarised from an article by Karen R. Long, entitled 'Movement Seeks to Curb Negative Tongue', published by the Religious News Service (and available in full on the web at www.religionnews.com/arc01/f_0108.html) and from other web items. This item was monitored for the Global Ideas Bank by Roger Knights.

Rabbi Chaim Feld in Cleveland has started a movement against verbal cruelty, gossip and slander. Jewish groups in Cleveland, Philadelphia, Miami, Cleveland and St Louis are taking up his public campaigns to curb gossip. "I want to create a social revolution, a shift in this society so that gossip is not acceptable," says Feld.

'The Talmud equates defamatory statements with murder'

"The Talmud equates *loshon hora* [defined as 'defamatory statements, insulting witticisms, disparaging anecdotes, idle mockery'] with murder," adds Feld. "If you've never met Michael, and someone tells you he is a jerk, then Michael has been murdered for you, before you even meet him."

Listening to *loshon hora* is, according to Jewish teaching, even more sinful than speaking it.

Unlike a thief who can make amends by returning or replacing property, the gossip cannot return a good name.

As Rabbi Joseph Telushkin puts it in his book *Words That Hurt, Words That Heal*, "This is an evil of such profound magnitude and consequence that Jewish law questions whether anyone who is guilty of this offence can ever fully repent."

Telushkin proposes an annual Speak No Evil Day.

"Thinking about the damage done by gossip is like learning a new word," says Feld. "Once you learn it, you see it everywhere."

Loshon hora

The rules of loshon hora seem almost untenably strict. Here they are as defined on the web at www.utexas.edu/depts/cjso/ChaiTimes/v2.2/loshon-hora.txt:

Loshon hora means the making of a derogatory or damaging remark about someone. The Torah forbids one to denigrate the behaviour or character of a fellow Jew or to make any remark that might cause him physical, psychological or financial harm.

Here are ten basic rules to remember:

'It is loshon hora to convey a derogatory image of someone even if that image is true and deserved'

(1) It is *loshon hora* to convey a derogatory image of someone even if that image is true and deserved (false derogatory statements are called *motzi shem ra*, slander).

(2) A statement which is not actually derogatory but can ultimately cause someone physical, financial, or emotional harm is also *loshon hora*.

(3) It is *loshon hora* to humorously recount an incident that contains embarrassing or damaging information about a person even if there is not the slightest intent that they should suffer an harm or humiliation.

(4) *Loshon hora* is forbidden even when you incriminate yourself as well.

(5) *Loshon hora* cannot be communicated in any way, shape, or form (ie through writing, body language, verbal hints, etc).

(6) To speak against a community as a whole is a particularly severe offence. Harmful remarks about children are also *loshon hora*.

(7) *Loshon hora* cannot be related even to close relatives, including one's spouse.

(8) Even if the listener has previously heard the derogatory account or the information has become public knowledge and the subject will suffer no further harm by its repetition, it nevertheless should not be repeated.

(9) It is also forbidden to believe that the derogatory statement is true. One should give the person the benefit of the doubt. Assume the information is inaccurate or that the person does not realise they are doing something wrong.

'Loshon hora is permitted when warning a person about a marriage partner'

Note: There are times when *loshon hora* is permitted or even required, ie when warning a person about potential harm, for example, a potential business or marriage partner, or to help someone deal with a difficult situation or person.

• *Rabbi Chaim Feld, Aish HaTorah, 14055 Cedar Rd., Ste. 309, Cleveland, Ohio 44118 (tel 321 7277; fax: 321 8844; e-mail: cleveland@aish.edu).*

20 Heber Road, London NW2 6AA, UK (rhino@dial.pipex.com), 2001, 300pp, ISBN 0 948826 58 4

• Words That Hurt, Words That Heal – How to choose words wisely and well *by Joseph Telushkin, published by William Morrow & Co (ISBN 0688163505, 240 pages, $14).*

Housing

A green building tax credit

Summarised from an article on the website of the National Resources Defence Council (www.nrdc.org/cities/building/nnytax.asp) and from an item by Guy Dauncey in Econews (September 30th 2000).

In New York, the state has started offering a 'green building credit' to developers in order to encourage them to build environmentally-sound buildings. The aim of the tax credit is to start laying the foundations for a shift to environmentally-progressive building materials and practices. By rewarding those developers who make commercial and apartment buildings with better indoor air quality, and which use recycled and recyclable materials, the state hopes to start a movement in the industry itself.

'The developers can claim back money per square foot for using environmentally friendly materials'

To receive the tax credit, developers have to meet certain criteria. In new buildings, for example, energy use cannot exceed 65 per cent of use as permitted under the state's energy code; for rehabilitated buildings, the figure is 75 per cent. Having met these criteria, the developers can then claim back money per square foot for using environmentally preferable materials. They can also recoup ten per cent of the cost of ozone-friendly air-conditioning, 30 per cent of the cost of hydrogen fuel-cells, and 100 per cent of the cost of built-in solar photovoltaic (PV) panels. It is just the kind of industry-centred initiative that is needed to create a truly green economy.

• *Related articles can be found at the National Resources Defense Council website (www.nrdc.org) and at the New York State Department's website (www.dec.state.ny.us/website/dar/ood/grnbldgtxcr.html).*

• *Guy Dauncey, Econews, Sustainable Communities Consultancy, 395 Conway Rd, Victoria, BC, V8X 3X1, Canada; (tel/fax Int.+1 250 8811304 (w); e-mail: guydauncey@earthfuture.com; web: www.earthfuture.com).*

Adopt volunteer homeless who live in their cars

Franis Engel

Adapted from a submission to the Global Ideas Bank.

At present, there is a severe housing shortage in the San Francisco Bay Area in California, USA. In my small town of 1800, there are over thirty residents who live in their cars since their flat or room was sold. In high-demand areas, people who work the low-paying service jobs cannot find even a room to rent at double their former rent. Rather than leave their jobs and friends by moving away completely, they move into their cars in the hope of saving money. And if something else goes wrong, these 'homeless by choice' people can often lose everything and become destitute.

> ## 'I have adopted a succession of car-dwellers, giving them limited access to my home in exchange for various chores'

To avoid this from happening, I have 'adopted' a succession of 'car-dwellers' (one at a time!) giving them limited access to my tiny home (showers, taking messages for job-seeking) in exchange for various chores. If I trusted them and enjoyed being around them, I sometimes charged them weekly 'rent' to sleep on my couch. Whenever I wanted them to leave, as a parting gesture, I gave all their rent money back to them without telling them I had saved it. With this help, most of them have managed to find housing.

Camaraderie seems to be high amongst homeless people as a group. So why not take advantage of their desire to help each other? Some of these 'recovered homeless' got together and rented a shared place. This household decided to start a twice-a-week evening pot-luck meal for their other friends who were still living in cars. The car dwellers bring extra food, prepare the food that's there, and clean up the kitchen. The renters get food prepared for them and their dinner dishes get washed; also, sometimes the kitchen gets a cleaning and sometimes the car-dwellers get showers. (Alcohol and telephone use is sometimes barred or limited by house members.) It may even occur that a car-dweller who gets a job moves into the house when a room becomes free. The key is community-minded thinking, and being aware of the hardship of others around you: small sacrifices can make a huge difference to the beneficiary, car-dweller or not.

* *Franis Engel (an8el@hotmail.com).*

20 Heber Road, London NW2 6AA, UK (rhino@dial.pipex.com), 2001, 300pp, ISBN 0 948826 58 4

TAXATION

Green tax yourself for a clear conscience

Summarised from an article by Lisa Jones, entitled 'Cabbage Patch Kid', in Grist magazine (www.gristmagazine.com; October 19th 2000). This item was monitored for the Global Ideas Bank by Tom Atlee of the Co-Intelligence Institute (see http://www.co-intelligence.org or http://www.democracyinnovations.org).

As someone with a highly defined environmental conscience, Dev Carey often felt pained by the consequences of things he did – such as taking occasional lifts in cars, eating non-local produce or buying from corporations. So he started taxing himself on what he consumes.

Here is an extract from his manifesto:

"Every time a dollar leaves my pocket, I classify it by two criteria: what is the environmental ethic of what I purchased and how far did it have to travel? The cabbage from Mexico (complete with pesticides and underpaid workers) gets a minus/minus. The local, organic cabbage gets a plus/plus, while an organic cabbage from California gets a plus/minus."

'Two dollars earned selling a corporate beer means another dollar to a non-profit, while two dollars earned teaching locally is not taxed at all'

For every minus/minus dollar spent, Dev then contributes another dollar to a deserving non-profit organisation. For every plus/minus, he contributes 50 cents, while for plus/plus items, he is tax-free. He applies the same system to everything, from Nike running shoes (minus/minus) to Ben & Jerry's ice cream (plus/minus).

Dev further extends the system to his earnings, although contributing at half the rate. Two dollars earned selling a big corporate beer will mean another dollar to a non-profit, while two dollars earned teaching locally is not taxed at all.

He claims the system works well for him, with his budget balanced and his conscience completely clear at all times. Buying local and organic produce now makes fiscal as well as environmental sense, and the amount Dev has contributed to charities has reduced his (actual) tax bill substantially.

WORK & EMPLOYMENT

A reward scheme for workers who recruit new employees

Summarised from an article by Julekha Dash, entitled 'Filling slots with inside referrals', in Computer World (10th July 2000), monitored for the Global Ideas Bank by Roger Knights.

The rewarding of employees who recruit new people to a company could be the way to avoid costly recruitment fees and worker short-termism.

At Minneapolis-based Carlson Cos., employees who refer IT workers receive $2,000 when the person is hired, and a further $1,000 every year for four years, providing both employees stay with the company. This not only encourages employees to refer friends or acquaintances, but also encourages them to look after their referrals once they have got the job.

As a result of the combination of a lump sum and a deferred payment tied to both employees remaining with the company, Carlson's scheme has been a great success. More than one-fifth of newly-hired IT employees have been from employee referrals in the first half of this year. Furthermore, as Lynne Carroll, an IT recruiter with the firm points out, the scheme "keeps everybody involved in making sure that people are happy with their jobs."

The idea works for everyone: the company saves on recruitment fees and ensures greater loyalty to the company, the original employee has a chance to make some relatively easy money, and the person being hired immediately feels more at home at a company where he knows people.

Prizes and rewards for those not taking sick days

Summarised from an article entitled 'No sick days? It can pay off' in the Seattle Times (December 22nd 2000), monitored for the Global Ideas Bank by Roger Knights.

Employees taking 'sickies' or skiving off work cost businesses millions of pounds a year, but they can do little about it. Some recently proposed a 'duvet day' in Britain to try and buck the trend of employee absence, the thought being that a scheduled lie-in might pre-empt an unscheduled one and give employees a well-earned rest. The Electric Boat shipyard in Groton, Connecticut may have a better solution. It has tackled the problem head-on by offering

20 Heber Road, London NW2 6AA, UK (rhino@dial.pipex.com), 2001, 300pp, ISBN 0 948826 58 4

cash prizes to those who have not used their sick days, with all salaried workers being eligible. And the number taking days off sick has halved as a result.

'20 workers received the top $2,500 cash prize, having not called in sick for two years'

Each salaried worker at the shipyard is entered into a lottery, with prizes including $2,500 cash prizes, gift certificates and free parking spaces. At the end of each year, the company hands out the prizes to the lucky few who haven't been off sick all year. In December 2000, for example, twenty workers received the top $2,500 cash prize having been drawn from a pool of 955 workers who have not called in sick for two years. Added to that, 75 prizes of $1,000 were handed out, plus free parking spaces and many $25 gift certificates – no-one went home empty-handed. And the result of this innovation? The average number of sick days taken by workers at the shipyard has fallen from 7.2 to 3.5 per year, and forty-one per cent of workers did not use a single sick day in the year 2000.

'The company pool together vacation time and sick leave into one big paid 'time-off' block'

There are other innovative approaches that can be taken to the problem of employee absences. Another company in the US, Aetna of Hartford in Connecticut, no longer give workers sick days. Instead, they pool together vacation and sick leave into one big paid 'time-off' grouping. That gives the workers the option of using the days in the ways they see fit, and the added flexibility is proving very popular at the company.

People with learning disabilities running their own projects

Dave Kirsopp

Adapted from a submission to the Global Ideas Bank. Dave Kirsopp lives and works in the Lancaster area, UK. He is a student at the School for Social Entrepreneurs this year; and is using this time to develop and launch Thumbprint.

Thumbprint is a new project which will enable people with learning disabilities to set up and run projects which they control – a radical departure from existing practice within services and charitable provision. With the right support there is no reason why someone with a learning disability cannot run their own project.

'Almost all existing opportunities for work are within what could be described as top-down organisations'

Why the need for Thumbprint? Because almost all existing opportunities for work are within what could be described as top-down organisations. I think often this can have the effect of reinforcing an individual's view of him or herself as dependent and devalued. The effect can be very subtle, say in tone of voice, linguistics or body language, but nevertheless it sends powerful messages about a person's status or perceived value. People absorb these messages even if their learning disability means that they cannot rationalise the underlying structures.

Also, there is no support system to enable people to take up the self-employment option. (I, for example, can go and work as a landscape gardener and there are people and organisations who will help me to organise my business, but someone with a learning disability would be very unlikely to access that sort of support.)

Being in charge of your working life can be hard work and risky, but it certainly develops you, gives you confidence and widens your outlook on the world – a very different outlook, I feel, than that provided by special schools, day centres and so on.

'My aim is to develop a support system to enable people to run their own working lives. Not to be a provider so much as a catalyst for change'

My aim is to develop a support system to enable people to run their own working lives. Not to be a provider so much as a catalyst for change.

How will I do this? I plan to work alongside people on ideas they may have, as well as identifying opportunities for possible projects. Together we will look at opportunities to see if they are viable and if so we will develop practical support systems to enable those people to take their idea and make it a reality.

I anticipate that much of my work will involve ensuring that formal and informal supports (such as parents, social services and day centres) share our vision and that support workers on the projects have the appropriate skills and attitudes to enable the clients to have a sense of ownership.

Though innovative, Thumbprint will employ well-tried skills currently in use for supporting people with learning disabilities. Approaches used to enable people to enter employment are adaptable to Thumbprint's aims in develop-

20 Heber Road, London NW2 6AA, UK (rhino@dial.pipex.com), 2001, 300pp, ISBN 0 948826 58 4

ing new projects.

I will establish the project on a small scale initially, using the first two years to work with just a few projects, gaining experience and building the organisation. Following this the project can be scaled up area-wide and nationally.

Without doubt, being in control of your working life is deeply empowering to all of us yet there is no formal organisation to enable people with learning disabilities to take the self-employed (paid or unpaid) route.

Thumbprint will develop that organisation; and in doing so will develop a model way of working which can be replicated and applied nationally.

This project is based on two premises:

(1) That people with learning disabilities are able to accomplish a great deal given appropriate support.

(2) That projects are set up by non-learning-disabled people according to what they perceive as a need rather than being devised and run by the people who would use them.

Why not provide the support system, the catalyst, which would enable people with learning disabilities to set up their own projects, truly own them, and develop the confidence to run them? Rather than assume inability, we could accept that we all need support and with the right support we can all achieve a great deal.

• *Dave Kirsopp (e-mail: davekirsopp@mailops.com).*

ECONOMICS AND BUSINESS

Wealth distribution is a law of nature

Summarised from an article by Mark Buchanan, entitled 'That's the way money goes', in New Scientist (August 19th 2000; New Scientist subs £97 or $140, tel 44 [0] 1622 778000).

Jean-Philippe Bouchaud and Marc Mezard, two French econophysicists, believe that wealth falling into the hands of a minority is not just a fact of life, but a law of nature. They have discovered a connection between the physics of materials and the movements of money, a link that could revolutionise the way we think about the distribution of wealth in society. It could also provide a mathematical basis to theories of free trade and competition.

That wealth is unevenly distributed is now widely accepted: in the US, 20 per cent of the people own 80 per cent of the wealth, and similar figures apply throughout western Europe. Most economists have struggled to explain this seemingly universal trend, usually putting it down to the distribution of people's abilities.

Bouchaud and Mezard started their analysis from the simplest possible basis, ignoring any economic theories and assumptions of previous years. Their one assumption was that life is unpredictable: returns on investments are random, trading is haphazard, profit and loss could come at any moment.

'Bouchaud and Mezard brought their knowledge of condensed matter physics into play'

While investigating the simple equations that make up an economy (of which there are millions, because there are millions of people), Bouchaud and Mezard discovered that they could bring their knowledge of 'condensed matter' physics into play. There is a model used in this area of physics concerned with 'ill-condensed' matter which is called a directed polymer. This model involves the imagining of a long wire lying on a landscape that undulates at random. The wire, which represents the polymer, is tethered at one end. Two forces then compete with one another: gravity wishing to pull the wire into the valleys of the landscape and the wire's desire to stay straight. The resultant path that the wire takes is a compromise between the two, and there is no 'best path' for it to take. Added in to this model is a third key factor of temperature: the hotter the temperature, the more the wire is buffeted by air molecules. The level of the temperature (and therefore the level of the buffeting) determines exactly how the wire manages its compromise between going straight across the landscape and staying in the valleys below.

Bouchaud and Mezard have now discovered that this physics model corresponds exactly to their economic model. The wire now represents the path of a quantity of money as it moves from person to person (with the number of wires crossing over a particular point representing the wealth of a particular person at that point). The irregularity of returns from investments is represented in the landscape: deep valleys correspond to places of more money, while peaks are where investors lose money and fare badly. And temperature is analogous to the vigour of trade, or how easily money moves between people.

'If an economy is 'cold' then wealth flows far less easily between people'

This shows, for example, that when trading is easy the economy is 'hot' and is not very strongly affected by the landscape below. Thus vigorous trading

20 Heber Road, London NW2 6AA, UK (rhino@dial.pipex.com), 2001, 300pp, ISBN 0 948826 58 4

enables wealth to flow easily from person to person which tends to spread money more easily. By contrast, if an economy is 'cold', by which is meant restricted trading and highly irregular returns, then wealth flows far less easily between people as it follows a path dictated almost entirely by the landscape. Wealth becomes even less fairly distributed, as its natural diffusion is overcome by the disparities of the economic landscape.

It follows, therefore, that a more equal society can not only be achieved through taxation and redistribution, but through the encouragement of freer and fairer trade, competition and exchange. The hotter the temperature of an economy, the more vigorous the rate and number of people trading, the more equal a society will become. This fits with most economists' experiences and expectations, but has now been given a mathematical basis. Also, the econophysicists' theory should mean that Internet trading proves to be an enemy of inequality, as more and more people take part in the random flows and movements of wealth.

• *For related articles and economic papers, see the website of the econophysicists:* www.unifr.ch/econophysics

A dozen policies for resisting globalisation, debt and the dollar empire

Goodbye America! – Globalisation, debt and the dollar empire, *by Michael Rowbotham, published by Jon Carpenter (Alder House, Market St, Charlbury OX7 3PQ, UK, tel 01689 870437, 2000, ISBN 1 897766 5 4, 210 pages, £11). Reviewed by Nicholas Albery.*

In this book, Michael Rowbotham quotes the head of Avis Car Rental as saying: "America is run largely by and for about 5,000 people, [including] maybe 2,500 mega-corporation executives" and he insists that the dollar empire created by these 5,000 people has been ruinous for developing nations.

'America is run largely by and for about 5,000 people'

America is to blame for third world debt by having imposed a trade ideology that favoured its political and economic desires, and by forcing developing countries to denominate their debts in US dollars rather than local currency.

Cancellation or repudiation of international debts carried by emergent nations would free them to set their own economic priorities. Thereafter, competition from new companies in these nations would lead to the slimming down and fragmentation of many corporate monopolies.

The author is even against setting environmental conditions on a nation's debt forgiveness. I think he is being too ethical here. Any lever for nudging a nation towards greener policies needs to be used, even abused.

But the author has a dozen or so unexceptionable policy proposals for downsizing corporate and political accumulations of power:

• Developing countries should adopt the Channel Islands model of creating newly-issued local money to fund new projects or public services, gradually taxing the money back in subsequent years.

• A graduated Tobin tax on stock market investment transactions.

• A ban on using leveraged hedge funds for currency deals.

'A ban on multinationals accepting cash inducements from governments'

• A ban on multinationals requiring or accepting cash 'inducements' from governments, unless equity ownership of the investment is granted to the government.

• Heavy fines for goods and services sold between or within corporations at rates that differ from those charged to the wider market.

• The right of national governments to subsidise domestic firms.

• The right of national governments to declare that chosen sectors of their economy must be wholly or partially owned by domestic companies.

'The right of governments to set their own environmental standards'

• The right of governments to set their own environmental standards.

• The right of governments to insist on patent transfers and the training of their own nationals as conditions of inward investment.

• The repatriation of corporate profits to be subject to international audit.

'An International Court of Commercial Conduct, for complaints against international corporations'

• The institution of an International Court of Commercial Conduct, for the hearing of complaints against international corporations.

These are worthwhile aspirations indeed, although the author is less forthright on how we are to get from the dismal here and now to this new utopia.

20 Heber Road, London NW2 6AA, UK (rhino@dial.pipex.com), 2001, 300pp, ISBN 0 948826 58 4

Companies offering telephone callbacks when busy

Gordon Grant

Adapted from a submission to the Global Ideas Bank. Gordon Grant is, he writes,"a retired Canadian living in Vancouver".

How often has this happened to you? You dial up a company and get a recorded message that puts you on hold for endless minutes or even hours, so you sit there fuming because they are wasting your time. So, why don't more companies offer a callback service?

'Leave your name and number, we'll call you back as soon as one of our agents is free'

How often has this happened to you? You dial up a company and get a recorded message that puts you on hold for endless minutes or even hours, so you sit there fuming because they are wasting your time. So, why don't more companies offer a callback service? All they have to do is have the recorded menu say something like: "Due to heavy call volume, we are unable to take your call. If you would prefer to leave your name and number, we'll call you back as soon as one of our agents is free ..."

You should then be able to hang up, go on to more important things, take their call when it comes, and save hours and hours of wasted time. IKEA does it. Why don't more companies do it?

• *Gordon Grant (e-mail: gogrant@telus.net).*

Adapt vending machines to accept cash deposits for savings accounts

Gregory Wright

Adapted from an e-mail to the Global Ideas Bank.

I suggest the introduction of vending machines adapted for making small cash deposits into a savings account. Instead of buying a chocolate bar or a soft drink, a person could then choose to put their loose change into their bank account on the spur of the moment.

Loose change contributed on a regular basis to one's investment, retirement or savings account adds up to real money over the long haul, provident individuals of all ages and incomes could benefit from the opportunity to turn small impulse purchases into impulse personal investments.

'The individual who chooses the saving machine over the snack machine will benefit doubly: in wealth and health'

The individual who chooses the saving machine over the snack machine for some of the time will benefit doubly: in wealth and health. The individual who opts to make the mini-investment and still buy the snack anyway was obviously hungry and ends up getting two rewards. If people started saving in this way when they were young, they could have a substantial nest egg by the time they are middle-aged, but everyone could benefit from such a system.

The same concept could also be applied to charitable micro-giving. Out-of-use vending machines could even be repaired and remodelled to give small packets of information and pictures about a charity in return for a cash donation. People might even end up smoking less as well.

* *Gregory Wright, Wright Thinking, 14161 Riverside Drive, #3, Sherman Oaks, CA 91423, USA (tel Int.+1 818 784 0325; e-mail: greg@newciv.org).*

WELFARE

Welfare in a cold climate is more all-encompassing?

Summarised from a two-sided A4 leaflet by Brian Micklethwait, entitled 'Can you sleep out all the year round?', published as Sociological Notes No. 27 (published by the Libertarian Alliance).

The conjecture put forward is this: in cold places, welfare statism is relatively easy to do, and is done a lot and believed in a lot. In warmer places, welfare statism is harder to do, and it is done less and believed in less.

'Can you sleep out in the open all the year round, or would sleeping out condemn you to death this winter?'

Ask of a country: Can you sleep out in the open all the year round, winter after winter, or would sleeping out condemn you to death this winter?

In Scandinavia, for instance, you must have a roof over you every night, all

20 Heber Road, London NW2 6AA, UK (rhino@dial.pipex.com), 2001, 300pp, ISBN 0 948826 58 4

winter long. In the West Indies, by contrast, you can sleep out all the year round. Scandinavian welfare recipients must follow orders or die. They must have a fixed and solid address to stay, before dark sets in. Which means that the government has you where it wants you, where it can always find out and learn all about you.

In a warmer climate, the welfare bureaucrat can't make welfare recipients do what is wanted in exchange for their welfare payments. The bureaucrat can't even know for sure the recipients' names, addresses or work. It is much easier to lie to a government official if you don't live anywhere in particular.

Does the extreme cold of the Russian winter perhaps help to produce a collectivism so ingrained that 'freedom' is, for other than a few globetrotting aristocrats, so silly an idea as to be unthinkable?

'If climate does influence enthusiasm for liberty, then what of climate change?'

If climate does influence enthusiasm for liberty, then what of climate change? England, for instance, endured its fiercest winter since World War II in 1946/7, just when the modern welfare state was being so confidently built.

(A further conjecture is that geography – rivers, shapes of coastlines and so on – in other words what makes Sweden so different from other parts of Scandinavia – may also influence the freedom-lovingness or lack of it of different places.) Any responses to these conjectures would be welcome.

• *Brian Micklethwait, Libertarian Alliance, 25 Chapter Chambers, Esterbrooke Street, London SW1P 4NN, UK; e-mail: admin@libertarian.co.uk; web: www.libertarian.co.uk).*

Curing depression could help tackle poverty

Summarised from an article by Andrew Solomon, entitled 'A Cure for Poverty', in the New York Times (May 6th 2001).

For some people, the best first step in alleviating their poverty could be to cure their depression, rather than to provide economic aid or welfare packages. It is generally assumed that the mental health of people who are poor improves if their economic conditions improve beforehand – that if they gain employment and greater prosperity, then they will recover from any depression that plagues them. But it could be more effective to treat the depression first, and thus give people the chance to change their own lives.

This is the theory which is gaining greater credence in the US, as help groups and psychiatrists find that treating depression first can completely revitalise the lives of people below the poverty line. If their mental health is improved, their outlook, ambitions and attitude to life can change, and that is often far more important than any amount of benefits or financial support.

'The depression rate among the poor is higher than that of any other social group in the US'

The depression rate among the poor is higher than that of any other social group in the US and the same is very probably true in the rest of the world. It is equally true that the poor are the least likely to have their depression recognised by themselves or others. After all, if you become depressed and can't work, who's going to notice the difference? If you become even less happy with your lot, will anyone recognise the change or just assume you're going through the same as them? The depressed poor see themselves as completely helpless and, as a result, very rarely seek support or help of any kind. And reaching out for help implies that you have diagnosed the problem in the first place, which is not the case for the vast majority of those living in poverty. Actually having the problem given a label or a name is half the battle – for what can be identified can be contained or dealt with.

'Consider the savings on welfare if just 15 per cent could have their lives turned around by anti-depression treatment'

Small programmes, such as group therapy and outreach self-help centres, have begun to sprout up, offering help to the poor who are depressed, but more are needed to fully tackle the problem. A national screening scheme, focusing on those who receive welfare, could begin the identification process, and that could be backed up by therapy schemes and pharmaceutical programs. Quite apart from the human benefits, a huge amount of money could be saved: consider the savings on welfare if just 15 or 20 per cent of those affected could have their lives turned around by anti-depression treatment. And whilst no one is suggesting that it is the only answer, the simple policy of making people feel better about their lives so they live better could save far more than a few billion dollars. It could save thousands from the twinned traps of poverty and depression.

• *For the full article by Andrew Solomon, see: http://www.nytimes.com/2001/05/06/magazine/06POVERTY.html*

20 Heber Road, London NW2 6AA, UK (rhino@dial.pipex.com), 2001, 300pp, ISBN 0 948826 58 4

Miniature guide horses live longer than guide dogs

Summarised from an item by Julie Rawe, entitled 'Seeing-Eye Ponies', in Time magazine (January 29th 2001), monitored for the Global Ideas Bank by Roger Knights.

Guide dogs have become a familiar sight on our streets in the latter half of the 20th century, but they often pass away just when their owner has come to rely on them. This then necessitates another dog and another period of training. But that need no longer be the case with a new friendly animal to help the blind: the miniature horse. The horses, which are about two feet tall, have excellent night vision, a good memory, and are calm in the midst of crowds and heavy traffic. Most importantly, though, they have a life span of between 25 and 35 years which is significantly more than the average guide dog. Dan Shaw, who received the first guide horse in May 2001 (named Cuddles) in the US, believes this will be their main advantage: "Instead of going through three or four guide dogs in my lifetime, I get to stick with one animal."

'They were impressed by the animals' calm negotiation of traffic'

The non-profit Guide Horse Foundation was founded by Janet Burleson, a retired horse trainer, after she and her husband rode through New York and were incredibly impressed by the animals' calm negotiation of traffic. On their return home, the couple taught their 24 inch high horse (Twinkie) to lead a blind woman through a shopping mall. Ten other horses are now in training to be donated to the visually impaired. There are two slight differences between owning a guide dog and a guide horse, though. Firstly, backyards or gardens are very important, particularly when nature calls; and secondly, the horses wear special trainers to give them traction indoors.

• *For more information, see www.guidehorse.com*

Help-My-Neighbour Bank
Natalie D'Arbeloff

Summarised from a submission to the Global Ideas Bank.

My idea would be to set up a network to enable people anywhere, at any time, to donate small (or large) amounts of money to help, anonymously, any person or project in their community which they feel is deserving of help. This would initially take place via the Internet and, eventually, via physical structures to be placed in every town, neighbourhood and village all over the world (in some distinctive shape and colour, like for example letter boxes).

The donation could be merely spare cash that is in their pocket, or regular amounts they can spare every month, or a proportion of some profit they have just made. It would be totally up to the person concerned.

'The system would consist of only person-to-person help'

The system would need to operate independently of any organised charities or institutions or government bodies but consist only of person-to-person help. A database would first be created where any individual or small group within a community would submit a description of their specific cash need. This would be entered on the database and held in a public-access place such as local library or café, where anyone could consult it and choose the 'cause' they wish to help.

A reference number would then be given for each cause, to which the donation would be directed, without passing through any administrative bodies.

This idea would initially require much setting-up effort but could, once up and running, provide an incentive for everyone, of even the most modest means, to put to helpful-to-neighbour use those small sums of money that could make a great difference to someone and which would otherwise go to waste like food left on a plate.

• *Natalie D'Arbeloff (augustine@freeuk.com)*

Donating unused mobile phones for domestic violence victims

Summarised from information on the Wireless Foundation's website. This idea was monitored for the Global Ideas Bank by Roger Knights.

A not-for-profit organisation in the US is collecting unused and unwanted mobile phones to give to domestic violence victims. A mobile phone is one of the most powerful tools in the fight against domestic violence, providing as it does the means for abuse victims to get instant help and support. As part of the 'Donate-a-Phone' program, the phones are cleared and pre-programmed to dial 911, a hotline, or the number of a local domestic violence shelter. Free emergency airtime is donated by the Cellular Telecommunications and Internet Association, so no-one donating a phone pays for any calls at all.

20 Heber Road, London NW2 6AA, UK (rhino@dial.pipex.com), 2001, 300pp, ISBN 0 948826 58 4

'Inactive phones are put to use, combining the need to recycle with the impulse to help others'

It has been estimated that there are more than 24 million inactive phones in US, because of the rapid changes in technology. As new phones come on the market, with new WAP technology or some such advancement, users simply buy a new one and either throw their old phone away or store it somewhere. This scheme puts these old phones to better use, and combines the need to help others with the need to recycle. Even phones that no longer work can be donated, either to be repaired or to be sold off to raise funds for other domestic violence charities.

• *For more information, see www.donateaphone.com*

CRIME & THE LAW

Community administration of Brazilian prisons to break the cycle of criminality

Summarised from information sent to the Institute by Roberto da Silva, who is the founder of the scheme detailed below.

A project in Brazil which puts the community in charge of its local prison is hoping to transform the way criminals are treated in the country, and to radically alter its flawed prison system. The idea is based on communities running their local prisons and taking responsibility for each prisoner's rehabilitation and care. In this way, the state prison system can be circumvented, riddled as it is with maltreatment and corruption.

The 'Citizenship in the Jail' project consists of an architectural plan for 30 prisons, each designed to house 210 prisoners and to be called a 'Centre of Resocialisation'. Then, in each city where the prisons are being built, an association made up of people from the local community has been formed to administer their prison. Each local association has signed an agreement with the government, under which the locals are responsible for the administration of the prison, with the government providing the budget for each prisoner. The community association is then fully responsible for running the prison, including the provision of security, healthcare, education, work, food, and even a chaplain. In the prisons in the state of Sao Paulo, this model was experimented with in 1995, and the success of the scheme should lead to the construction of 15 prisons in 2001 and 15 more in 2002 if all goes as planned.

The scheme is the brainchild of Roberto da Silva who is also an advisory expert to the United Nations (Latin America Section) on the prevention of crime and the treatment of the criminal. He has become a human rights scholar and expert despite having spent 12 years of his life in care and a further six years in jail. Whilst in prison, he met many other adolescents from the care system who had had similar experiences to his own. Da Silva gradually came to believe that the internment of such young children in the draconian care system leads directly to criminal behaviour, and on his release he set out to prove this.

'36 per cent of them had become criminals, committing over 400 crimes between them'

Having studied a sample of 370 children who were his contemporaries in the state care system, he found that 36 per cent of them had become criminals, committing over 400 crimes (including 40 murders) between them. He found that at the root of their criminal behaviour was the government's system which interned children under the legal condition of 'moral abandonment' but only provided them with food and a place to live. Furthermore, the levels of education in the system were very poor, and children could often find themselves arbitrarily sent away for little more than minor mischief, only unsettling the child in question further. The government also never informed many of the children of their brothers and sisters who lived elsewhere in Brazil. Da Silva himself found two of his brothers through his own research, but they knew nothing of him nor of a long-since disappeared elder brother. As well as being kept in prison-like homes, the children were (and are) denied any sort of familial support.

Da Silva went on to pursue legal proceedings against the government, and published a thesis entitled 'The Formation of Criminal Identity in Orphan Children', arguing that the treatment of teenagers and children needs to be a priority if the level of crime in Brazil is to fall. This belief engendered the prison project, which places an emphasis on education and human rights for prisoners rather than just suspicion and punishment of them. The idea has already won a Social Enterprise award from the Ashoka-McKinsey Centre for Social Entrepreneurship, and with an agreement already signed with the state government of Sao Paulo, a full implementation is imminent.

- *For more information on the project, see Roberto da Silva's website (in Portuguese) at www.webtrade.com.br/histpresente or contact him at Roberto da Silva, Rua Tapes 57, Apt. 182 Liberdade, Sao Paulo, Brazil, Cep 01527-050.*
- *Details of the Ashoka-McKinsey Social Entrepreneurship Centre can be found at www.ashoka.org/fellows/global_net_center.cfm*

20 Heber Road, London NW2 6AA, UK (rhino@dial.pipex.com), 2001, 300pp, ISBN 0 948826 58 4

Pay earned in jail later given to non-recidivists only

Hans-Peter Voss

Adapted from an e-mail to the Global Ideas Bank. Hans-Peter Voss is a physicist and head of the Department of Academic Staff Development at the University of Applied Sciences Karlsruhe in Germany.

The work of criminals in jail should be adequately paid. The money or a certain major amount of it should be kept by the state and only be paid out over several years on condition that the former convict reintegrates into society and does not offend again during that period. If he or she does re-offend, he or she would lose the whole salary earned in prison (or at least some part of it)

'If the ex-convict does re-offend, they would lose the whole salary earned in prison'

The justice of this is easy to convey to those reconvicted in this way, because they will appreciate that a new offence creates new expenses for society.

The longer people have been inmates, the more money they will have accumulated and the stronger their desire will be not to fall back into crime. During their imprisonment the inmates can plan systematically (maybe with the support of mentors) for their time after jail and they know that thanks to the salary they have accumulated during their imprisonment, they have a fair chance of starting a legal business.

The incentive to develop an optimistic and constructive perspective on life will be very strong. Falling back into crime would mean to lose the fruits of years of hard work and would become extremely unattractive.

• *Hans-Peter Voss (e-mail: hans-peter.voss@fh-karlsruhe.de)*

Navajo peacemaking emphasises restitution not punishment

Summarised from an article by The Honourable Robert Yazzie, entitled 'Navajo justice', in YES! A Journal of Positive Futures (Fall 2000 Issue). For subscriptions, at $24/year, contact YES!, PO Box 10818, Bainbridge Island, WA 98110, USA (tel: 001 800/937-4451; e-mail: subs@futurenet.org; web: www.yesmagazine.org)

The Navajo Nation have begun an experiment in which peacemakers take the place of judges, prosecutors and prisons. In January 2000, the Navajo Nation Council changed their criminal code to eliminate jail time and fines for 79 offences, to require the use of peacemakers in all criminal cases and to require the courts to see to the rights of victims. They also incorporated the traditional Navajo concept of "nalyeeh" into the code, a word which refers to the process of confronting those who have hurt others with a demand that they talk things out. It is in this area that the peacemakers become involved.

'The accused might give a symbolic object as part of the restitution process'

In Navajo peacemaking, a session is held involving the person accused of an offence and the person who suffered from it. The relatives of the accused and the person hurt by the accused are also invited along. A community leader (or peacemaker) moderates the session, and the people talk about what happened and how they feel about it. Navajos believe that a harmful act is "something that gets in the way of living your life", and their method of peacemaking deals with such an act by identifying it, discussing it and thinking of a plan to deal with it. For example, the relatives of the accused might be asked to watch over their relative to be sure he does not reoffend, or the accused might be asked to give a symbolic object as part of the restitution process. Horses, for instance, are prized possessions of the Navajo people and they are a form of restitution for serious sexual insults. Such a symbol might mean anything from "I'm sorry" to "Let this be a symbol and something tangible to remind us that we have talked this hurt out and entered into good relations with each other."

'The Navajo Nation courts see 28,000 criminal cases every year, but have enough jail space for only 220 people'

This experiment could prove to be an invaluable one. The Navajo Nation courts see 28,000 criminal cases every year, but have enough jail space for only 220 people at any one time. By returning to a traditional method of justice that concentrates on the effects of a crime rather than how to punish its perpetrator, the Navajos could be offering a lesson to the rest of America and the western world. It is simply not viable to keep locking up a major part of the population, and peacemaking could be a way of reducing that prison population while letting the offenders see the effects of their crimes. Most importantly of all, perhaps, it puts the victim (or the person harmed by the crime) at the centre of the justice process.

20 Heber Road, London NW2 6AA, UK (rhino@dial.pipex.com), 2001, 300pp, ISBN 0 948826 58 4

Stopping crime through wanted ads on TV

Dennis Wright

Summarised from a submission to the Global Ideas Bank.

Crime has reached an all time high in America. One effective tool in preventing the rapists, the murderers and drug pushers from getting away with their deeds, is exposure on television. 'America's Most Wanted' and 'Justice Files' have not only proven effective but have helped to catch such people. If governments funded adverts on television, in an updated version of 'Wanted' posters from the Wild West, then the effect could be remarkable. And although the featured criminals would have to be limited for legal reasons, perhaps to those who are indisputably guilty or on the run, the power of television to bring results can never be underestimated.

• *Dennis Wright (www.bigbopper201@aol.com)*

Scientific research ideas to reduce eyewitness errors

Summarised from an article by Atul Gawande, entitled 'Under suspicion', in the New Yorker (January 8th 2001), monitored for the Global Ideas Bank by Roger Knights.

The elements that make up a police case have changed little over the years: the line-up identification, the alibi, the confession. Yet mistakes continue to be made, with wrongful convictions occurring due to eyewitness error, or to an innocent person not having a good enough alibi. There could be changes, though: the solution to these errors could lie with science, if only the legal establishment would allow it. For researchers working outside the legal profession have found that simple changes to procedures can substantially reduce misidentification. The proposed changes emerged from scientific experiments not from received convention. For example, the technique of showing the people in a line-up individually rather than all at once has been shown to reduce errors by over 50 per cent, but few police departments give the idea even cursory attention.

'Putting two suspects in one line-up greatly increases the incidence of errors'

Gary Wells, the leading figure in the US in the field of eyewitness research, has been conducting experiments and research in this area for over 20 years, but he continues to be marginalised by those who work in the business of justice. Other research by Wells and his colleagues found that many misidentifications occur because the witness is not told that the line-up may not contain the actual perpetrator of the crime. Research at the State University of New York discovered that the witness is substantially more likely to make a misidentification if they are not explicitly told of this possibility, probably because they feel they have to pick someone. Another police technique which was found to greatly increase the incidence of errors is putting two suspects in one line-up, something that is routine in many police departments.

Yet only a handful of people take notice of Wells' research, primarily a few police departments in Canada. Even when a report from the US Department of Justice stated that scientific evidence had established the superiority of the sequential line-ups, the selfsame report also stated that it had no preference between the traditional method or Wells' superior sequential one. The fact is that science is not trusted by the people who enforce the law: they prefer to rely on convention and precedent rather than experimentation and progress. But the scientists continue to research and make their results available, and Gary Wells for one is not giving up: he's now turning his attention to the alibi, and how reliable our memories are as to what we were doing at a certain time. Perhaps he'll be listened to this time.

Legal forms online cuts cost and paperwork

Summarised from a submission by Stephen Russell, from the SmartAgreements website (www.smartagreements.com) and from an entry in Brill's Content (July/August 2000). The latter item was monitored for the Global Ideas Bank by Roger Knights.

Stephen Russell's suggestion is that printable legal forms for such things as filing motions, planning court dates and for general court use should be available via the Internet. Thus, for small claims and the like, no lawyer would be needed, and working people could organise legal matters at any time of the day or night. The online resource could be extended to provide legal glossaries, a facility to e-mail forms to court, and perhaps even advice on how to proceed in different legal matters. Legal fees could be slashed, as could the huge amount of paperwork often involved in court proceedings. Lawyers could find work in online advice or putting together do-it-yourself law websites, or as consultants in planning such a system.

20 Heber Road, London NW2 6AA, UK (rhino@dial.pipex.com), 2001, 300pp, ISBN 0 948826 58 4

'Downloadable forms direct the user through the ins and outs of the issues involved'

One American firm has already had a similar idea, although its focus is on providing legal forms for the home user, rather than having any direct links to the court or its motions and proceedings. SmartAgreements.com have taken the do-it-yourself law idea into the technological age by offering downloadable forms that direct the user through the ins and outs of the issues involved. Each form costs a small fee to download, and has the obvious benefit of being delivered straight to your computer.

One such form is for a pre-nuptial agreement, an area of law that often involves substantial costs. The form is allied to a program (also downloadable) which takes the user through 54 individual decision points which change from green to red text as they are completed. And though the firm strongly advises some lawyer input, the form only costs $10, which could mean a great reduction in the cost if lawyers were doing everything for you from the start. The site also has forms covering many and varied aspects of law, from personal estate planning through to all aspects of business. Piles of paperwork and massive legal costs could be a thing of the past, especially as more sites begin to offer this type of service.

• *Stephen Russell (steveventure@yahoo.com)*

A textbook with legal advice for whistle-blowers

Summarised from a review by William Sanjour of Stephen Kohn's book, Concepts and Procedures in Whistleblower Law *(published by Quorum Books, 2001; ISBN 1-56720-354-X), in Rachel's Environment and Health News Issue 715 (January 4th 2001). To subscribe to Rachel's e-mail newsletter, e-mail listserv@rachel.org with the words SUBSCRIBE RACHEL-WEEKLY [YOUR NAME] in the message (or contact them at Environmental Research Foundation, PO Box 5036, Annapolis, MD 21403-7036, USA). This item was monitored for the Global Ideas Bank by Matthew Mezey.*

As corporations grow in their influence and power, governments are increasingly relying on voluntary compliance with laws from those corporations. As a result, the role of the whistle-blower is becoming more and more crucial in protecting the public against violations of the law. As recently shown by the film *The Insider*, a whistle-blower is someone in a corporation or firm who speaks out publicly against their employers' illegal practices, be they against public health or wasting public money. But the law in such cases can be something of a minefield, and that has prompted whistle-blower lawyer Steve Kohn to write his new book.

Kohn, who also founded the National Whistleblower Center in Washington, has written the book to aid lawyers and laymen to pick their way through the labyrinthine statutes and precedents that make up whistle-blower legislation. The book contains a great deal of advice, including, for instance, the importance of an employee keeping good records of their employment. This can later be used as evidence if a whistle-blowing disclosure leads to a transfer, termination, a demotion, a change in attitude or some other obvious change in the employee-employer relationship.

Far from the burden of proof being on the whistle-blower, it is the firm or corporation who must prove that they would have taken the same action against an employee even if they had not made their whistle-blowing disclosure. Furthermore, the action taken by the employer does not have to be sacking or firing – other adverse action can include blacklisting, a reassignment to a less prestigious position, or even a circulation of a bad-mouthing memo.

'Employees are under no duty to demonstrate the accuracy of their safety allegations'

It is also a misconception that the allegations made by the whistle-blower must necessarily be an actual breaking of the law. Kohn writes that the whistle-blower must be acting in 'good faith', and that "this 'good faith' belief must be based on 'reasonably perceived violations' of the applicable law or regulations. Employees are under no duty to demonstrate the underlying veracity or accuracy of their safety allegations." So the employee in question should not be overly concerned that they are alerting the authorities to an actual violation of the law, although obviously that would make a subsequent court case stronger.

The major pitfall for the whistle-blower in the US is the 30-day statute of limitations, which is a law specifying that anyone who feels that they have been wrongly treated following a disclosure must file a complaint within 30 days of the employer's action. The problem is that the moment when the employer starts acting differently is not always clearly definable, making that 30-day period a very short one. But with Steve Kohn's book and the assistance of a lawyer, the prospective whistle-blower may have far fewer fears about the process than previously.

 • *The National Whistleblower Centre's website is at www.whistleblowers.org/ index.html*

 • *For details of recent whistle-blowing cases, see www.oalj.dol.gov/libwhist.htm and www.hcn.org/servlets/hcn.Article?article_id=578*

20 Heber Road, London NW2 6AA, UK (rhino@dial.pipex.com), 2001, 300pp, ISBN 0 948826 58 4

Car labels invite police to pull them over if seen at strange hours

Summarised from an article by Linda Ashton, entitled 'Decal would let officers pull car over', in the Seattle Times (June 5th 2001), monitored for the Global Ideas Bank by Roger Knights.

A new scheme in Washington will allow car owners to put up registered permanent transfers on their windscreens which invite police to pull the car over if it is being driven in the early hours of the morning. The 'Watch Your Car' scheme is an anti-theft program funded by the US government, and it hopes to reduce the number of stolen cars in the city. Vehicle owners in the city are being encouraged to register with their local police force, stating that their car is very rarely used at certain hours of the late night and early morning. They then receive the 'Watch Your Car' official transfers for the front and rear of the vehicle. If police then see a car with the transfers (or 'decal', as it is know in the US) on it being driven between 1am and 5am, they can stop that car for no other reason than to verify that the right person is behind the wheel.

'Police have come across several kids sneaking out in the family car for a spin at night'

In a country where a car is stolen every 20 seconds, any such initiatives are welcome. In Washington alone, there were almost 35,000 cases of vehicle theft in the year 2000. Other regions have claimed to have reduced the number of cases by up to 50 per cent with similar schemes, although the success rate is always dependent on the number of people who volunteer to register their car. Some parents might find it doubly worth their while, because police have come across several cases of kids sneaking out at night and going for a spin in the family car without permission.

'Some states offer free etching of Vehicle Identification Numbers on car windows'

In addition to the decals or transfers, some states are also offering free etching on windows and windscreens of the Vehicle Identification Number (VIN) as a further disincentive to car thieves.

• *For more information on 'Watch Your Car' see, for example, www.state.ma.us/ccj/watch.htm*

Institute for Social Inventions, £15 subs, £17 from abroad by credit card, tel London 020 8208 2853

HEALTH & THERAPY

Health Tips of 2001 from recent medical research

The following is an update supplementing the far more comprehensive book published by the Institute for Social Inventions, entitled **1,001 Health Tips –** from recent medical research *(£7.14 inc p&p from www.globalideasbank.org/bookorder.html). These updates are summarised from literature and cuttings sent to the Institute by correspondents in the UK and the USA. Wherever the correspondent remembered to provide a date and source, this has also been included. The focus here is not on the latest drugs or treatments but on tips that empower the average person, enabling them to do something for themselves about staying healthy or about regaining their health.*

Food & diet

• **Occasional coffee-drinkers** may be more at risk from **heart disease** than habitual drinkers, due to the sudden strain on the heart. Roberto Corti, a Cardiologist at the University of Zurich, told the European Society of Cardiology conference in Amsterdam that non-habitual drinkers would do better to avoid coffee completely, even the decaffeinated varieties (the London Times, August 22nd 2000).

'Three large cups of coffee a day can significantly decrease the risk of getting Parkinson's disease'

• A study carried out by Hawaiian researchers and reported in the Journal of the American Medical Association, has shown that drinking about three large cups of **coffee** a day can significantly decrease the risk of getting **Parkinson's disease** (US News and World Report, June 5th 2000).

• **White tea** may be even more effective than green tea in preventing the cell mutations that can cause **cancer**, according to research carried out at Oregon State University (Simon Crompton in the London Times, August 1st 2000).

'Tea can stave off heart disease and cataracts, and may even help women conceive'

• **Tea** can not only stave off heart disease, cataracts, and even help women

20 Heber Road, London NW2 6AA, UK (rhino@dial.pipex.com), 2001, 300pp, ISBN 0 948826 58 4

conceive, it can also prevent **colon cancer**. Researchers in Britain and Italy have found that if rats are given extracts of black Assam tea – the equivalent of three or four cups a day – their guts are protected against the effects of a known carcinogen (New Scientist, October 2000).

• Substances called polyphenols present in unsweetened **black tea** make it effective in destroying cavity-causing bacteria or suppressing their growth, a US study has found. Christina Wu, of the University of Illinois, said: "It's going to stain your teeth, but it's good for **oral health**" (the London Metro, May 25th 2000).

'Chocolate contains double the quantity of antioxidants found in a glass of red wine'

• Research presented to the European Society of Cardiology confirms that **chocolate** is good for the heart. According to Dr Harold Schmitz, a nutrition expert from the University of California at Davis, a 40g block of dark chocolate contains double the quantity of **antioxidants** found in a glass of red wine. Antioxidants reduce the risk of blood clotting, protect against stress on the heart, and relax blood vessels (the London Times, August 22nd 2000).

• Alberto Bertelli and his colleagues at the Universities of Milan and Pisa studied the effect of tyrosol (also present in extra virgin olive oil and a known anti-inflammatory) on white blood cells and concluded that a glass and a half of **white wine** a day could help protect against autoimmune diseases such as **rheumatoid arthritis** (New Scientist, April 21st 2001).

'Honey protects against heart disease and cancer'

• Scientists at the University of Illinois who investigated seven varieties of **honey** made from different flowers, found that each contained antioxidant compounds which mop up dangerous free radicals, protecting against **heart disease and cancer** (the London Metro, June 25th 2001).

• Foods previously dismissed as unhealthy may actually have protective properties, according to researchers at Australia's science body, CSIRO. **Baked beans, white bread** and badly cooked pasta contain starch which releases chemicals in the intestine thought to prevent bowel cancer, while curry was found to contain high levels of anti-oxidants which combat cancer-causing free radicals (the London Metro, July 4th 2001).

• **Tomatoes** are not only rich in antioxidants: Professor Asim Dutta-Roy and colleagues at the Rowett Research Institute in Aberdeen have proven that they contain an ingredient – codenamed P3 – which reduces the **blood's tendency to clot** (the London Times, September 2000).

• Lycopene may have other benefits: researchers at the University of North

Carolina showed that it reduces the risk of **heart attacks**. And a study at Harvard Medical School discovered that eating more than two tomato products a week reduces the risk of prostate **cancer** by up to 34 per cent (New Scientist, 23rd December 2000).

'Lycopene, found in watermelons, grapes and tomatoes, may boost male fertility'

• Lycopene, found in **watermelons, grapes and tomatoes**, may boost male fertility, claim researchers at the All India Institute of Medical Sciences in New Delhi. An experiment involving 30 men diagnosed as infertile resulted in six of their partners falling pregnant (the London Metro, January 2001).

• Researchers studying the effects of **tomato juice** and vitamins C and E on **LDL oxidation** found that commercial tomato juice increased plasma lycopene levels and boosted LDL resistance to oxidation almost as effectively as a high dose of vitamin E (Upritchard, Sutherland and Mann, Department of Human Nutrition, University of Otago, Dunedin, New Zealand, published in Positive Health, March 2001).

'Tomato products can reduce the risk of breast, pancreas, prostate and intestine cancer'

• A team led by Betty Schwartz, a biochemist at the Hebrew University of Jerusalem, found that lycopene – the pigment that makes **tomatoes** red – may destroy **cancers** in the mouth. Peter Bramley of Royal Holloway, London, believes this contributes to a growing body of evidence (see above also) that lycopene in the diet can reduce the risk of breast, pancreas, prostate and intestine cancer and recommends eating tomato products which also have some fat content, such as ketchup and tomato pizza toppings.

• Men whose diets include 1.8 mcg of **boron** daily have a 62 per cent lower risk of developing **prostrate cancer** than men who consume half the amount, a recent US study indicates. Boron is found in nuts, wine, fruit and vegetables, and especially in prunes, grapes and avocado (Time, April 16th 2001).

'Brazil nuts, kidney beans, liver and shellfish are all mood-enhancing foods'

• Recent studies have shown that a diet low in **selenium** may have a negative effect on mood, and even cause depression, according to Margaret Rayman, of the Centre for Nutrition and Food Safety at the University of Surrey Selenium rich, and consequently mood-enhancing foods, include **brazil nuts, kidney, liver and shellfish** (the London Times, May 22nd 2001).

• Evidence would suggest that lutein and zeaxanthin, which are members

20 Heber Road, London NW2 6AA, UK (rhino@dial.pipex.com), 2001, 300pp, ISBN 0 948826 58 4

of the carotenoid family, might be important in maintaining **eye health** and preventing cataract formation; the are chiefly found in **kale, spinach, broccoli** and collard greens. However, Professor Alan Bird, of Moorfields Hospital in London, advises against eating only dark green leafy vegetables. Cataracts, caused by free radicals, may be prevented by eating highly coloured fruit and vegetables, such as **cantaloupes, carrots, blackberries and cherries**, while damage may also be inflicted by **smoking and sunlight** exposure.

'Blueberries are especially beneficial to younger persons who risk eye damage'

Studies have concluded that long-term intake of **vitamin C** supplements, sometimes combined with **vitamin E**, may reduce cataract risk. Bilberries (or European **blueberries**) are also gaining recognition for their importance in eye health. Alison Johnson, a nutritional therapist at Bioforce, claims they work if used continuously for more than two months. They are especially beneficial to younger persons who risk eye damage due to long hours spent driving or staring at a computer screen. A high-sugar diet is also known to adversely affect eye health (Suzannah Olivier, *A Diet for Your Eyes*, the London Times, May 22nd 2001).

• A new study led by Amy Howell, a research scientist at the Rutgers University Blueberry and Cranberry Research Center, has discovered that both **blueberries** and **cranberries** contain condensed tannins which make them effective in preventing urinary tract infections. A daily ten-ounce glass of cranberry juice or a fistful of blueberries is recommended for women with recurrent **urinary tract infections** (US News and World Report, October 19th 2000).

'Cranberry juice may prevent oral infections, gingivitis and gum disease'

• Research has found that the anti-bacterial property in **cranberry** juice may prevent oral infections, gingivitis and periodontal **gum disease** (the London Times, October 9th 2000).

• All varieties of **winter squash** are low in cholesterol and fat and high in potassium, vitamin C and the antioxidant vitamin A, thereby fortifying the immune system against winter **colds** (Catherine S. Gregory in New Age, November 2000).

• Researchers report that eating **beans** four times a week can reduce the incidence of **heart disease**, including heart attack, by 20 per cent. The findings, reported by the American Heart Association, claim any legume, even peas, peanuts and soy, are effective in lowering cholesterol and blood pressure (Time, March 13th 2000, monitored for the Institute by Roger Knights).

- A trial on buddhist monks has shown that vegetarians have a level of salicylic acid in the blood 12-fold higher than meat-eaters. **Salicylic acid** is a component of aspirin considered protective against **heart disease and cancers**, and abounds in fruit, vegetables, herbs and spices. John Paterson of the Dumfries and Galloway Royal Infirmary believes these results may indicate why vegetarians are generally less susceptible to these diseases (New Scientist, July 7th 2001).

'Folic acid supplements are an effective way of minimising risk of coronary heart disease'

- A recent study from the University of Otago in New Zealand suggests that eating **folic-acid-enriched cereal** could lower the risk of **coronary heart disease** (CAD) by up to 30 to 40 per cent amongst those in the high-risk category. The results showed that eating fortified cereals and taking folic acid supplements are the most effective ways of minimising risk of CAD (New Age magazine, October 2000).
- An English study reports that it may take about twice the current US Dietary Reference Intake of **folic acid** – eg 0.8 mg a day – to ward off a **heart attack** (Time, November 27th 2000, monitored for the Institute by Roger Knights).
- Curcumin, found in the spice **turmeric**, has been proven by J. L. Arbiser and colleagues at the Department of Dermatology, Harvard Medical School, Boston, to inhibit the progression of chemically-induced **colon and skin cancers** (Positive Health, October 2000).

'Cinnamon could significantly help people with type II diabetes'

- Taking between a quarter and a full teaspoon of **cinnamon** every day could significantly help people with type II, or non-insulin dependent **diabetes**. Researchers at the Agricultural Research Unit in Maryland, USA, found that cinnamon recovers the ability of fat cells in diabetics to respond to insulin and may even help prevent the onset of the disease (the London Metro, August 10th 2000). However:
- An article published in Gezond, a health and food newsletter published by the Dutch Consumer Organisation in The Hague, claims **cinnamon** has been found to contain coumarin, a recognised **carcinogen** and genotoxic agent in animal studies (New Scientist, September 2nd 2000).
- Eating a **high-fat diet** when young increases the risk of **Alzheimer's disease** by up to 30 times, researchers informed a congress in Washington. For those with an identifiable genetic marker, the risks are seven times higher (the London Times, July 12th 2000).

20 Heber Road, London NW2 6AA, UK (rhino@dial.pipex.com), 2001, 300pp, ISBN 0 948826 58 4

- A **reduced-calorie diet** may be instrumental in warding off the onset of age-related neurological diseases such as **Alzheimer's** and Parkinson's, according to Dr Brian Merry and colleagues at Liverpool University. Research suggests that a low-calorie diet slows the metabolism and thereby reduces the transmission of free radicals, highly reactive molecules known to cause cell damage (the London Times, July 13th 2000).

- Canadian scientists believe eating a **high-fat diet** may impair **memory**. In their trial on rats given a diet in which 40 per cent of their calories came from fat, equivalent to the proportion of fat calories in many adolescents' diets, the rats demonstrated critical impairment in memory tests. Gordon Winocur and Carol Greenwood of the Baycrest Centre for Geriatric Care in Toronto believe developing neural pathways may be permanently damaged by a high-fat diet during adolescence (New Scientist, March 3rd 2001).

'High-protein diets increase the risk of osteoporosis four-fold'

- Scientists at the University of California in San Francisco have discovered that **high-protein diets** increase the risk of **osteoporosis** four-fold. The acid produced by high-protein diets leads to the stripping of the essential minerals calcium carbonate and calcium phosphate from bones. This causes the thinning of bone tissue, which results in increased brittleness. The research suggests that older women, the highest risk group for the disease, should seriously consider replacing some of their meat intake with fruits and vegetable and cheese with yoghurt and milk. Foods such as spinach, apricots and bananas are helpful (the London Times, November 2000).

- A **high-fibre diet**, long recommended as a preventative measure against **bowel cancer**, may actually increase the risk of developing the disease, according to research conducted by the European Cancer Prevention Organisation. However, Dr Tim Key, a nutrition specialist with the Imperial Cancer Research Fund, suggested that the high-fibre beverage used in the trials was not necessarily identical with natural dietary fibre, and that natural fibre in the diet should not therefore be regarded as harmful (the London Times, October 14th 2000).

- Recent findings support belief in the protective role of **carbohydrate** and **beta-carotene** intake against **colorectal cancer**. Breuer-Katschinski and colleagues at the Department of Gastroenterology, University Hospital Essen, Germany, also found high **meat** consumption linked to an increased risk of colorectal cancer (Positive Health, July 2001).

- **Soy** can cause **low thyroid activity**, of which weight gain, hair loss, depression and water retention are all symptoms, reports the People's Pharmacy (the London Times, September 10th 2000).

- Taking a high dose of an **isolated vitamin** may prevent the absorption of another vitamin or mineral in the body, leading to other symptoms of **deficiency** (the London Times, July 18th 2000).

• Boosting your intake of **vitamin E** – found in dark-green leafy vegetables, wheat germ, almonds and whole grains – can lower the risk of miscarriage in the early weeks of pregnancy, claim Britain scientists, while researchers in Chicago found that it reduced cognitive decline in the elderly. Australian scientists also claim the vitamin is able to improve blood flow in patients with Type 1 diabetes (Catherine S. Gregory in New Age, November 2000)

• The American Cancer Society reports that large doses of **vitamin C** may be detrimental to **cancer treatment** and warns patients to avoid doses of 1gm or more daily. Many cancer therapies work by releasing free radicals that damage cancerous (and healthy) cells; vitamin C devours free radicals, thereby counteracting the effectiveness of the treatment (Janice M. Horowitz, reporting in Time, April 10th 2000).

• Research teams at Leicester and Pennsylvania Universities in the US have found that large doses of **vitamin C** can damage DNA, potentially increasing the risk of **cancer and rheumatoid arthritis**. Dr Astley, who commented on the findings, said that one should be able to absorb the necessary vitamins from a balanced diet, and this is infinitely healthier (the Independent, June 21st 2001).

• On the other hand, **vitamin C** reduces the **risk of stroke**, say scientists at the Tokyo Medical and Dental University. "The risk of stroke was 70 per cent higher amongst those in the lowest vitamin quarter than those in the highest", said Dr Tetsuji. Among those who ate fruit and vegetables six days a week the risk of stroke was 58 per cent lower than among those who ate them twice a week (The UK Week, October 14th 2000).

• Boosting your intake of **plasma vitamin C** reduces the risk of developing **diabetes**, conclude Sargeant and colleagues at the Department of Community Medicine, University of Cambridge (Positive Health, March 2001).

'Low levels of folate and vitamin B12 make dementia twice as likely'

• In an investigation of 370 randomly-selected elderly persons, Swedish researchers discovered that those with the lowest levels of **folate and vitamin B12** in the blood were twice as likely to develop symptoms of **dementia** after three years as those with normal levels. Folate abounds in leafy greens, orange juice and fortified cereals, while vitamin B12 is found in fish, meat and dairy products. Elderly people may sometimes require injections to boost their blood levels to those attained by younger adults (Newsweek, May 21st 2001).

• Foods rich in **live bacteria** may help to counter the effects of **stress**, poor diet, alcohol or antibiotics, all of which upset the balance of intestinal flora in the gut. Susanna Cunningham-Rundles and colleagues at Cornell Universi-

20 Heber Road, London NW2 6AA, UK (rhino@dial.pipex.com), 2001, 300pp, ISBN 0 948826 58 4

ty's Weill Medical School in America, recommend, however, that the average healthy person take probiotic supplements only when under particular strain (the London Times, October 3rd 2000).

• A study in which American children with AIDS were given a daily course of **probiotic bacteria** has lent weight to the belief that the bacteria can significantly boost the **immune system**. Susanna Cunningham-Rundles, of Cornell University's Weill Medical School in America, who led the study, found that the children gained weight and their yeast infections cleared (New Scientist July 8th 2000).

'People whose diets are rich in refined carbohydrates, such as processed foods, sugar, cakes and biscuits, had a lower IQ'

• Research from the Massachusetts Institute of Technology in the US has shown that people whose diets are rich in **refined carbohydrates**, such as processed foods, sugar, cakes and biscuits, had a **lower IQ** than those who ate more healthily. The difference between the scores of the high and low sugar-eaters in their study was almost 25 per cent (Best of Health, December 2000).

• Neuroscientists from the University of New Mexico in Albuquerque have found that higher concentrations of the chemicals **N-acetylaspartate (NAA) and choline** in the brain are linked to **higher IQ**. You can increase your intake of choline by sprinkling some lecithin granules on your cereal in the morning, while research has shown that upping your intake of B-complex vitamins – particularly pantothenic acid – can increase the production of NAA (Best of Health, December 2000).

• Paul Knekt and colleagues at the National Public Health Institute, Helsinki, found evidence in their research to suggest that the consumption of **apples** is related to a decreased risk of **thrombotic stroke** (Positive Health, October 2000).

'Eating a single piece of fruit daily could cut the risk of death in middle age by a fifth'

• Eating a single piece of **fruit** daily could cut the risk of death in middle age by a fifth, new research from Cambridge University indicates. The effect on **heart disease** was the most dramatic, but effects on cancer were also significant (the London Times, March 2nd 2001).

• Research at Wolverhampton University claims that **garlic** powder can kill the bacteria that cause **stomach ulcers**, while a study conducted by Pennsylvania State University, USA, shows that the sulphurous compounds in garlic can not only suppress tumours, but help to prevent **cancer** (the London Times, July 11th 2000).

'Garlic can help prevent the growth of cancerous cells'

• A protein called **lectin**, extracted from **garlic**, inhibits the growth of **cancerous cells** while leaving healthy cells unharmed, according to a discovery made by Yuji Karasaki and colleagues at the University of Occupational and Environmental Health in Kitakyushu (New Scientist, March 2001).

• A recent study conducted by The **Garlic** Centre in which 72 volunteers took one Allimax capsule (with active ingredient allicin) daily whilst the other 72 took a placebo, found that the placebo group had almost three times the number of **colds** over a three month period and took longer to recover from each cold than those taking Allimax (Positive Health, May 2001).

• Deficiencies of **omega-3s** in the diet could be a contributing factor to **depression**, according to Andrew Stoll, a Boston psychiatrist. When he supplemented the medications of 30 bipolar patients with ten grams of omega-3s, their improvement compared to the placebo group was remarkable, while causing virtually no side effects.

'Oily fish such as anchovies, mackerel and salmon proved a powerful adjunct to Prozac'

Dr Josepph Hibbeln, a National Institute of Health psychiatrist, suggests the evidence may explain why heart disease and depression often occur together. Though many factors play a part in modifying mood, and omega-3s are unlikely to replace standard treatments such as Prozac, they may be a powerful adjunct, and at least contribute to a healthy heart. Oily fish such as anchovies, mackerel and salmon, as well as flaxweed, wheat germ, walnuts and spinach are all rich sources of omega-3 (Newsweek, April 23rd 2001, monitored for the Institute by Roger Knights).

• **Fish oils** are vital in maintaining **cardiovascular and mental health**, says Professor Michael Crawford, of the Institute of Brain Chemistry and Human Nutrition at the University of North London. They may also be instrumental in the prevention of **cancers**, including breast, prostrate and colon cancers, whilst suppressing tumour growth if cancer does occur, claims Professor Steven Hays who heads the breast clinic at Aberdeen Royal Infirmary. Nutritionalists advocate eating three meals of oil-rich seafood a week for optimum health (the London Times, January 16th 2001).

• The presence of essential fatty acids (known as omega-3s) in **cod liver oil** make it highly effective in the prevention and treatment of **arthritis**, according to research by Bruce Caterson of Cardiff University. Additional studies have shown cod liver oil to be important in treating heart disease, kidney failure and even schizophrenia and depression (Financial Times, September 2000).

20 Heber Road, London NW2 6AA, UK (rhino@dial.pipex.com), 2001, 300pp, ISBN 0 948826 58 4

'The pain caused by osteoarthritis may be significantly eased by glucosamine'

• The pain caused by **osteoarthritis** may be significantly eased by the natural chemical, **glucosamine**, while the latest Belgian study found that it also slowed cartilage deterioration. Other complementary therapies include the use of Devil's Claw, bromelain and stinging nettle (the London Times, April 24th 2001).

• A **snack** and a **soft drink** before a flight can cut the risk of **economy class syndrome** and other circulatory problems by raising the volume of blood circulating in the body, thereby preventing heart attacks, fainting and deep-vein thrombosis, all of which have been linked to long-distance air travel, say cardiologists from the Saitama Medical School in Japan (the London Times, November 16th 2000).

'Broccoli sprouts are a rich source of Sulforaphane, which boosts the responsiveness of immune organs'

• **Broccoli sprouts** are a rich source of Sulforaphane, which boosts the responsiveness of immune organs; it functions as the most powerful antioxidant, with longer-lasting effects than any other antioxidant. Tony Talalay, M.D., professor of pharmacology at John Hopkins University School of Medicine and leader of the research, claims "sulforaphane may help the body to disarm **cancer**-causing agents at an early stage". Sulforaphane is present in kale, cabbage and broccoli, with the highest level occurring in broccoli sprouts (Best of Health, February 2001).

'Drinking whipped blender drinks helps one to feel fuller and so guards against overeating'

• Incorporating more **air in**to your **food** – by eating air-popped popcorn, puffed cereals, or drinking whipped blender drinks – can help one to feel fuller on fewer calories and so guard against **overeating**, says Dr Barbara Rolls, who led the Penn State research (New Age, January 2001, monitored for the Institute by Roger Knights).

• Drinking **excessive water** can be dangerous because it dilutes the minerals, including sodium, that the body requires to balance its fluids, says Susan Clark in the Sunday Times; in extreme cases it can cause heart attacks. Unless you consume sufficient salt, drinking water is ineffective, as the cells lose their fluids if sodium levels are too low. Dr Peter Mansfield of the Good Healthkeeping organisation, recommends people take in the equivalent of a teaspoon of **salt** each day, so that the extra fluids they are drinking really make a difference (The UK Week, November 25th 2000).

• The effects of **lutein supplementation** on visual acuity and subjective visual disturbances in **retinitis pigmentosa (RP)** has been researched at John Hopkins University School of Medicine, Baltimore, USA. Their results indicate short term vision improvements in individuals suffering from RP, especially those with blue eyes (Positive Health, March 2001).

• Wasabi, the fiery green horseradish paste used in **sushi** and sashimi, contains isothioccyanates which help to prevent **tooth decay** by retarding the growth of plaque bacteria, a new study indicates. Hideki Masuda research director at Ogawa & Co in Chiba, Japan, says "eating sushi will help the teeth". Cabbage and broccoli, which also contain isothioccyanates, may likewise be tooth-friendly (New Scientist, December 23rd 2000).

Men

• The **husbands of women who work full-time** may risk a reduction of up to 25 per cent in their chances of being in **good health**, according to a recent survey conducted by Ross Stolzenberg of the University of Chicago. This has been attributed to a lack of 'health nagging' by the woman (whose own health, incidentally, remained the same whether working or not), but other factors to blame include the woman's lack of time for organising social events with friends and family (New Scientist, September 9th 2000).

> ### 'The husbands of women who work full-time may risk a reduction of up to 25 per cent in their chances of being in good health'

• **Cannabis** may slow down **sperm**, helping to explain low fertility rates among men who smoke marijuana, claims Herbert Schuel of the State University of New York at Buffalo. In the study, low levels of a chemical similar to that found in cannabis caused increased rapidity in sperm activity, while high levels caused sluggishness in the sperm and inhibited their ability to bind to the egg (New Scientist, December 23rd 2000).

• Research has found that regular **jogging** and other vigorous exercise helps to prolong life and wards off **impotence** in men. The Massachusetts Male Ageing Study concluded that men who did the equivalent of a two-mile brisk walk a day were three times less likely to become impotent (the London Times, September 8th 2000).

• A recent study claims that **short bursts of exercise** can be just as beneficial to men at risk from heart disease as a more arduous and lengthy session, as long as the total amount of exercise is the same. The research, carried out at the Harvard School of Public Health and led by the epidemiologist, Howard

20 Heber Road, London NW2 6AA, UK (rhino@dial.pipex.com), 2001, 300pp, ISBN 0 948826 58 4

Sesso, indicated that physical activity need last no longer than 15 minutes to reduce the risk of **heart disease** (the London Times, August 22nd 2000).

Women

• Isoflavones – chemicals present in **soya** – may be toxic and could lead to **breast cancer**, brain damage in men and abnormalities in babies, according to senior scientists at the US Food and Drug Administration (the London Metro, August 14th 2000).

• **Sage** is a natural remedy long known as effective in treating both **hot flushes** and night sweats due to its anhidrotic (sweat-reducing) properties (the London Times, July 25th 2000).

'Abortion could increase the risk of developing breast cancer by up to 30 per cent'

• A survey completed by Professor Joel Brind, of the University of New York, indicates that having an **abortion** could increase the chance of developing **breast cancer** by as much as 30 per cent (the London Times, August 14th 2000).

• **Eating less** and taking more **exercise** could reduce a woman's risk of **developing breast cancer**, according to research carried out by Grazyna Jasienska of Jagiellonian University in Cracow, and Inger Thune of Norway's Tromso University (the London Times, March 9th 2001).

• **Women smokers** are **twice as likely to develop lung cancer** as men who smoke the same number of cigarettes (due to difference in lung tissue and the presence of the hormone oestrogen), claims Diane Stover, head of the lung unit at Sloan-Kettering Cancer Center in New York (the London Times, May 22nd 2001).

'Ecstasy encourages the body to retain water and lowers sodium levels to a critical level'

• **Young women** – in fact, any women of reproductive age who are still menstruating – have a much higher risk of dying from taking **Ecstasy** than any other group, according to a recent study led by Mary Forsling, Professor of Neuroendocrinology at King's College, London. When broken down, Ecstasy stimulates the release of vasopressin, a hormone which encourages the body to retain water and lowers the sodium levels in the body to a critical level; drinking a lot of water further exacerbates the condition. Professor Forsling stressed that the drug was highly unpredictable, because a number of factors peculiar to each individual determines one's response to the drug: "the consequences could be fatal" (the London Times, November 20th 2000).

- The rising **age of mothers** may go some way towards explaining the increase in **diabetes**, according to Edwin Gale and colleagues, at the University of Bristol. They found that a mother over 45 was more than three times as likely to have a child with diabetes as those under 20, and that for every five years in age, the chance of the mother's child developing diabetes increased by 25 per cent (the London Times, August 11th 2000).
- **Hormone Replacement Therapy** (HRT) may keep ageing womens' **memory** in good shape. Elizabeth Hampson at the University of Western Ontario tested the memories of 96 menopausal women and found that those taking oestrogen performed significantly better on verbal and spatial tasks (New Scientist, January 6th 2001).
- Although **asthma** is not common in postmenopausal women, a new study documented in Time magazine reveals that those who take **HRT** increase their risk of developing the illness by 60 per cent (Time, November 6th 2000).

'Oestrogen could prove beneficial in helping people with schizophrenia'

- The female sex hormone **oestrogen** could prove beneficial in helping people with **schizophrenia** recover from psychotic episodes, according to a preliminary study by Jayaashri Kulkarni, a psychiatrist at the Dendenong Psychiatry Research Centre in Melbourne (New Scientist, March 3rd 2001).
- A study of women over 65 has found that even a little physical activity such as **walking** protects against loss of **mental function**. Kristine Yaffe and her colleagues from the University of California discovered that a quarter of the least active women observed suffered cognitive decline (New Scientist, May 12th 2001).
- In a study of men and women with **bladder cancer**, Ronald Ross and colleagues at the University of Southern California School of Medicine, Los Angeles, discovered a threefold increase of risk among women who used **permanent hair dyes** regularly for 15 years or more; temporary or semi-permanent dyes were found to pose no risk (New Scientist, March 2001).

'The contraceptive pill may interfere with a woman's ability to select a suitable mate'

- Research has revealed that where women usually sniff out mates with genes for immunity that differ from their own, thereby increasing their chances of healthy offspring, those on the **contraceptive pill** unknowingly select men whose genes for immunity are closest to their own. The study, by Claus Wedekind, a Swiss scientist from the University of Bern, indicates that the pill may interfere with a woman's ability to select a suitable mate (New Scientist, February 10th, 2001).

20 Heber Road, London NW2 6AA, UK (rhino@dial.pipex.com), 2001, 300pp, ISBN 0 948826 58 4

'Agnus castus fruit – the fruit of the chaste tree – has proved effective in the relief of pre-menstrual symptoms'

• Dry extract of **agnus castus fruit**, better known as 'the fruit of the chaste tree', has been shown to be effective in the relief of **pre-menstrual symptoms**. Rued Schellenberg from the Institute of Care and Science in Frankfurt, found that women taking the extract over three months suffered less from mood swings, sore breasts and headaches than the control group (http://news.bbc.co.uk, January 19th 2001).

• The anti-depressant **Prozac** has been proved effective in the treatment of severe pre-menstrual symptoms. The study, led by Dr Meir Steiner at McMaster University, St Joseph's Hospital, Hamilton, gave half the women sufferers 20mg or 60mg of Prozac and the other half a placebo. The former group reported a 30 per cent improvement in mood and physical symptoms including tension, depression, tender breasts, bloating, and muscle and joint pain, compared with improvements of less than ten per cent amongst the placebo group (the London Independent, June 21st 2001).

Conception, pregnancy & birth

• Recent research suggests that **vegetarian mothers** are more likely to give birth to **girls**. Pauline Hudson, a pregnancy expert at the University of Nottingham, also found that vegetarian mothers had a significantly lower risk of giving birth to premature, underweight, or stillborn babies. High magnesium, potassium and calcium levels were also shown to have an effect on gender, producing more boys, although there is no evidence to suggest that a vegetarian diet is deficient in these elements (the London Times, August 7th 2000).

• In addition to the research at the University of Nottingham, a study carried out at Bristol University last year found that **vegetarians** were five times as likely to give birth to boys with a rare **genital deformity** called hypospadias (Helen Rumbelow in the London Times, August 7th 2000).

'Ginger is effective in treating sickness in pregnancy'

• An investigation has found **ginger** to be effective in the treatment of **nausea** and **vomiting** during pregnancy. Vutyavanich and colleagues of the Department of Obstetrics and Gynaecology at Chiang Mai University, Thailand, treated the women with one gram of oral ginger a day. 28 of the 32 treated experienced a significant improvement in their symptoms, while no adverse effects were detected (Positive Health, July 2001)

- **Nursing mothers** with family members who suffer nut allergies should avoid eating **nuts** altogether during the breast-feeding months, as peanut protein in the milk can sensitise susceptible babies to peanut allergens, potentially triggering a peanut allergy later in life, caution doctors. Mothers should beware of the peanut protein hidden in tomato sauce, chilli con carne and Chinese takeaways (Time, April 16th 2000).

'Aromatherapy can relax mothers and render them better able to control labour pains'

- A study has discovered that those mothers whose **weight** was normal prior to pregnancy and who gained more than the recommended 25lbs to 35lbs, were twice as likely to fail at **breastfeeding** (Time, April 16th 2001).
- Women with **older partners** are significantly **less likely to conceive** in less than six or 12 months, according to the Avon Longitudinal Study of Pregnancy and Childhood (the London Times, August 1st 2000).
- 'The Use of **Aromatherapy** in Intrapartum Midwifery Practice' (published by Oxford Brookes University), the result of an eight year study involving more than 8,000 mothers who gave birth in Oxford between 1990 and 1998, reveals that aromatherapy can relax mothers and render them better able to control pain. Compared with the women who did not have aromatherapy during labour, fewer women ended up with emergency Caesarean sections or had their labours stimulated because contractions were weak. 88 per cent of women who had aromatherapy rated it most effective in transition, the stage when contractions are almost continuous (the London Independent, October 21st 2000).

'Painkillers given to women during labour increase five-fold the likelihood of the child growing up to be a drug user'

- **Painkillers** given to women during labour increase five-fold the likelihood of the child growing up to be a drug user. New research undertaken at Gothenburg University suggests that exposure in the womb to high-dose medication may be an important and preventable risk factor for later **substance abuse** (the London Metro, October 19th 2000).
- **Analgesics** taken during labour may numb the baby, preventing them from feeding normally and consequently impeding the release of a hormone which facilitates **bonding** between mother and baby, says Anna-Berit Ransjo-Arvidson of the Karolinska Institute in Stockholm (New Scientist, March 31st 2001).

20 Heber Road, London NW2 6AA, UK (rhino@dial.pipex.com), 2001, 300pp, ISBN 0 948826 58 4

'A bacterial infection common among adults but rare in British babies may be the major cause of cot death'

• A study by Dr Jonathan Kerr and colleagues at Manchester Royal Infirmary found evidence that a **bacterial infection** common among adults but rare in British babies may the major cause of **cot death** or Sudden Infant Death Syndrome. 28 of the 32 babies examined showed signs of infection with Heliobacter pylori (H pylori) a gut bacteria linked to ulcers, stomach cancer and heart disease in adults, and which would induce vomiting and ammonia poisoning in babies. The theory is compatible with other known risk factors, as babies who sleep on their fronts are more likely to inhale their vomit, while mothers who smoke are more susceptible to contracting the H pylori infection (the London Times, October 24th 2000).

• Babies that become too warm are at risk of **Sudden Infant Death Syndrome**. The Foundations for the Study of Infant Deaths advises parents to keep a thermometer in a baby's room to ensure the correct room temperature of between 16C and 20C (60F-70F) is maintained. Dr Levene warned that parents should also be cautious about **overheating** on buses and in shops. Further advice includes the use of lightweight sheets and layered bedclothing (instead of duvets), which should be tucked in, and sleeping the baby with its feet to the foot of the cot. Touching a baby's tummy is a good way of assessing temperature (the London Times, November 23rd 2000).

'Babies whose mothers do not sing to them could suffer from an inability to communicate emotion effectively'

• Babies whose mothers do not sing to them could suffer from an inability to **communicate** emotion effectively, claim Dr Marwick and colleagues at the University of Edinburgh. As the most expressive form of language, **song** accelerates the process of recognising voice pitch, and teaches a child self-expression (the London Times, August 7th 2000).

• The health-giving effects of **lactobacillus** – the bacteria found in live yoghurt cultures – on the gut microflora are generally well known. However, The Lancet recently carried a report of research proving that when taken by pregnant women who had a close relative or partner with **allergies**, lactobacillus reduced by 50 per cent the incidence of eczema, rhinitis (runny nose) and asthma in their children (the London Times, April 16th, 2001).

• Mothers who take **ecstasy** during pregnancy risk producing children who suffer considerable **impairment** of basic learning processes, a trial on rats led by Charles Vorhees at the University of Cincinnati College of Medicine has indicated (the London Times, January 2001).

'The children of mothers who ate oily fish achieved significantly higher scores in brain development'

- The children of mothers who ate **oily fish** – such as sardines or mackerel – once a fortnight during pregnancy achieved significantly higher scores in **brain development** tests than the children of women who went without. Cathy Williams, who undertook the study at the University of Bristol, claimed even occasional fish eating made all the difference (New Scientist, February 10th 2001).

- The dangers of smoking during **pregnancy** have long been established, but the implications of **passive smoking** may be more serious than one imagines. Researchers at the Nordic School of Public Health in Gothenburg, Sweden, measured the levels of nicotine in the hair of non-smoking mothers who had recently given birth. Jouni Jaakkola and colleagues found that those with the highest levels were six times as likely to give birth more than three weeks prematurely (New Scientist, June 23rd 2001).

Children

- A growing number of parents are refusing to get their children vaccinated against **measles**, with an increased risk of epidemic. Research by the World Health Organisation shows that the population can be protected only if 95 per cent of children are vaccinated (the London Times, August 10th 2000).

- Children due for **vaccinations** might benefit from a drink containing the live bacterium Lactobacillus plantarum 299v, as it could reduce susceptibility to infection, advises Susanna Cunningham-Rundles, of Cornell University's Weill Medical School in America (the London Times, October 3rd 2000).

'A germ-free childhood could expose children to a higher risk of cancer'

- Research carried out by a team from cancer institutes and universities in Italy have found that a **germ-free childhood** in a small family could expose children to a higher than average risk of **cancer.** The study found that young children in a family are less likely to have allergy problems than older siblings, as it is believed they are exposed to more bugs and consequently develop an immune system less sensitive to allergens (the Sunday Times, November 19th 2000).

- Tests carried out by AA in conjunction with the German motoring

20 Heber Road, London NW2 6AA, UK (rhino@dial.pipex.com), 2001, 300pp, ISBN 0 948826 58 4

organisation ADAC reveal that 15 out of 17 **child safety seats** tested were unsatisfactory in guarding against head and neck injuries (the London Metro, May 23rd 2001).

• A recent study by the Institute of Optimum Nutrition and University College Swansea found that after eight months, the **IQ** of children given the optimum amount of **vitamins and minerals** had risen by ten points (Positive Health, November 2000).

'Zinc may aid the recovery of children suffering severe diarrhoea'

• Supplementing the diet with **zinc** may aid the recovery of children suffering severe **diarrhoea,** a study in India has shown. Sick children between 35 months and six years of age, who took 20 mg of zinc daily, got better faster than those who went without the treatment (the London times, October 3rd 2000).

• Recent studies reveal that some genetic **learning disorders** in people are caused by a defect in their metabolism of essential fatty acids, found in salmon, mackerel, tuna, trout, sardines, bluefish and organ meats. Children suffering from such disorders and treated with **fatty acid supplements** over three months showed dramatic improvement in their attention span and ability to learn, while dyspraxics improved in dexterity and balance. The study, carried out by B. Jacqueline Stordy and Malcolm J. Nicholl, has been extended and published as 'The LCP Solution: The Remarkable Nutritional Treatment for ADHD, Dyslexia & Dyspraxia', published by Ballantine (the Seattle Times, November 9th 2000, monitored for the Institute by Roger Knights).

'Children may have a higher risk of asthma if they are overweight'

• In a recent study of more than 15,000 children aged between four and 11 conducted by scientists from King's College, researchers concluded that children may have a higher risk of **asthma** if they are **overweight**, though it was unclear whether the obesity or the asthma came first. However, children who exercised less could suffer more as their airways narrow. Swimming, yoga and team **sports** are recommended especially for asthmatics (BBC News Health (news.bbc.co.uk), January 18th 2001).

'Babies not introduced to solid foods between six and nine months are likely to become fussy eaters'

• If babies are not introduced to a range of **solid foods** between six and nine months, they are likely to become **fussy eaters**. Pauline Emmett, the dietician who led the research at Bristol University, said parents should not wait for their babies to develop teeth before starting them on adult food as "having something to chew on actually helps teeth" (the London Times, February 2001).

• Babies who are **breastfed** for more than four months are more likely to develop **damaged arteries** that can cause heart disease, scientists from the Medical Research Council have discovered (the London Times, March 16th 2001).

Lifestyle

• **Smoking** quadruples the risk of **gum disease**, according to new evidence published in the Journal of Periodontology. Quitting, however, can bring the smoker's risk down to that of someone who has never smoked at all – though it may take ten years (Time, June 12th 2000).

• Research has proven that **smoking** does indeed cause **wrinkling** of the skin, according to scientists from the Guy's, King's and St Thomas' Schools of Medicine in London. Tobacco triggers a protein which attacks collagen, the substance responsible for the skin's elasticity; and causes irreversible damage (the London Times, March 23rd 2001).

'Men who drank moderately had an IQ 3.3 points higher'

• Research at the Japanese Institute for Longevity Sciences in Aichi Prefecture found that men who drank moderately – defined as 540 millilitres of wine and spirit a day – had an **IQ** 3.3 points higher than their non-drinking counterparts; women **drinkers** scored 2.5 more points than women teetotallers. The type of alcohol did not influence results. Scientists were quick to stress that the findings must be treated with caution. Indeed, the research proved that alcohol binges dull the brain. Professor Hiroshi Shimokata, who led the study, agreed that it was difficult to show a cause-effect relationship and believes other factors such as lifestyle and diet may be significant (the London Metro, December 7th 2000).

'People cannot make up for a lost night's sleep by sleeping late on other days'

• Researchers at Harvard Medical School have proved that a good night's **sleep** is invaluable to the formation of **memory**. Having given young people a visual response task, they then divided them into two groups, allowing one

20 Heber Road, London NW2 6AA, UK (rhino@dial.pipex.com), 2001, 300pp, ISBN 0 948826 58 4

to sleep as normal after the task, while keeping the other group awake that night and the following day. Even though this group was allowed to sleep as much as they liked the following two nights, they showed no improvement in skills when re-tested, unlike the group that had slept normally. The study indicates that during sleep, the connections are established which transform information into memory and that people cannot make up for that critical night's sleep by sleeping late on other days. Steffen Gais and colleagues at the Medical University of Lubeck, Germany, found that the 'early' or slow-wave sleep – as opposed to REM sleep – was particularly important to learning (Yahoo News, November 21st 2000).

'A power nap is a better remedy for afternoon tiredness than an extended night's sleep'

• A ten-minute **'power nap'** is a better remedy for **afternoon tiredness** than an extended nights sleep, says Professor Horne, of the Sleep Research Centre at Loughborough University. He warned that anything more than ten minutes sleep, after which the body adjusts to proper sleep processes, would result in the person feeling groggy. Watching television, chatting or reading may be equally restorative as a nap, Professor Horne explained, as more nutrients are available to the cells when awake than during sleep when cells are 'fasting' (Time, April 16th 2001).

• A College of Nursing at the University of South Carolina, USA, has investigated the relationship between pain and **sleep** quality in sufferers of HIV. Phillips and Skelton of the Department of Administrative and Clinical Nursing, reported a significant improvement in sleep activity and quality in all of the 21 subjects, following five weeks of individualised **acupuncture** (Positive Health, July 2001)

'Betel nut may alleviate the symptoms of schizophrenia'

• Chewing on the **betel nut** may alleviate the symptoms of **schizophrenia.** Research carried out by Roger Sullivan and colleagues from the University of Auckland found that sufferers of schizophrenia who chewed more than ten betel nuts a day suffered far milder symptoms than those without the habit (New Scientist, August 5th 2000).

• **Ecstasy** can seriously deplete the brain's supply of **serotonin**, a neurotransmitter linked to mood swings, according to Stephen Kish of the Centre for Addiction and Mental Health in Toronto. The brain has difficulty in replenishing the supply of serotonin released by the drug, leaving levels in the brain 80 per cent lower than those in a healthy brain (New Scientist, July 29th 2000).

- The number of serious head injuries among cyclists of all ages has fallen due to increased use of **cycling helmets**, report Dr Aziz Sheikh and Adrian Cook of the Department of Primary health Care and General Practice, Imperial College School of Medicine. However, while head injuries fell during the study period of increased helmet wearing, other cycling injuries increased, suggesting that greater action needs to be taken to improve safety for cyclists (Imperial College London Press Release, October 27th 2000).

'Reduce duration and frequency when exercising, and increase intensity'

- The proponent of a new science called evolutionary fitness, Art de Vany is a professor of economics at the Institute for Mathematical Behavioural Sciences at the University of California, Irvine. He advises people to reduce duration and frequency when exercising, and **increase intensity,** to improve general **health and fitness** (New Scientist, July 29th 2000).
- Playing a 90-minute **bridge game** can be enough to tone up the **immune system**. A study conducted at the University of California at Berkeley shows that bridge-playing stimulates the dorsolateral cortex of the brain. This area of the brain influences the immune system. The study showed how the presence of CD-4 positive T cells in the blood of bridge players increased significantly after a 90-minute game (Times, November 9th 2000).

'Worrying about weight may lead to lower bone density'

- It is far better to take the time to teach yourself to be **ambidextrous** now than to wait until a time in the future when you may lose the use of your working hand. **Stroke** sufferers often find they are too busy learning how to stand up, walk, eat and even speak with one side of the body to teach their one hand to do simple things such as do up buttons, type a letter, open a door, etc (from a letter by Alan Watling, Colchester, to the London Guardian, October 11th 2000).
- **Worrying about weight** may lead to **lower bone density**, a condition linked to osteoporosis. Susan Barr and Jerilynn Prior of the University of British Columbia in Vancouver, Canada, studied healthy pre-teen girls and found that worry and the consequent release of bone-weakening hormones was a determining factor in bone density (New Scientist, July 15th 2000).

'Laughter is a good way of protecting yourself against a heart attack'

- **Laughter** is a good way of protecting yourself against a **heart attack**.

20 Heber Road, London NW2 6AA, UK (rhino@dial.pipex.com), 2001, 300pp, ISBN 0 948826 58 4

People who have had heart attacks, or who have been treated for heart disease, are up to 40 per cent less likely to laugh in various situations, say American cardiologists at the University of Maryland in Baltimore (Times, November 16th 2000).

• The health benefits of **self-esteem** have been confirmed by a study of the longevity of Oscar-winning film stars. Compared with non-winners, a single oscar win was found to **increase life expectancy** by an average of 3.9 years, while multiple winners gained an average of six years. Professor Redelmeier, who participated in the University of Toronto study, highlighted the significance of the findings: "if you could cure all cancers in all people, you would merely have a 3.5 years increase in life expectancy" (the London Times, May 16th 2001).

'Feeling guilty about vice is bad for your health'

• People exposed to **power lines and electrical machinery** are more vulnerable to **suicide**, according to a study carried out by Dr David Savitz and his colleagues from the University of North Carolina. They believe this may be because electromagnetic fields induce depression, caused by the reduction of the 'mood hormone' melatonin (the London Times, August 22nd 2000).

• A study conducted at Emory University in Atlanta, Georgia, has offered the first solid proof that long-term exposure to **pesticides** and **toxins** may cause **Parkinson's disease** in old age. Earlier studies had already shown that those who often used pesticides at home had a 70 per cent higher risk of getting Parkinson's and that Californian counties with the most pesticide use also had the most deaths from the disease. The study in question suggests that we need to look again at the way we assess the safety of pesticides (New Scientist, November 2000).

• An investigation into **immune system response** suggests that **feeling guilty** about vice is bad for your health. The research, carried out by Dr Geoff Lowe and John Greenman of the University of Hull, indicates that whilst feeling guilt may disable the immune system, feeling good boosts the production of the antibody immunoglobulin A, which protects against infection (the London Times, July 18th 2000).

'Watching Richard and Judy's *This Morning* TV show increased IQ by five points'

• **Watching television** may **boost intelligence**, new research claims. Professor Kevin Warwick, from Reading University, found that watching Richard and Judy's *This Morning* TV show increased the IQ by five points, whilst it was lowered by more stimulating tasks including reading, chatting or listening to classical music (the London Metro, August 14th 2000).

• A recent report confirms that **hands-free mobile phone kits** substantially limit exposure to **radiation**. Unlike the Consumer's Association report, SARtest Ltd measured the 'specific absorption rate' (SAR), which tells how much radio frequency energy is absorbed by the brain over a period of time. Their findings show that absorption levels when using a hands-free set are significantly lower than when one is not used. SARtest Ltd suggest that "users of kits should allow the earpiece cable to hang down naturally from the ear, that the cable should be kept away from the antenna of the phone, and that the phone should not be placed directly against the body" (the London Times, August 8th 2000).

An Australian report advised mobile phone users that the use of **hands-free kits** could reduce the effects of **electromagnetic radiation** by 92 per cent (Metro, August 8th 2000).

'On long flights, massage your legs from feet to thigh every hour'

• The dangers of **deep-vein thrombosis** (DVT), highlighted by the recent House of Lords select committee report, can be reduced by a number of preventative measures, including taking an aspirin before a long flight, moving around on board for at least five minutes every hour, massaging your legs from feet to thigh every hour and wearing support socks to improve circulation (monitored by Yvonne Ackroyd, Sunday Telegraph, November 25th 2000).

• Drinking plenty of **fluid** may help to reduce the risk of **deep-vein thrombosis** on long flights. A research team from the Saitama Medical School in Moroyama, Japan, put two groups of volunteers in a pressure chamber which simulates in-flight conditions. At that pressure, the body usually responds by lowering blood pressure and reducing circulation; these effects were seen in the control group, while the blood pressure of those given fluids did not drop. They had more oxygen in their brains and the blood flow in their carotid arteries was five per cent greater than in the non-drinking group. Toshiro Makino, director of the clinic at Tokyo's international airport agreed: "the biggest problem is dehydration, and that is made worse by drinking alcohol. My advice is to keep off the alcohol and drink lots of water" (New Scientist, January 13th 2001).

• Crossing several time zones on **long-haul flights** impairs **memory** and reaction time by causing shrinkage of the brain, claims a research team from Bristol University, led by Kwangwook Cho. "A greater gap between long-haul flights would prevent cabin crew and frequent flyers suffering such difficulties," says Cho (New Scientist, May 26th 2001).

• The chemical **phenylpropanolamine (PPA)**, found in many cold and flu remedies such as Benylin Day & Night, Contac 400, Day Nurse, Sinutab and Vicks Coldcure, has been linked to hundreds of **strokes** among young women

20 Heber Road, London NW2 6AA, UK (rhino@dial.pipex.com), 2001, 300pp, ISBN 0 948826 58 4

and has been banned in the United States. American consumers have been warned to avoid all products containing PPA, but it will remain on sale in chemists in Britain while the Department of Health review the evidence (the London Times, November 7th 2000).

• To reduce **eye damage** caused by prolonged use of **Video Display Units**:

* look away from your computer screen every 20 minutes and take regular breaks

* place your computer screen a comfortable distance from your eyes – around 60cm (two feet) – and keep the copy you work from the same distance away to avoid continual refocusing

* position your screen so that windows and lights are to the side of it, not behind

* ensure walls and desk surfaces are non-reflective (Lindsay Barnes in Best of Health, Winter 2000).

'High impact activities such as jogging, tennis, squash and football build healthier bones'

• **High impact activities** such as jogging, tennis, squash and football build **healthier bones** than lower impact sports such as swimming and cycling, a Cambridge study reports. Sports which involve "an element of airborne projection and impact" build bone mineral density and make fractures of the hip less likely (the London Times, January 19th 2001).

• Moderate **aerobic exercise** three times a week is as effective as Zoloft in the treatment of **depression**. The research, at Duke University Medical Center, found that after ten months, only eight per cent of those exercising had relapsed into depression, compared with 38 per cent of patients on medication, and 31 per cent of those who were both exercising and taking medication (Time, October 9th 2000, monitored for the Institute by Roger Knights).

'People with a positive attitude to life are less likely to develop Alzheimer's disease'

• People with a **positive attitude** to life are less likely to develop **Alzheimer's** disease, a study of over 100 nuns in America has ascertained. David Snowden, of the University of Kentucky, who led the study found that essays written as early as when the nuns were in their 20s could predict their susceptibility to the disease (the London Times, May 2001).

• People who take part in **recreational activities**, whether physical or intellectual, are less likely to develop **Alzheimer's** disease than those who are inactive, according to a study by Robert Friedman and colleagues at the

University Hospitals of Cleveland in Ohio (the London Times, March 6th 2001 or see www.uhhs.com/uhc/).

'UV-screening chemicals in sunscreens have triggered accelerated cancer cell growth in rats'

• Common UV screening chemicals in **sunscreens** are hormonally active and have triggered accelerated **cancer** cell growth and uterine development in rats, according to Margaret Schlumpf from the Institute of Pharmacology and Toxicology at the University of Zurich. They cannot say yet whether the doses are high enough to cause problems in humans, but Schlumpf advises that sunblocks with **zinc oxide** may be a healthier alternative (New Scientist, April 14th 2001).

Young people

• Teenage girls with diets deficient in **iron** risk lowering their **IQs**, claims Mike Nelson, of King's College, London. He found that a quarter of the 11-18 year olds studied suffered from anaemia, and had lower IQs than their counterparts with normal iron levels, although their IQs increased when given additional iron. Those most at risk were girls who were both vegetarian and dieting (the London Times, July 26th 2000).

'Teenagers who smoke are four times more likely to develop symptoms of depression'

• A new study appearing in the October issue of Pediatrics, has found that **teenagers who smoke** are about four times more likely to develop symptoms of **depression** than non-smokers. Dr Elizabeth Goodman, an adolescent-medicine specialist at Children's Hospital Medical Centre of Cincinnati, who led the study, believes that the effectiveness of anti-depressant drugs in treating nicotine addiction further supported the results (the London Times, October 3rd 2000).

Miscellaneous

• **Vomit** is exceptionally effective in spreading **viruses**, public health scientists have discovered. Roy Fey and colleagues suspect that virus-infected vomit may be the cause of many food-poisoning outbreaks, as people within the vicinity of the vomit seem to inhale or swallow the infection agent (New Scientist, September 9th 2000).

    • A study comparing sick leave taken amongst two groups of fit, working

20 Heber Road, London NW2 6AA, UK (rhino@dial.pipex.com), 2001, 300pp, ISBN 0 948826 58 4

adults and cited in the New England Journal of Medicine, found that the group vaccinated with the **flu jab** took almost half the amount of sick leave as those who were not vaccinated. The vaccine only offers 80-90 per cent protection, but may be potentially life-saving for the frail. Dr Joe Neary, a GP and chair of the clinical and special projects network for the Royal College of General Practitioners, believes "it is worth having a flu jab if you are a fit, healthy adult" (the London Times, Summer 2000).

• A study by the CSIRO in Australia has found high levels of toxic chemicals leaking from furniture, paints and floors in **new houses** which, though unlikely to pose a serious threat to most people's health, could lead to **headaches** and other symptoms (New Scientist, March 10th 2001)

'Tea bags can assist in neutralising the toxicity of chemicals from fresh paint'

• **Tea bags** scattered around a newly decorated house can assist in **neutralising the toxicity of chemicals** from fresh paint and glue by up to 90 per cent, Japanese research has shown. The Tokyo Metropolitan Consumer Centre has found that the scattered teabags (dry black or green tea were more effective) soak up formaldehyde in the air from paints and glue, aided by tannin in the tea (New Scientist, 22nd July 2000).

• A link has been drawn between **serious head injuries** in early adulthood and the onset of **Alzheimer's disease** in later life. Richard Havlik, of the US National Institute on Aging, in Maryland, who led the study of WW2 veterans, with colleagues at Duke University, North Carolina, found that of the risk of developing the disease was increased fourfold in those who had sustained severe head injuries in the past, leading to unconsciousness or amnesia. The findings support evidence that Alzheimer's is a long illness that develops over many decades (the London Times, October 24th 2000).

'Place the banana peel on the wart, tape it in place and leave it to work its magic'

• **Banana peel** is effective in the treatment of **warts**, according to Joe Graedon and Teresa Graedon, PhD, People's Pharmacy columnists of The Seattle Times. Place the inside surface of the peel on the wart, tape it in place and leave it to work its magic for a few hours – preferably overnight (the Seattle Times, December 17th 2000).

• A new design of **protective sunglasses** with lenses infused with melanin protect against the damaging effects of blue-violet high-energy visible (HEV) radiation, cited as a contributing factor to **retinal disease**. New Code Melanin-XP sunglasses provide progressive protection relative to the damage potential of both UV and HEV radiation and are available by calling (001) 800

786 4527, or by visiting www.sunglasshut.com (New Age, January 2001, monitored for the Institute by Roger Knights).

• Smoothing out wrinkled foreheads may relieve **migraines**, claims plastic surgeon Bahman Guyuron of Cleveland, Ohio, who found that 31 of 39 of his patients who had suffered from migraines and undergone **'forehead rejuvenation'** surgery experienced complete or significant relief (New Scientist February 10th, 2001).

Mandatory right to know all the ingredients in cigarettes

Dennis Wright

From a submission to the Global Ideas Bank.

There needs to be a law requiring the listing of all the ingredients in cigarettes – such as acetone, ammonia, butane, methanol, arsenic, formaldehyde, nicotine tar and carbon monoxide.

We need to be warned of these toxic and slow death ingredients – maybe it will discourage people from picking up the cigarette habit.

• *Dennis Wright (www.bigbopper201@aol.com)*

Voice recognition of suicide cases

Summarised from an article by Ian Sample, entitled 'Voice from the grave', in New Scientist (August 19th 2000; New Scientist subs £97 or $140, tel 44 [0]1622 778000).

Recent research has shown that the earliest sign that someone is seriously considering committing suicide could be a slight change in the sound of their voice. The change is distinctive, and psychiatrists are planning to use the change in sound as a kind of early warning system to distinguish between those who are actually suicidal and those who are just depressed.

Stephen Silverman, a psychiatrist from Yale University, noticed that he could infer from a patient's voice if they were likely to make a suicide attempt. With this unscientific hunch, he went to see Mitchell Wilkes, an electronics engineer at Vanderbilt University in Nashville, to see if there was any empirical evidence for such a change in voice sound. So they recorded interviews with a number of depressed patients and compared the recordings with others who were not depressed. A further comparison was then made between the recordings and the history of the patients.

20 Heber Road, London NW2 6AA, UK (rhino@dial.pipex.com), 2001, 300pp, ISBN 0 948826 58 4

After conducting these tests and analyses, Wilkes noted that the voice became "slightly hollow and empty" in suicidal patients, a character which people call "the voice from the grave." More scientifically, he noticed that those who were seriously suicidal used a narrower range of frequencies when saying vowels than those who were merely depressed. Added to this, the voices of the seriously suicidal patients had a noticeably higher pitch.

'You get changes in moisture and elasticity of the vocal tract when anxious or stressed'

The reasons for these changes are unclear, although Wilkes believes it could be due to stress-induced physiological changes. Changes in muscle-tone quality can occur in times of stress, which might affect the vocal cords. Wilkes adds that "you get changes in moisture and elasticity of the vocal tract" when anxious or stressed.

The reasons for these findings are less important than the findings themselves, though, which could potentially aid helpline volunteers in their assessment of a depressed caller's mental state. The eventual result of the research could be to have a diagnostic device for helplines and emergency rooms. Volunteers could then have a better idea of whether the person is truly suicidal or not – lives could be saved. As Emma Charvet from The Samaritans says, "If there's any way of finding out earlier the level of someone's risk of suicide, it'd be a great help."

Web donations of hospital medications nearing expiry

Paul Christy

From a submission to the Global Ideas Bank.

My hospital destroys thousands of dollars worth of medications monthly because these medications have less than one month to go before the manufacturer's expiration fate.

'Hospitals could post inventories and receive donation requests'

Consider the possibility of an Internet website, possibly open source, where such facilities could post their inventories and receive requests for donations – donations for the benefit of indigent consumers or inmates on the public pay.

• *Paul Christy (Reensure@BellSouth.net)*

Patient feedback letters to be kept with medical records

Summarised from an article by Andrew Herxheimer, entitled 'Write a letter to your doctor', in the British Journal of General Practice (July 2000 issue, p.598-9), which was submitted to the Global Ideas Bank by the author.

Andrew Herxheimer proposes that a triangular correspondence could be set up between patients, GPs and specialists in order to promote the involvement of patients in their own care. The problem with the system at the moment is that all written records are made by health professionals. This idea could solve that problem by providing the patient with some direct input.

A typical correspondence could proceed as follows:

• The general practitioner writes a referral letter to the specialist (or consultant) which the patient may see.

• The consultant reports back to the GP, and sends the patient a copy of the letter. At the same time, the patient writes to the consultant about her or his experience of the illness and its management, sending a copy to the GP.

• The consultant may reply to some points raised by the patient in their letter.

'Doctors could find the letters a way of improving rapport with patients, and as an aid to self-audit'

The idea would then be that this triangular correspondence becomes part of the records wherever they are held. The feedback on the patients' experience of the consultation and/or operation could then prove helpful to the consultant, the GP and to the patient themselves. As Dr Herxheimer writes, "Doctors could find [the letters] a useful way of improving rapport with patients, and also as an aid to self-audit." They would also allow the patient to "communicate ... convincingly to their doctors about their state of mind and what they consider important."

'Would help to promote a more patient-centred approach'

While there are undoubtedly problems with the idea (not least the extra burden on doctors and their secretaries, and the cost of collating all the letters), such a correspondence would improve the communication between the involved parties, and help to promote a more patient-centred approach to medicine.

20 Heber Road, London NW2 6AA, UK (rhino@dial.pipex.com), 2001, 300pp, ISBN 0 948826 58 4

DIPEx – a database of patients' experiences of medical treatment

Summarised from an article by Andrew Herxheimer, Ann McPherson, Rachel Miller, Sasha Shepperd, John Yaphe and Sue Ziebland, entitled 'Database of patients' experiences (DIPEx): a multi-media approach to sharing experiences and information' in The Lancet (29th April 2000; Vol. 355; No. 9214; p.1540-3), and from the Dipex website (www.dipex.org).

To fill a major gap in healthcare information, a specialist medical team in Oxford have begun compiling a database of patients' experiences (DIPEx) which is accessible via the Internet or by DVD/CD ROM. Their aim is to improve understanding of people's experience of illness and promote a more balanced encounter between patient and health professional. Patients can use the database as a resource which will provide them with some indication of the feelings of others who have experienced similar procedures. Health professionals, on the other hand, can get an indication of patients' priorities and details of many procedures of which they may not be as experienced.

'DIPEx combines a collection of interviews with people about their experience of illness with other appropriate resources'

DIPEx combines a systematic collection and analysis of interviews with people about their experience of illness with evidence of the effects of treatments, information about support groups and other appropriate resource materials. The idea of the database is that it provides a range of patient stories, so that people looking for information can understand the different experiences possible with each disease. And that information is freely available to doctors, researchers and members of the public alike, both on the website and also, in the future, on DVD in GPs surgeries, public libraries and outpatient departments.

Interviews with patients are being collected and analysed for each illness, and the sampling method used aims to represent the fullest possible range of experiences. For each condition, a steering group (consisting of clinicians, support group members, academics etc) is responsible for identifying and approving the information included. This is just part of a rigorous monitoring process of DIPEx to ensure the quality and current nature of the information contained in the database.

Thus far, the scheme has received backing from the Department of Health and Macmillan Cancer Relief, and has collated stories of people with prostate cancer and high blood pressure. Before the end of 2002, they aim to add experiences of patients with breast, bowel, and cervical cancer. In the future, people diagnosed with an illness need not feel as if they are stepping into the unknown. The isolation and fear that comes from lack of knowledge on the patient's part, and lack of understanding from medical professionals, should be greatly reduced in the future by this database of patient experiences.

• *To contact DIPEx for information, or with questions and suggestions, write to: DIPEx, Department of Primary Care, Institute of Health Sciences, University of Oxford, Headington, Oxford, OX3 7LF, UK (tel. Int.+44 [0]1865 226672; fax Int.+44 [0]1865 227137; e-mail: dipex@dphpc.ox.ac.uk; web: www.dipex.org).*

A one-size standard prescription dosage is dangerous

Summarised from an article by Jay S. Cohen M.D., entitled 'The one-size dose does not fit all', in Newsweek magazine (December 6th 1999), monitored for the Global Ideas Bank by Roger Knights.

A major cause of many adverse medication reactions could be an error in dosage, because a standard dose applied to all takes no account of differences in weight, age or drug sensitivities.

'Adverse reactions to medications cause more deaths than AIDS, accidents and infectious diseases in the US'

For just as people differ in their ability to drink coffee or alcohol, they differ in the amount of drugs they can cope with. It seems like common sense that a seven-foot, 25-year-old basketball player should not receive the same dosage as a five-foot, 90-year-old grandmother, but with many prescriptions today, that is exactly what happens. Standard methods of prescribing drugs ignore such variations in height, weight, age, and metabolism. When adverse reactions to medications cause more deaths than AIDS, accidents and infectious diseases in a country as developed as the US, surely something has to change?

'54 per cent of patients needed only 5mg a day for Prozac to work, but the lowest recommended dose is 20mg a day'

The standard dosage system is as it is because of two main reasons:

20 Heber Road, London NW2 6AA, UK (rhino@dial.pipex.com), 2001, 300pp, ISBN 0 948826 58 4

Firstly, pharmaceutical companies often exclude medical findings from their labelling information. The key for them is drugs being effective, and a higher dose is more likely to be effective, even if it brings higher risks with it. Testing of Prozac, for example, had shown that 54 per cent of patients needed 5mg a day for the drug to work; the lowest recommended dose of Prozac is 20mg a day, as given by the manufacturers who commissioned the same testing.

The second reason is that doctors prefer drugs that are quick and simple to prescribe. With doctors under the pressure that they are today, it is perfectly understandable that they opt for the one-dose-for-all option, when they have little time to give thought to matching doses to different patients.

'If the illness isn't serious, they can ask to be started on a lower dose'

Yet the consequences of the one-size dose can be very serious. Millions of people each year are affected by adverse medication reactions, and most of those reactions occur at the doses the manufacturers recommend. Individually, people should monitor their own drug sensitivities. They can tell their doctor about side effects or about sensitivity to drugs in their family. If the illness isn't serious, they can ask to be started on a lower dose: the medication can always be increased if it is unsuccessful. Alternatively, a higher dose may be required than is recommended, although this is rarer. Lower doses are not necessarily better than high doses, but individualised doses must surely be better than standardised ones.

Ketamine as a treatment for alcoholism

Ketamine – Dreams and realities *by Dr Karl Jansen, published by MAPS (2105 Robinson Avenue, Sarasota FL 34232, USA, tel 888 868 6277; web: www.maps.org), ISBN 0 9660019 3 1, $14.95. Reviewed by Nicholas Albery.*

Ketamine is a anaesthetic drug which at lower doses has been used in the treatment of alcoholism. Since the early 1980s, as the author of this book recounts, ketamine has been given by Dr Evgeny Krupistsky and colleagues at St Petersburg's National Institute of Drug Abuse to a total of more than 1,000 patients. One year after treatment, 67 per cent of the patients were dry, 27 per cent had relapsed (and data could not be obtained on the other seven per cent). In the control group, only 24 per cent were sober and 69 per cent had relapsed.

'One year after treatment, 67 per cent of the patients were dry'

In one such trial, the method used was as follows: During three months in hospital (undergone by the control group as well), the patients' anxiety and depression were treated, as well as any physical problems. Individual and group therapy took place to examine their relationships and general outlook and to foster negative attitudes towards alcohol.

'They might have out-of-the-body experiences which they would not be able to resist'

The ketamine group were told that they would undergo a treatment which would allow them to see the underlying roots of their problem, that they were to expect positive changes in their personality and that they might have out-of-the-body experiences which they would not be able to resist. The therapist helped them to tailor individual plans, with their ideas of the causes of their addiction and their goals of how they wanted to be in their sober life.

The drug sessions themselves, lasting 45 minutes to one hour, with a recovery period of one to two hours, involved injections of aethimizol, bemegride and then ketamine in doses of 2-3 mg/kg (i.m). The bemegride was provided for enhancing the emotional aspects and visions, and the aethimizol for improving memory of the ketamine trip. A therapeutic dialogue took place during the session, emphasising, in a personalised way, the positive aspects of sobriety and the negative aspects of alcoholism. During intense moments, the patient was given alcohol to smell to help establish a deep aversion to it. Afterwards, discussion and interpretation took place, and the patients wrote a detailed account that evening.

'Ketamine can reconnect the ego with denied part of the self'

In group therapy the following day, people interpreted their sessions. On tests of personality change, there were improvements on many scales – including those measuring depression, anxiety and ego strength. Patients became less anxious and more emotionally open, mature and responsible. Dr Jansen concludes that "ketamine can reconnect the ego with denied part of the self. It can also lead to a perception of reconnection with wider fields such as the family, community, planet and universe in general – a form of spiritual experience".

20 Heber Road, London NW2 6AA, UK (rhino@dial.pipex.com), 2001, 300pp, ISBN 0 948826 58 4

Ketamine as an addictive drug

The irony of ketamine's value in the treatment of addiction is that it is itself a remarkably addictive drug, with one PhD student reporting in this book that overcoming his ketamine problem was "harder than heroin". A number of highly intelligent independent researchers have come to grief in their investigations into ketamine. Dr Jansen estimates that ten per cent of those using ketamine for its psychedelic effects lose control over their usage.

'Dr John Lilly was found floating face down in his pool, resuscitated and taken to hospital by helicopter'

Dr John Lilly's report of his ketamine and other adventures – *The Scientist – A novel autobiography* (published by Bantam Books) – acknowledges the staff of no less than five hospitals; at one point he was found floating face down in his pool, resuscitated and taken to hospital by helicopter. D. M. Turner, the author of *The Essential Guide to Psychedelics* (published by Panther Press), died in a bathtub with a bottle of ketamine at his side. Marcia Moore, the author of *Journeys into the Bright World* (published by Para Research) was found frozen to death in a tree, where she had repeatedly injected herself with ketamine. A year or two before, she had written that "in the right hands this unique substance could be safely, easily and advantageously applied toward the psychospiritual regeneration of planet Earth ... if captains of industry, leaders of nations could partake of this love medicine the whole planet might be converted into the garden of Eden."

Therapy invoking altered states of being

Dr Jansen believes that altered states of being induced by ketamine can be therapeutic. "Some [psychiatric] symptoms," he writes "arise from a failure of parts of the mind to talk to other parts, as if they were walled castles with the drawbridge raised. Transcendence of the usual patterns may produce a weakening of these walls so that at least some communication occurs, to reduce inner conflict."

'Allowing a deeper and faster apparent return to the womb'

He describes how Dr Alberto Fontana Y Col in Argentina used ketamine to treat depression and anxiety by inducing death-rebirth experiences. "He found that ketamine was the most effective substance to aid this process, allowing a deeper and faster apparent 'return to the womb' than could be achieved using other methods."

One ketamine user, identified only as P. F., reports that "I've had an interest in altered states of consciousness since I was 15 years old, when a head injury resulting from a bicycle accident produced a dissociative state that I years later identified as a Near-Death Experience. ... The first time I tried ketamine I immediately recognised the state as being nearly identical to the Near-Death Experience state."

'Intertwined with hundreds of billions of other beings in a thin sheet of consciousness that was distributed around the galaxy'

Other ketamine users go further: "That 22-minute journey to becoming the intelligence at the heart of the universe remains the most powerful and cosmic experience of my life". Another writes: "I had stumbled into the blast furnace at the heart of the cosmos, the engine that drives the process of creating manifest reality out of the thoughts of the mind of God". Or as Dr John Lilly put it: "I experienced 'myself' as melded and intertwined with hundreds of billions of other beings in a thin sheet of consciousness that was distributed around the galaxy: a membrain."

Such experiences lead Dr Karl Jansen to fascinating speculations as to the nature of consciousness: "Some of the more recent reports in physics journals use similar terms to those describing ketamine trips ... Extended objects called p-branes, which are types of membranes. A string is called a one-brane as it has length but no other dimension. The real interest lies in other fundamental entities with higher dimensions, other types of 'branes'. The experience of actually becoming an across-the-universe membrane or fabric is a typical ketamine effect."

Ketamine is evidently not a drug to be trifled with, and deserves the well-written, encyclopedic, balanced and thought-provoking investigation that Dr Jansen has provided.

• *Dr Jansen (e-mail: K@BTinternet.com) plans a follow-up volume,* Ketamine reconsidered, *and solicits contributions.*

Easy stress relief

Wally Evans

Adapted from a submission to the Global Ideas Bank.

This is a simple process I learned from Nelson Zink back in 1993. You need to follow the directions exactly, with someone to guide you through it.

20 Heber Road, London NW2 6AA, UK (rhino@dial.pipex.com), 2001, 300pp, ISBN 0 948826 58 4

(1) Get in touch with a feeling of stress (anxiety or whatever label you use). The most useful way to do this is by closing your eyes, centering yourself and paying attention.

(2) Calibrate this feeling on a scale of one to ten. This is your 'present state memory' level.

(3) Get a ball (the size and weight of an apple or orange). Start tossing the ball from hand to hand at about shoulder width and at a slow pace and shallow arc.

'Tossing the ball with your eyes closed'

(4) Now, the important aspect is to do this tossing with your eyes closed. While doing this, *with your eyes closed*, go back in your mind to the thing you thought about and recalibrate.

How much did your comfort level change?

Most people will take a deep breath as soon as they close their eyes when tossing the ball. That's OK!

I have used this in clinical and non-clinical situations. It appears to be extremely useful in eliminating phobias.

I hope that this will spread and help many become more calm and healthier. Please contact me with any questions or results, as feedback is appreciated. If you would like a printed sheet, please e-mail me your address.

• *Wally Evans (e-mail: easychange@hotmail.com)*

Stress-relieving rocking chairs in public places

Summarised from an item by Lini S. Kadaba in The Philadelphia Inquirer (March 5th 2000), monitored for the Global Ideas Bank by Roger Knights.

Rocking chairs, invented for the elderly and nursing mothers in America in the 18th century, are now making their way into airports, city halls and urban parks as stress-relievers for modern-day travellers and city workers.

'It takes you back to your mother rocking you as a baby'

In Pittsburgh, city types queue in the local park at lunchtime to sit in 30 chairs placed there by the Market Square Association; at Philadelphia International Airport another 30 white rockers are used by passengers; in Orlando, Florida, City Hall workers share 25 chairs placed outside the building by local government.

"It takes you back to your mother rocking you as a baby," said police officer Janice Roska as she rocked away her wait for a flight home.

Sit on the floor – for health, humility and the environment

Summarised from an article by Brad Lemley, entitled 'Down to Earth', in New Age magazine (January/February 2001), monitored for the Global Ideas Bank by Roger Knights.

In a western world increasingly filled with bad backs, poor posture and arrogance, it may be time to look to a simple idea from the East: using the floor. For sitting on the floor not only gives better posture, but also makes one feel more humble: it is difficult to look down on people metaphorically if you are looking up to them literally. In Japan, there is great respect for the floor, with shoes taken off before entering the house. In the cheaper restaurants there, one generally sits in a chair; in the more exclusive noodle-houses, sitting on the floor is the chosen position. On top of humility and posture, there is also the environmental angle to consider: imagine if even ten per cent of the US or UK population decided they could do without their plastic chair at work or home, and how much that would save in terms of raw materials, waste etc. Going back to the floor should not be limited to the boss checking on his workforce.

'Modern pieces of furniture from the sofa to the toilet induce bad posture–'

The best reason of all for getting back in touch with the floor may be a health one. Man used to live without chairs, sofas or beds off the ground, and thus had to stretch hundreds of times a day up and down. Nowadays, people are often on the same level (from bed to chair to sofa to bed etc) and do not exercise the muscles as much. Added to that, pieces of furniture from the sofa to the toilet induce bad posture in the person using them. Virtually every medical expert who has written on defecation and toilet habits has concluded that squatting is the best physiological position for the process, so why still have our chair-like thrones? Over half of the world's population doesn't.

'When people are all sitting on the floor, the conversation is noticeably more warm and intimate'

20 Heber Road, London NW2 6AA, UK (rhino@dial.pipex.com), 2001, 300pp, ISBN 0 948826 58 4

More intuitively, it could also be argued that there is a link between the amount of distance a person keeps from something and the amount they like something: people tend to get close to things they love and vice versa. So standing and walking on the floor could contribute to having a lack of respect for the earth, and could be seen as trying to distance oneself from what supports and creates us. It is also noticeable that when people are all sitting on the floor, the conversation is noticeably more warm and intimate than when they are all positioned in separate chairs. As the people come down to earth, their attitude does the same.

And if less chairs were needed, there would be less strain on the environment. Fewer trees would need to be cut down, tons of steel need not be smelted, miles of fabric need not be stitched and dyed, and masses of petrochemicals need not be produced. And thousands of non-biodegradable plastic chairs need not be discarded every year. For health, humility and eco-friendliness, it could be time to head back to childhood: back to the floor.

Brushing to help dyslexia

Summarised from an article in the London Mirror (March 8th 2001).

Brushing 30 reflex points on the body (on the face, hands, back, arms and legs) with a fine-haired paintbrush can help those with dyslexia, phobias, anxiety and panic attacks, says neurodevelopmental consultant David Mulhall, who trained at the Institute of Neurophysiological Psychology in Chester and who has treated 450 children and adults with the new method.

'The brushing stimulates the nerve endings and thus improves the reflexes'

The brushing, which needs to be done ten minutes every day for six to 18 months, stimulates the nerve endings and gradually improves the reflexes. If some of a person's 70 reflexes are not fully developed while they are a baby (perhaps because of a difficult birth) they may grow up with problems – such as eyes unable to move smoothly when reading (dyslexia) or malcoordination (dyspraxia). Other signs of damage can be vertigo, being not very good at map reading or sports, over-anxiety, or tripping over your words when speaking. The British Dyslexia Association comments: "If specialist treatment such as multi-sensory teaching is accompanied by reflex work this can have a very positive effect."

• *The David Mulhall Centre, 31 Webbs Road, London SW11 6RU, UK (tel Int.+44 [0]20 7223 4321).*

• *The British Dyslexia Association, 98 London Road, Reading RG1 5AU, UK (tel Int.+44 [0]118 966 8271).*

Using the stairs improves health

Summarised from an item by Linda Ciampa, entitled 'Skip the elevator in favor of stairs, CDC says', on CNN (October 9th 2000).

New research has shown that taking the stairs instead of the lift on a regular basis could radically improve health over a substantial period of time. Researchers at the Center for Disease Control (CDC) in the US have found that spending ten minutes on the stairs each day could result in losing ten pounds of weight over the course of a year. The CDC encouraged people to take the stairs by making them more interesting places to be: colourful artwork and upbeat signs were used to this end. And making the staircases more interesting and attractive led to a 14 per cent increase in their use.

'When the stairs were more attractive, stair use increased by 14 per cent'

The research followed on from a European study which found that young women who used the stairs for seven weeks had lower heart rates and better cholesterol levels. The key to the American research was that it promoted exercise to people in a completely passive way: just by making the stairs a more positive and upbeat area, a significant number used them more. And in a country where it is thought that up to 60 per cent of people get almost no physical activity, that is no small success. As researcher Nicole Kerr puts it: "Small changes can lead to a bigger impact, and if you do this on a daily basis over the course of a year, you can significantly impact your health". So next time the escalator on the subway is broken, or the elevator is out of order, don't curse the technicians: thank them for the exercise.

Honesty better than false optimism for cancer patients

Summarised from an article by Mark Henderson, entitled 'Honesty best for cancer patients', in the Times (December 11th 2000), and from a paper in the British Medical Journal by Anne-Mei The et al, entitled 'Collusion in doctor-patient communication about imminent death: an ethnographic study' (December 2nd 2000 issue).

A study by a team of Dutch researchers has found that more honesty from doctors as to cancer patients' chances of recovery would be more useful than engendering false optimism. The research demonstrated that doctors and patients collude in a 'recovery plot', in which both parties concentrate on

20 Heber Road, London NW2 6AA, UK (rhino@dial.pipex.com), 2001, 300pp, ISBN 0 948826 58 4

short-term treatment instead of long-term prognosis. The doctor is often unwilling to deliver a 'death sentence', and the patient is understandably unwilling to hear it. This can lead to a situation where the patient feels a lot of regret when they eventually admit the gravity of their condition, because they have little time to organise their affairs or say proper goodbyes to their relatives and loved ones. It can also be very painful for all involved when it becomes clear that the optimism was based on illusions. Most importantly of all, such false optimism can affect the patient in making sensible and well-considered treatment choices.

'The false optimism can arise from ambiguities in medical terminology'

The study, based on observation of 35 consultants and their patients, goes against the idea that positive thinking plays an important role in recovery from illness. Whilst this is undoubtedly the case for some patients, those with little or no chance of recovery might actually find it better to discuss honestly with their doctor how long they have got left, and then plan accordingly. Instead, the researchers found that it was not unusual for a patient to tell their friends and relatives that the doctor had told them they were cured, even when the cancer was not cured and the patient's life expectancy was two years at best. This arises partly from the false optimism from doctor-patient collusion, but also from ambiguities in medical terminology. For example, when a doctor tells a patient that a tumour "can be treated", the patient may understand that simply as "something can be done about the tumour", whereas the doctor may have meant merely that there are treatments that can prolong life.

'The patient and doctor collude in not facing up to the long-term realities of the situation'

By focusing on short-term treatment and intermediate results (one clear x-ray after chemotherapy interpreted as being cured), the patient and doctor collude in not always facing up to the realities of the situation in the long-term. The key to solving this is a more honest doctor-patient relationship, not one that is either unduly pessimistic or falsely optimistic. And if this proves too difficult to achieve, the study recommends the introduction of outside 'treatment brokers' who can clarify information for patients, giving them the confidence to discuss things more openly with their doctor.

• *The full paper of the study can be read on the British Medical Journal website at www.bmj.com/cgi/content/full/321/7273/1376*

Double beds in hospitals

Summarised from an idea by Justin Hawkins on the idea-a-day website (May 21st 2001).

The introduction of double beds in hospital would allow relatives to be closer to patients at important times. For example, people with terminal illnesses could have their partners with them for the last days, day and night. Equally validly, young children in hospital could have their parents near them, making them feel secure and comfortable at different times. The main problem would be space, but the provision of double beds could be limited to the areas suggested above, to those patients (and, indeed, relatives) who would really appreciate the facility.

• *For more ideas every day, see www.idea-a-day.com*

Laziness – the key to longer life

Summarised from an article, entitled 'Relax – laziness is good for you', on Yahoo News (http://uk.news.yahoo.com; April 18th 2001), and from an item entitled 'New theory divulges longer life formula' in Serendib News (www.serendibnews.com).

New research from a German scientist has concluded that laziness is good for health. Professor Peter Axt, of the Fulda college, wrote in his article that "People who would rather laze in a hammock instead of running a marathon, or who take a midday nap instead of playing squash have a better chance of living into old age". His theory, based on the work of early 20th century physiognomic research, states that those who burn up energy quickly live for a shorter time, while those who conserve energy are more likely to live longer. There is nothing wrong with moderate exercise, says Professor Axt, and avoiding overeating is also advised; but the best antidote to stress (particularly work-induced stress) is indolence, or aimless sloth.

'Early risers live shorter lives than those who lie in bed longer'

The research also criticises those who get up too early, with Axt and his team having accumulated evidence that shows that early risers (getting up before 7.20am) live shorter lives than those who revel in a lie-in. Further proof given by the German researchers included countless examples of top sportsmen who had died in middle age. For example, Jim Fixx, the American who wrote the best-selling *Complete Book of Running* and inspired the jogging revolution, died at the age of 52. Professor Axt, in conjunction with his daughter

20 Heber Road, London NW2 6AA, UK (rhino@dial.pipex.com), 2001, 300pp, ISBN 0 948826 58 4

Michaela, state that there are three keys to long life: to play less sport (particularly those placing a heavy strain on the body), to reduce stress, and to eat less food.

So for those looking for the perfect excuse for laziness, or for a 'wasted' evening in front of the television, look no further. Professor Axt's prescription for reducing stress and being healthy is simple: "Waste half your free time. Just enjoy lazing around."

NEIGHBOURHOOD

International Neighbourhood Day

The first Monday in May each year is International Neighbourhood Day, a day to get to know your neighbours. Put a leaflet out to everyone in your street inviting them over for a cup of coffee, organise a get together or dance in your local hall, or whatever else you can think of.

'Put a leaflet out to everyone in your street inviting them over for a cup of coffee'

The non-profit Institute for Social Inventions in London, UK and www.DoBe.org who are publicising this day, urge you to post up details of your events on www.DoBe.org (in its 'Neighbourhood' section) as an inspiration for others.

In the Christian bible, Jesus talks about loving your neighbour, but it's got so bad nowadays, as the Rev John Papworth (who first proposed International Neighbourhood Day) has pointed out, that most people, Christian or other, don't even know who their neighbours are. There is nothing more vital today than to rebuild our sense of community – evidence shows it leads to increased health, less crime, etc.

'Jesus talks about loving your neighbour, but most people don't even know who their neighbours are'

John Papworth writes:

"There is an increasing awareness that many problems of modern life are stemming from the general dissolution of community ties and structures. Young people especially are afflicted with a sense of divorce from a rooted and defined sense of reality which gives their own lives the necessary coordinates of a meaningful framework of existence in terms of relationships, rituals, traditions and common objectives.

"One result of the stresses this imposes on people is an increasing resort to drugs, tranquillisers, fundamentalist forms of religion or politics, a growing spirit of amoral unconcern for social support factors such as family ties, care of the aged, financial and other obligations and a general decline of caring and sharing. The results, in terms of family breakdown, lawlessness, violence and sickness of mind, body and spirit had become part of the commonplaces of 20th century life. The same factors will surely characterise life even more in this 21st century – unless we take remedial action."

So International Neighbourhood Day is a positive step to commemorate and celebrate the life and spirit of the local neighbourhood.

On this day each year (a bank holiday Monday in the UK), celebrations will be held to signify the importance of neighbourhood ties and traditions; these can include, besides inviting neighbours in for a drink:

- Street parties
- Beating the bounds
- Dancing
- Presentation of neighbourhood civic awards
- Evening banquet
- Tree planting

In our societies today we lack Vitamin T, the tribal vitamin (where even a nod from a neighbour counts as one unit of Vitamin T and you need at least a hundred units a day).

- *For more on the philosophy behind this day, see John Papworth's journal* Fourth World Review *; subscriptions cost £20 from John Papworth, The Close, 26 High St, Purton, Wiltshire SN5 4AE, UK (tel Int.+44 [0]1793 772214; fax 01793 772521; john.papworth@btinternet.com).*

- *For more on Vitamin T, see the next item.*

- *Media, etc can contact the editors of www.DoBe.org, the sponsors for International Neighbourhood Day, at www.DoBe.org, 20 Heber Road, London NW2 6AA, UK (tel Int.+44 [0]20 8208 2853; fax Int.+44 [0]20 8452 6434; e-mail: rhino@dial.pipex.com; www.DoBe.org).*

Vitamin T – the tribal vitamin

Nicholas Albery

The questionnaire that follows is designed to help people to take note of the extent to which they are detribalised and rootless and whether or not they are getting their Recommended Daily Allowance (RDA) of what I term Vitamin T, the tribal vitamin. My rating today, as I type this, adds up to 69 – so I am

20 Heber Road, London NW2 6AA, UK (rhino@dial.pipex.com), 2001, 300pp, ISBN 0 948826 58 4

getting a mere 69 per cent of the Vitamin T RDA, although I suspect I am getting a good deal more than the average person.

Most people do not seem to realise that they have near-starvation levels of Vitamin T. I know that I'm deprived of Vitamin T simply because I was lucky enough as a young man in the 1960s and 1970s to experience feeling part of a tribe as an active participant in community-based organisations in London's Notting Hill. So I feel what I'm missing now in my middle aged isolation. For others, the nearest equivalent may be looking back fondly on their time at university when their immediate surroundings were suffused with the possibility of interesting casual social encounters; and socialising didn't involve making appointments and getting in a car to visit friends in distant places.

What I miss most is the possibility in the evening of just dropping in on a convivial neighbour for a chat and a meal.

'Each nod they receive from a neighbour counts towards their RDA of Vitamin T'

Solitary elderly people trying to survive on a state pension are amongst those most in need of such informal neighbourhood contacts. Each nod they receive from a passing neighbour in the street, each chat with a local shopkeeper, counts towards their RDA of Vitamin T.

In our evolutionary past, we lived in small groups of 50 to 250 or so people, and we still need that intense level of inter-communication and sense of place and neighbourhood. The Rev John Papworth who edits Fourth World Review (with its slogan of 'small nations, small communities and a human scale') used to give sermons on the theme of Jesus' commandment to "love your neighbour" whilst complaining that nowadays most people don't even know who their neighbours are.

There's no word in the English language which quite means *lonely* – lonely despite having your happy nuclear family around you – lonely in the sense of feeling without a tribe, isolated, rootless and alienated. A new word such as *kithless* – as in without kith and kin – is needed. For kithlessness is, I believe, today's most unrecognised feeling. Almost every urban dweller feels it deep in themselves, but hardly anyone recognises or verbalises the feeling.

Some people even go to great lengths to keep apart from their neighbours. They believe that their tribe consists of those who share the same interests as them, in however far flung places they may live, or just the people they work with, or just their cosy nuclear family. No doubt in the past people could feel very trapped in their isolated, stultifying village culture, but now the pendulum has swung the other way, and we have only too many ways of escaping from our locality, through travel, work, holidays, telephone, television and the web.

But Vitamin T is based on the assumption that we have an inbuilt need for a tribe we live in proximity to, for kith and kin living co-operatively within a geographical neighbourhood.

'A strong social network is a predictor of long life'

Doubtless Vitamin T is essential for our health too. There is accumulating evidence that a strong social network is a predictor of long life – and a stronger predictor than our smoking and drinking habits (see for instance www.globalideasbank.org/wbi/WBI-70.HTML).

In the future that's rapidly arriving, where computer programmers and web designers and their ilk will be the aristocrats lording it over the rest of us, who will be either out of work or providing them with their luxuries, it will be ever harder to feel part of society, and it is only within cohesive neighbourhoods that we will be able to receive recognition for who we are as people, whatever our job or lack of one may be.

Please note that in this questionnaire, 'nuclear family' means 'you, your spouse and your children'; and 'local' means 'within 15 minutes' walk from your home'. The questions only address encounters in your neighbourhood or at work which take place within this 15 minutes' range and which are outside your nuclear family. It is a neighbourhood rating, not a test of how many friends you have in distant places or how happy you are with your partner and children.

Vitamin T questionnaire

• Roughly how many local people (neighbours, local shopkeepers, waiters, hairdressers, local co-workers, etc) have you chatted with in the last week (apart from your partner and immediate nuclear family)?

   • Roughly how many others have you nodded to or greeted whilst, for instance, passing them in the street? (For scoring purposes, divide this total by 2.)

   • How many local people (apart from your partner and immediate nuclear family) would be likely to notice and regret your death, if you were to die now (only include those whose deaths you would also notice and regret)? (For scoring purposes divide this total by 3.)

   • If you were seriously ill, roughly how many local people (apart from paid carers, your partner and immediate nuclear family) could you count on to visit you, to do your shopping for you, etc? (For scoring purposes double this total.)

   • How many households locally do you feel you could drop in on for a chat or a meal, almost on impulse, without it being a big deal? (For scoring purposes multiply this total by 5.)

20 Heber Road, London NW2 6AA, UK (rhino@dial.pipex.com), 2001, 300pp, ISBN 0 948826 58 4

• How many local people are there (apart from your partner and immediate nuclear family) whom you tend to treat as confidantes, people you can discuss and share your innermost fears and worries with? (For scoring purposes multiply this total by 10.)

• How many local people (apart from your partner and immediate nuclear family) care about your goals in life and actively support you in trying to achieve them? (For scoring purposes double this total.)

• Last week, how often did you engage in the equivalent of a tribal ritual – eg religious service, meal with local friends or local co-workers, drink at the local tavern or coffee shop with friends – occasions, in other words, where there was active participation by all those present? (For scoring purposes double this total.)

• In general, to what extent do you feel that you are part of a local neighbourhood or tribe who care for each other? (Score on a range from 0 to 20, where 20 = 'Just one big extended family' and 0 = 'no contact at all'.)

'How about inviting your neighbours for a social meeting in your home?'

Add up your total to arrive at your personal very rough-and-ready percentage of the RDA of Vitamin T. And if you're over 100 per cent, don't worry, there's no danger of overdosing. A friend of mine rated himself on this questionnaire as regularly over 1,000 per cent for one of the most interesting and stimulating periods of his life when he lived in Christiania community in Copenhagen. If your score is low, how about taking up John Papworth's suggestion – photocopying a notice and putting it through the letterboxes in your neighbourhood, inviting people for a social meeting either in your home or in a neutral venue? We have an annual tea party in our street, meeting in a different house each year, which I initiated, and even this small token event is beginning to make a difference to the sense of neighbourhood and the way we help each other out when we have problems.

I would be interested to receive feedback and suggestions for improvements from anyone who tries this questionnaire out.

• *Institute for Social Inventions, 20 Heber Road, London NW2 6AA, UK (tel Int.+44 [0]20 8208 2853; fax Int.+44 [0]20 8452 6434; e-mail: rhino@dial.pipex.com; web: www.globalideasbank.org).*

• *www.DoBe.org and the Institute for Social Inventions are co-sponsoring International Neighbourhood Day (see the previous item).*

• *John Papworth, editor, Fourth World Review (£20 p.a. subs), The Close, 26 High St, Purton, Wiltshire SN5 4AE, UK (tel Int.+44 [0]1793 77221; fax Int.+44 [0]1793 772521).*

Comment from Rabbi Mimi Weisel

As a group of us were sitting together and enjoying dinner on New Year's eve, we took your Vitamin T quiz and discovered that we have a large dose of Vitamin T in our lives. We attributed our relatively high score to our explicit, conscious choice to live as observant Jews, a choice which provides each of us with a great variety of the connections author Nicholas Albery says are lacking in most urban settings today even though we live in Los Angeles, one of the largest, most spread-out cities on earth.

As Jews committed to following the laws of our tradition, our lifestyle fosters community connections outside our immediate families, thereby providing us with networks for socializing and for nurturing. Perhaps the best example is our weekly observance of Shabbat, the Jewish Sabbath. We do not drive or ride in cars on Saturday, so we need to live within walking distance of a synagogue.

Part of our weekly ritual is saying "Shabbat Shalom" to others we pass on the way to and from the synagogue. On Shabbat we share meals and drop in on one another so our families can interact. Furthermore, living in a close neighbourhood such as ours also means that an infrastructure to support our observance is created: there are kosher restaurants and bakeries, Jewish bookstores and gift shops. Walking into these establishments, one is bound to run into friends and acquaintances and to create casual relationships with the shop owners.

Being part of an observant Jewish community, we are also involved in synagogue life, which promotes visiting the sick, comforting those who are in mourning, and welcoming others into the community. We work together to support schools, a variety of charitable causes, and social justice issues. We talk together and discuss our concerns for our community, our families, and the world as we sit together at shared meals and celebrations.

'Jewish tradition helps us to achieve balance and connection, community ties and support'

My friends and I are aware that many might consider our lifestyle to be restrictive and confining. Nonetheless, though we live in an open society with its plethora of choices and freedoms, all of us have chosen to live a life of observance. Each of us could have opted out of this life choice, yet we have all embraced it. Why? As modern individuals involved in careers and families, we are just as apt as others to be isolated by our computers, cell phones and cars, or to face the anonymity of the malls and movie theatres. In contrast, Jewish tradition helps us to achieve balance and connection, community ties and support.

Most organized religions offer strong support for creating communal

20 Heber Road, London NW2 6AA, UK (rhino@dial.pipex.com), 2001, 300pp, ISBN 0 948826 58 4

connections. Not only synagogues but also churches and mosques provide networks for caring and friendship on an on-going basis. I and my friends feel blessed to have these resources as well as the tenets of our tradition, which have resulted in the physical creation of a small community within a large metropolis.

    • *Rabbi Mimi Weisel, Assistant Dean, Ziegler School of Rabbinic Studies, University of Judaism, 15600 Mulholland Drive, Los Angeles, California 90077, USA (e-mail: mweisel@uj.edu).*

Neighbourhood Walkability Index
Chris Bradshaw

Chris Bradshaw writes: "I am co-owner of Vrtucar, the Ottawa Car-sharing organization, having retired early from my community relations position with the Regional Municipality of Ottawa-Carleton. I also work on traffic issues with my community association (the Glebe C. A.), do yardwork for seniors, am working on a new company to promote urban modeling simulation software, and am interim leader of the Green Party of Canada. I have a BA from Oberlin College in Political Science and live car-free with my wife of 31 years in central Ottawa. Our two daughters have 'flown the coop'."

    The following is from Bradshaw's paper entitled 'Creating – and using – a rating system for neighbourhood walkability – towards an agenda for 'local heroes' ' which he presented to the 14th International Pedestrian Conference in Boulder, Colorado, in October 1993. In 2001 Bradshaw submitted the paper to the Global Ideas Bank.

Abstract

'Walkability' is a quality of place, one that is being eroded by the day throughout the world. Although the term has been appearing in literature for some time, the author, a pedestrian rights activist and public consultation practitioner, knows of no attempt to measure it. This paper attempts to do that, as well as give three practical purposes for using the 'walkability index'. One such use is to provide a motivation to induce more people to become 'local heroes', by re-establishing their links with their streets and neighbourhoods and committing personal resources to rebuild their local physical and social infrastructure, so necessary to human life and the ecology of 'the commons'.

Why measure walkability?

I believe that I live in one of North America's most walkable neighbourhoods.

Unfortunately, its housing is also among the highest priced in the city. Last year, its homeowners and business owners faced steep increases in property taxes which are based on market values. Many of my neighbours challenged the market-value-based property taxes with the argument that market value of one's property does not necessarily reflect one's ability to pay taxes. Others argued differently: that the average person in our neighbourhood is more likely to walk and therefore has less need for the municipal-level infrastructure paid for by property taxes.

'Walkability could be used in calculating property taxes'

This got me thinking. I had always liked the idea of being able to measure this quality called 'walkability'. But now there might be a very important use for it. What if a collection of such measurements – in the form of a rating system or index – could be used in calculating property taxes and, for new buildings, the initial development fee? This may seem unfair, since it comes close to being an example of user-pay, but would be applied not to the individual or the household, but to the basic unit of walkability, the street block and the neighbourhood.

'The index could also be useful to homebuyers: are the streets safe? Will we need a car?'

The index could also be useful to homebuyers who could use the index to settle matters such as: Are the streets safe? Is transit service good? Will we need one car, two cars, or even no car?

Finally, there is the use of the index's indicators as an agenda for collective action. Since the index would apply to an entire neighbourhood, the action would naturally be collective. A neighbourhood could improve its rating through changing itself: its physical form and amenities, its range of businesses, its local services, and collective programmes. Therein lies the reference to the 'local hero', the person who enjoys the local scale, has affection for his or her particular surroundings, and commits time and resources to doing something to improve it by working with and through others to improve the conditions for a sense of community: economic, social and cultural commerce.

What is walkability?

Walkability has four basic characteristics:

(1) A 'foot-friendly' man-made, physical micro-environment: wide, level sidewalks, small intersections, narrow streets, lots of litter containers, good lighting and an absence of obstructions.

20 Heber Road, London NW2 6AA, UK (rhino@dial.pipex.com), 2001, 300pp, ISBN 0 948826 58 4

(2) A full range of useful, active destinations within walking distance: shops, services, employment, professional offices, recreation, libraries, etc.

(3) A natural environment that moderates the extremes of weather – wind, rain, sunlight – while providing the refreshment of the absence of man's overuse. It has no excessive noise, air pollution, or the dirt, stains, and grime of motor traffic.

(4) A local culture that is social and diverse. This increases contact between people and the conditions for social and economic commerce.

Proposal for creating the Walkability Index

Note: Like in golf, the lowest score is best. Each question gives the demerits to features or qualities that work against walkability.

(1) Density (persons per acre, up to centre-line of bordering features)

over 15	1
10-15	2
5-10	3
fewer than 5	4

(2) Parking places off-street per household (unrestricted street access)

less than 1	1
1-2	2
2-3	3
more than 3	4

(3) Number of sitting spots on benches per household (include seating in front yards)

more than .75	1
.5 to .75	2
.25 to .5	3
.25 or fewer	4

'Chances of meeting someone you know while walking'

(4) Chances of meeting someone you know while walking

10 or more per mile	1
3-10 per mile	2
fewer than 3 per mile	3
'Are you kidding?!'	4

Institute for Social Inventions, £15 subs, £17 from abroad by credit card, tel London 020 8208 2853

(5) Age at which a child is allowed to walk alone

Age 6 or younger   1
Ages 7-9   2
Ages 10-13   3
Age 12 or older   4

(6) Women's rating of neighbourhood safety

"I walk alone anywhere anytime"	1
"I walk alone, but am careful of routes"	2
"I must walk with someone at night"	3
"I never walk, except to car visible from entrance"	4

(7) Responsiveness of transit service

Within ten minutes   1
10-20 minutes   2
more than 20 minutes   3
no service   4

(8) Number of neighbourhood 'places of significance' (significant to the respondent) named by average respondent

10 or more   1
5-10   2
3-5   3
fewer than 3   4

(9) Parkland (measurement)

More than 50 acres per square mile and per average residence and less than 1,500-foot walk   1

More than 50 acres per square mile and per average residence and more than 1,500-foot walk   2

Less than 50 acres per square mile and per average residence and less than 1,500-foot walk   3

Less than 50 acres per square mile and per average residence and more than 1,500-foot walk   4

(10) Sidewalks (single point each)

Not on both sides of 90 per cent of streets
Dips at each driveway
Widths less than 5 feet on residential streets; 8 feet on shopping streets
More than discontinuity (1 inch or more) per block

The final score divided by 20 will produce a walkability index between 0.45 and 2.00

20 Heber Road, London NW2 6AA, UK (rhino@dial.pipex.com), 2001, 300pp, ISBN 0 948826 58 4

Scale in human activity

We live life on different scales:
- global
- national
- city/region
- neighbourhood
- street/project
- household/family
- individual

Until recent times, few people lived their lives at scales above the city/region level. In fact, although many people have jobs that operate in the loftier orbits, or favour international news to local news, or buy few locally-produced goods, life is still lived locally.

Think of the seven scales as a hierarchy inside a thermometer. As energy and cognitive capacity increases, the mercury expands up the scale as the individual has the ability to operate at larger scale. Over the normal course of a person's life, the scale starts low, climbs into adulthood, then drops slowly until death. If plotted against time, it would be like a bell curve. But no matter how large a domain we can master, we continue to need to function comfortably at lower scales.

'We are losing the infrastructure for the street and neighbourhood scales'

The problem is this. We are losing the infrastructure for the street and neighbourhood scales. The streets have become automobile feeders for the city-scale roads. City agencies have replaced neighbourhood and street-level visiting of the sick and elderly. The child, who needs to have ever-widening contiguous spaces to freely explore as he or she grows, is not allowed independent access to the street until after he or she is old enough not to have much use for it. How many of us in our work produce for a local market or purchase local goods or services?

'Cities designed only for AAAs: active, affluent adults'

The result is cities designed only for AAAs: active, affluent adults. If you are young, old, or disabled, you stay inside or go out only with a guardian in tow, usually ferried about in a car or bus. If you are poor, transit and long walks under inhospitable conditions are your lot. These people are not only denied the human scale and lively streets they need, but they now need more income to buy the 'solutions': a car and a 'better' neighbourhood.

Why has this happened?

(1) The automobile – a vehicle more suited to freeways and rural roads – has taken over all streets. As a society we now accept that streets are dangerous and dirty. Drivers are not held responsible for pedestrian deaths and injuries; the pedestrians or their guardians are. The streets reflect 'might makes right', rather than, 'the more you wield, the more you yield' that exists between boats on waterways.

'Women – traditional nurturers of the local scale – are adopting men's love of the large scale'

(2) Women, the traditional nurturers of the local scale, including the household, have joined the workforce and are adopting men's love of the large scale, which they believe equals power. Unfortunately, street and neighbourhood relations have suffered. (The solution, of course, is not for men and women to go back to their own separate 'domains', but for all adults to re-establish local links.)

(3) We are moving towards globalism: economy, government, and even environmentalism. There is little in-between that is not owned or controlled by global interests: no sinew, no connecting tissue. Why? The large-scale interests want it that way: local interests, loyalties, goods, values, etc are redundant in the modern world.

Urban life, too, is disdained. Life is to be lived only after leaving the city job far behind each day and driving as far away to a non-urban home as money and time will afford.

'Exotic vacations in places where safe civic spaces and human-scale streets still exist'

The result is an imbalanced infrastructure: people buying private solutions to public problems. There is no civic life occurring in civic places anymore. We are told to expect only negative experiences in these places. They are replaced by larger private yards, membership in health clubs, and exotic vacations in places where safe civic spaces and human-scale streets still exist. When they must be used, one takes along protection. We buy evermore sophisticated home and car alarms, rather than spend time rebuilding common, local space. The self-regulating civic culture of the Commons is fast disappearing. In those spaces we now see the 'weeds' of crime, litter, unkempt buildings and grounds, noise and grime, and abandoned people.

20 Heber Road, London NW2 6AA, UK (rhino@dial.pipex.com), 2001, 300pp, ISBN 0 948826 58 4

How broadly does walkability impact on local government costs?

Applying the walkability index to taxes and development charges raises the question, "Should it not be limited only to the portion that applies to transportation infrastructure?" No. The effects of walkability are beneficial over a far broader area.

The walkable neighbourhood makes less demand on several services and resources:

• roads and parking facilities: Because of shorter trips and smaller modes (space and weights), they make lower use of roads and parking, and the real estate and maintenance costs they represent.

• transit: Transit subsidies are lower (or perhaps non-existent) for those living in walkable neighbourhoods: (a) more riders per mile; (b) shorter trips and therefore more fares per mile; (c) more transit use in off-peak; and (d) more bi-directional travel during peak period.

'The walkable neighbourhood provides a great deal more of its own surveillance'

• police protection: The walkable neighbourhood provides a great deal more of its own surveillance, provides more jobs and activities for youths, has fewer new, expensive cars to be stolen; and fewer off-street parking lots where assaults are most often committed.

• density-sensitive services: Garbage collection, underground pipes, fire protection, and general administration are services that cost more where development is less dense.

• social and health services: Besides being sensitive to density, these services are also sensitive to the presence or lack of informally provided community services, best illustrated by neighbours visiting sick neighbours or providing babysitting or even a ride for a neighbour having a doctor or job appointment.

• economic development: The higher-density, the mixed land use, the availability of a larger and more diverse work force, and the availability of marginal, incubator spaces and services makes these neighbourhoods more powerful generators of economic vitality.

Enter local heroes

I have started to invest more of my time into my local communities: my street and my neighbourhood. I am starting to see the need – and the opportunities – for this involvement, and am trying to find a way to support myself doing it. Here are my ideas and initiatives. I predict that, due to the downturn in the economy (and the poor expectations for early recovery) and the arrival of the baby boomers in the empty-nester stage of life, many more people will find their local interests growing.

'I have started to invest more of my time into my street and my neighbourhood'

What are 'local heroes'? The term local heroes comes from a movie of the same name in which the main character successfully resists the moves of Burt Lancaster working for a multinational company to convert the local economy and resources to a 'higher use'. In my mind, a local hero is simply loyal to that scale and to the specific people and places within his or her community, in the same way a mother is loyal to her family.

An agenda for local heroes

Local heroes need to spend time and mental energy getting to know their community and street better and sympathetically. And that takes time. Our employer pays us to spend 40 hours a week focusing on his or her scale, and if we have a family, we will tend to spend most of the remainder on the household and ourselves. Our personal time will tend to be spent with larger-scale information and entertainment sources available in print and electronically.

The first local heroes will need to be real leaders. They will need to conceive and create new institutions and infrastructure for these scales. Here are some ideas that I am working on:

(1) Start a 'co-transportation' club. This is the way to provide fractional access to a car and break the need to use a car a lot in order to justify the high fixed costs.

'Hold a walking festival with all the walks offered as part of a multi-day blitz'

(2) Local stories and maps. Get local people to record and share local knowledge, develop local maps, design neighbourhood walks for newcomers and visitors. Then hold a walking festival with all the walks offered as part of a multi-day blitz.

(3) Visions. Organize street and neighbourhood visions or plans and bring together resources to coordinate future changes to conform.

Try a Visual Preference Survey (developed by A. Nelessen) to focus people on their communities as place. It gets people mentally out on foot in the settings they usually only drive through.

(4) 'Be a PESt!' (Pedestrian Environment Steward) and animate – and care for – the streets and parks.

(5) Start a 'DePoT' (corner store, recycling centre, laundry or photo drop-

20 Heber Road, London NW2 6AA, UK (rhino@dial.pipex.com), 2001, 300pp, ISBN 0 948826 58 4

off, and postal station, and delivery point for larger stores and catalogue shopping). Hire teenagers to help with pickup and delivery.

(6) Be a 'johnny greenseed' and restore your neighbourhood's ecology.

'Encourage locals to produce for your store'

(7) Get local merchants to localize: (a) cater to local customers (the ones who don't use parking spots and don't expect you to sit on a busy road and advertise city-wide, (b) encourage locals to produce for your store, (c) hire locally and help current employees to move into neighbourhood, (d) reduce outbound wastes.

(8) Start a neighbourhood BBS (computer bulletin board system) for local information and commerce.

(9) Determine your community's walkability.

Conclusions

I hope I have related a context for recreating the missing links in the continuity of urban life, the scales that are closest to the commons, the economic incubators, the cultural breeding ground, the feedback systems necessary for reducing humankind's footprint on the earth and on each other. Walkability is pretty close to livability, to healthy communities, to sustainability, but it's not as abstract. We can all relate to it. And it relates so much to quality of life: health, community, social equity, enjoyment, attachment to place, environment, fitness, low stress.

Let's look at walkability as a positive indicator of what we all want – to replace pollution, crime, traffic accidents as indicators of what we don't want – and thus become a focus for action, the collective action, action and involvement that re- creates community and caring for each other and the places we share.

Let me close with the words of Wendell Berry in his essay, 'Words and Flesh'.

'The heroes of abstraction keep galloping in on their white horses to save the planet – and they keep falling off in front of the grandstand'

"The favourite adjective of [the environment] movement now seems to be 'planetary'. This word is used, properly enough, to refer to the interdependence of places, and to the recognition, which is desirable and growing, that no place on earth can be completely healthy until all places are. But the word "planetary" also refers to an abstract anxiety or an abstract passion that is desperate and useless exactly to the extent that it is abstract. How, after all, can anybody – any particular body – do anything to heal a planet? The suggestion that anybody could do so is preposterous. The heroes of abstraction keep galloping in on their white horses to save the planet – and they keep falling off in front of the grandstand."

We cannot save the world by riding white horses, heroically or otherwise, or by duplicating global marketing. It will be done locally in the places we know and love, where we live and work and walk and play. It will occur within the dynamics of community and immediate, useful feedback on our own actions.

Bibliography

Berry, Wendell, *What are People For?*, San Francisco: Northpoint Press, 1990
Jacobs, Jane, *The Death and Life of Great American Cities*, Vintage, 1961
• *Chris Bradshaw, 6 Howick Place, Ottawa, Ontario, Canada K1S 3S5 (tel Int.+1 613 230 4566; e-mail: chris@ties.ottawa.on.ca).*

Parish councils for community democracy in large cities

Summarised from information supplied to the Global Ideas Bank by John Crewdson, Chair of the Home Rule movement in Bradford.

The Home Rule campaign in Bradford was begun in June 2000 with the aim of establishing parish and town councils throughout the Bradford Metropolitan District. The Home Rulers wish to do this because they believe that Bradford is too large to cater for the individual and distinct needs of its constituent neighbourhoods.

The Home Rule movement, as its name suggests, therefore hopes to bring about genuine self-governance across Bradford, with communities having more control over their own affairs and a stronger sense of their own identity. The parish councils will allow local people to elect their own democratic body, one accountable to them and solely created for their interests. As each community elects its own council, be it a rural village or an inner-city estate, a new political infrastructure will gradually be formed, with the devolution of power giving them real control over issues that concern their own area.

'The first community within the borders of the city of Bradford to have a parish council'

The Home Rule campaign is aiming to achieve this local devolution by using the petitioning process laid down in Section 11 of the Local Govern-

20 Heber Road, London NW2 6AA, UK (rhino@dial.pipex.com), 2001, 300pp, ISBN 0 948826 58 4

ment and Rating Act of 1997. Already this is well under way, with a petition for a Sandy Lane Parish Council nearly complete; this means that it will soon be the first community within the borders of the city of Bradford to have a parish council.

Campaigns are also under way in the suburb of Bierley and the inner-city neighbourhoods of Barkerend, Little Horton and Manningham. Many other areas are showing interest in the movement, and there are independent campaigns for new parish councils in Wilsden, Bingley, Queensbury and Clayton Heights. A petition has been collected for a Keighley Town Council, which will be the largest parish or town council in England if it is ratified by the government. Home Rule is currently gauging interest in forming new parish councils in the townships of Heaton, the rural village of Baildon and the town of Shipley.

'Neighbourhood forums will be a key factor in involving the community in the process'

The Home Rule campaign is also spreading the word using neighbourhood forums run by Bradford Council. At these forums, representatives of Home Rule can lay out the benefits of parish councils and how to begin the process of setting one up. This will help to let more people know about the possibilities for community democracy, and it will also be an ideal platform for reaching those who are already active in their communities. This will be a key factor if more progress is to be made, with local people necessarily being at the heart of the movement. If that begins to happen across Bradford, along with the campaigning and support of the Home Rule organisation, then community democracy could truly be established in what is presently a disparate sprawling city.

Home Rule has established links with the Welsh Communities Campaign, the London Community Alliance, the Association for Neighbourhood Democracy and the Campaign for Yorkshire, all of which are campaigning for devolution in different parts of the UK, with the latter seeking a Parliament or Assembly for the Yorkshire region. The agenda is a common one, that of seeking a more decentralised society where power is distributed according to the principle of subsidiarity.

• *www.homerule.org.uk aims to provide a sort of 'tool-kit' for those interested in neighbourhood democracy, which will include guidelines on campaigning for a parish council, as well as downloadable templates of petitions, leaflets and posters. Home Rule, 118 Bierley Lane, Bierley, Bradford, West Yorkshire BD4 6AS, UK (tel Int. 44 [0]1274 681479; e-mail: info@homerule.org.uk).*

• *John Crewdson, 17 Sandymoor, Sandy Lane, Bradford, West Yorkshire BD15 9LF, UK (tel Int. 44 [0]1274 681479; e-mail: john@crewdson.net).*

What America can learn from the English village

Civility in an English village, *by William Stephens, published by Severn Books (30 Amberwood Parkway, PO Box 388, Ashland, OH 44805, tel 419 281 1802; fax 419 281 6883; e-mail: wstephens00@hotmail.com; ISBN 0 9679738 0 5, 2000, 280 pages, $19.95).*

This book, by an American writer aided by his English wife, aims to show the American reader what can be learned by observing an English village – in this case an unnamed village with a population of 700 (or 1,200 including outlying farms and hamlets) in Worcestershire.

This is a village of half-timbered houses (some of them thatched), Georgian houses, small housing estates, some council houses, a church, a primary school, an award-winning pub, a butchers, a village shop with a post office inside it, a bakery and a village hall. The village seems to have managed to avoid the slow decline that so many rural communities in the UK are now suffering from. The author's wife, Edna Ward Stephens, was perhaps the saviour here, as she went out and recruited gypsy children from the nearby encampments so as to prevent the village school closing, a closure which would have been the beginning of the end.

'This English village has solved most of our American social problems'

"This English village has 'solved' most of our American social problems," writes William Stephens. "The village is not perfect, and some problems remain. But in many ways it stands as a lesson for us all. The village is safe. Women can walk at night. People are trusting. Conflict is kept down. ...

"People are considerate of their neighbours, and they do what has to be done for the community. There is an intense caring about matters of civic concern. Citizen groups are powerful because they can count on grassroots support. The environment, and historic buildings, are protected by this citizen vigilance.

"People take care of each other. The elderly, especially, are cared for by the village at large. Trades people take care of their customers.

'Death is handled in a humane manner'

"The doctors take pains to care for their patients. Medical care is virtually free. Death is handled in a humane manner."

He is starry-eyed about Britain as a whole: the well-preserved ancient landscapes, the system of public footpaths, the lack of billboard and commer-

20 Heber Road, London NW2 6AA, UK (rhino@dial.pipex.com), 2001, 300pp, ISBN 0 948826 58 4

cial signs along the roads, the less intense advertising on TV and radio, the reduced profile of lawyers and government, the lower frequency and level of damage awards for medical negligence, the "simplified" income tax forms ("an ordinary householder can fill out his tax return in a few minutes, with no need for an accountant") and the "vastly superior medical service" – surely some exaggerations have crept in here.

'Reputation rewards the generous public-spirited persons. There is a sort of group memory in the village'

He proceeds to examine how this Utopian situation arises. Partly, he argues, but only partly, it comes about as a result of the smallness of the community. In a small village, it was "easier to get started with volunteer work, it took less courage; it was harder not to volunteer. People solicited you and there was no place to hide". Persons of all ages scored higher on life-satisfaction in smaller communities. You attended a village event because your presence was needed, not simply because you thought you might enjoy it. Everyone was needed in order to have activities, so even incompetents and eccentrics were made welcome. In a small community, "reputation rewards the generous, giving, public-spirited, kind persons. There is a sort of group memory in the village."

But basic to all this, the author maintains, are moral standards. "The moral code is similar to our own. However, trust – and the rest – is as it is, because the people are at pains to do the right thing."

'A child is usually expected to be quiet and not to interrupt in the presence of adults; he would not be permitted to dominate the conversation'

He insists that the fundamental aspect that makes the village work is the disciplined way in which children are brought up. "Children are taught self control by rather controlled, disciplined parents. This prepares them for school, in which competition and aggressiveness is downplayed. Being mindful of others' needs, and of one's obligations to other people, is emphasised." Edna Ward Stephens suggests that all this starts in the first months of life, through "speaking quietly to the child, setting a regular routine of living, having regular hours [and] quiet mealtimes at set times." A child is usually expected to be quiet and not to interrupt in the presence of adults. "Adults would speak to him; he would be included in the conversation. However, he would not be permitted to dominate the conversation. ... Then you can take the child to places outside the home. Such a child can go places and not be unwelcome, not spoil it for others."

'A sense of mutual obligations develops'

Through this self-control, a sense of mutual obligations develops that sustains and underlies the trust and co-operation that holds the village together.

But despite all that the author says to the contrary, it does seem always to come back to the issue of scale and small community advantage: "Parents prepare their children to be well-behaved and attentive in school. The school takes off from that point and furthers this style of socialisation. In the surrounding larger towns and in the city, ... the schools tend to be different. This manner of step-wise development is no longer possible."

The author maintains that sophisticated, well-read and well-travelled English people under-appreciate the qualities of the English village. Here at the Institute for Social Inventions we plead not guilty, but perhaps this simply reveals our lack of sophistication.

• *For further items on the importance of (and tactics for) preserving small-scale community life, see www.globalideasbank.org/neighbourhood.html*

Neighbourhood sponsors techie kids

Aaron Campbell

Adapted from a submission to the Global Ideas Bank.

We all know the tech guru at our office – the person who seems to live and breathe in acronyms and bytes – but do we know who that person is when our home iMac needs the dreaded paper-clip and we don't know where the secret spot is located? I suggest that neighbourhoods pitch in the proceeds of a bake sale or two and 'sponsor' a youngster in the technology field. If there are more than a few kids up to the task, sponsor a group of kids.

The money (no more than $200 to start with, in order to buy Norton Utilities or Internet for Dummies) would have a cap and be used only if the neighbourhood didn't have the software or peripherals needed.

A kid like this would grow to be more responsible, similar to the way kids in my old neighbourhood used babysitting. It's another good excuse to have a community meeting (so you can organise flowerplantings, block-watch programs, etc) and get neighbours to look out for each other.

The kid or kids would gain valuable skills and could eventually teach other kids those same skills (or their lazy parents!). Any sort of neighbourhood

20 Heber Road, London NW2 6AA, UK (rhino@dial.pipex.com), 2001, 300pp, ISBN 0 948826 58 4

sponsorship would be beneficial, but the kids can get into the tech or computer stuff quickly and see results in personal pride and civic accomplishment.

• *Aaron Campbell (aaroncampbell@netscape.net)*

Planning cities for a small country

A review of the book Cities for a Small Country *by Richard Rogers and Anne Power (published by Faber, London; 310pp; £14.99; ISBN 0-571-20652-2). Additional information summarised from an article by Anne Power, entitled 'City Limits', in the Guardian (October 25th 2000). Reviewed by Nick Temple.*

To be told that the cities in Britain have problems is nothing new for anyone who has ever lived in one. Crime, congestion, and inequality in the inner cities lead to suburban sprawl, 'developed' green field sites, and full blown abandonment of the urban space, as well as being problems in their own right. As a small country, this cannot continue ad infinitum: something has to change, and our cities have to be at the core of that change. This is the belief of Richard Rogers and Anne Power, whose new book, *Cities for a Small Country*, aims to combine their twin fields of expertise: architecture and design with social policy and exclusion. And while their suggested solutions may be nothing groundbreakingly new, (such as green belts and higher density of buildings) they are more likely to be effected than other ideas in many a theoretical book on planning: for the authors were asked to head up the Urban Task Force in the UK. They therefore have the ear of a government desperate for answers to Britain's depleted inner cities.

'Sprawling green-field suburban development has direct consequences for the inner city'

Their main point is that cities need to be improved, and that an efficient, inclusive and compact city can be a cohesive, alluring place. They also point out that sprawling green-field suburban development has direct (and reciprocally poor) consequences for the inner city, and that that has knock-on consequences for the inner city's economic and social conditions. Moreover, they argue that the physical form of cities and the social conditions within them are inextricably linked, and both can be affected and changed by human action. The main suggestions of the authors as to what should be done are as follows:

• to **create green belts** around all built-up areas to prevent suburban sprawl
• to **double the density of new urban development** to levels equivalent to a popular village high street

Institute for Social Inventions, £15 subs, £17 from abroad by credit card, tel London 020 8208 2853

- to **prioritise public spaces**: streets, squares, parks; and public transport, especially buses
- to **make city streets both safe and attractive** by controlling traffic and employing wardens

'Stop the release of green field sites for development until all available brown field has been used up'

- to **stop the release of green field sites for development** until all available brown field land has been used up; and to re-use brown field sites at the city's core
- to give **equal incentives to those wishing to restore and repair** existing buildings as well as those planning new developments

In essence, their plan is one of environmentally-friendly density: compact, well-designed cities that are less wasteful and less stressful for all. And the design is a key factor: density is all well and good, but a packed estate with darkened nooks and crannies is a recipe for danger not security, as the recent killing of Damilola Taylor has shown. Rogers and Power's blueprint for change places an emphasis on the interaction of the architectural with the social, of the structured with the inclusive. As Anne Power has written elsewhere, "To overcome the long legacy of social exclusion, cities must hold on to both richer and poorer residents. Their interests coincide. They both want good quality, spacious homes in a pleasant, safe environment, close to work, good schools, shops and transport". This book provides a plan for achieving such a city – it deserves to have notice paid to it.

Global Neighbourhood Watch via the Internet

Summarised from an article by Neal Stephenson, entitled 'Global Neighbour-hood Watch', in Wired Magazine (Wired Scenarios issue; to subscribe, call 415 222 6200 or e-mail: subscriptions@wired.com). This item was monitored for the Global Ideas Bank by Roger Knights.

People from the other side of the world can watch out at night for crime on your street by using video cameras and the internet.

Such a system will allow people working on their computer in other countries to alert that particular neighbourhood to any crime. By using video cameras with motion detectors, the cameras will only transmit digitised output when something is actually happening. Then the video can be put online, once

20 Heber Road, London NW2 6AA, UK (rhino@dial.pipex.com), 2001, 300pp, ISBN 0 948826 58 4

the neighbourhood's computers are linked to the internet. Meanwhile, in the UK or Australia, while the crime-ridden neighbourhood in America sleeps, the computer user could be alerted when something is moving on screen.

'A red button clicks on and sounds an alarm on the American's computer'

If the movement is innocent (a stray cat, a piece of litter in the wind), a green button could be clicked on; if a crime is in progress, a red button could be clicked on which sounds an alarm on the American's computer to wake the person up. The reverse could happen during night-time in Australia or the UK.

Obviously, this idea relies on a few important factors. Firstly, the street (or streets) in question would have to be in a neighbourhood with several computer-owning households. Secondly, the people taking part in the scheme would have to have their computers on all the time, unless some sort of shift system could be devised. Thirdly, connection failures and poor visual images could lead to communication problems, although as hardware and software continues to improve, this will be less of a problem. Finally, the people watching have to be completely trustworthy, not just jokers who enjoy waking you up every five minutes.

The potential in the idea is clear, though. If enough people in enough countries were interested in taking part, the concept of a 'Global Neighbourhood Watch' could become reality. Rather than peeking out of the windows at home at anyone suspicious, we could soon be looking into the Windows on the screen.

Brazilian city where neighbourhood groups allocate budget

Summarised from an e-mail from Tom Atlee to the Institute (contact: The Co-Intelligence Institute, PO Box 493, Eugene, OR 97440; e-mail: cii@igc.org; web: www.co-intelligence.org) and from an article, entitled 'The Experience of the Participative Budget in Porto Alegre, Brazil', on the UNESCO website (www.unesco.org/most/southa13.htm).

In 1989, the city of Porto Alegre came up with a radical solution to its major problems of unaccountability and extreme poverty: a participative budget. For the last decade, the people of the city have been deciding how the budget for public works should be allocated. Neighbourhood groups propose projects, and people from community groups and non-profit organisations, who have been elected by their neighbours, decide which projects will go ahead. In some cases, the community delegates also oversee implementation of the final projects. This has had the triple result of avoiding corruption and mishandling funds, improving concrete matters on the ground, and increasing democratic participation in the process by a huge amount.

'65,000 more homes have a basic water supply'

Since this budget system came into force, there have been some startling results. 65,000 more homes have a basic water supply, and the percentage of the population served by the sewerage system has leapt from 46 per cent to 85 per cent. In the poorest sections of the city, 25 to 30 kilometres of street are paved each year, while drainage and public lighting have both risen to the head of the priority list. The participative budget has had a massive impact in education, too, with new focused funding resulting in a doubling in the total number of enrolments between 1988 and 1995 alone. Perhaps the most dramatic effect of all, though, has been on the number of people involved in the whole process. Tens of thousands of people regularly attend the two public assemblies each year which elect the delegates and check up on last year's achievements, and there are a huge quantity of local associations and popular organisations who have received overdue representation.

'50 other South American cities are putting the budget system into place'

The system is not only viewed as a success by its citizens, (who recently gave it an 85 per cent approval rating in a poll), but by other cities in South America. 50 other cities in Brazil, Argentina and Uruguay are putting the same budget system into place, and the trend looks sure to spread. Porto Alegre should be an example to everyone of what can be achieved when the people whom policies affect are truly involved in the making, funding and effecting of those policies.

• *Porto Alegre Council can be contacted at Porto Alegre City Hall, Praca Montevideo 10-11/4 andar, Porto Alegre, Rio Grande do Sul, Brazil 90010-170 (tel Int.+55 [0]51 224 4400; fax Int.+55 [0]51 228 8725; e-mail: zanotta@procempa.tche.br).*

20 Heber Road, London NW2 6AA, UK (rhino@dial.pipex.com), 2001, 300pp, ISBN 0 948826 58 4

A summer leisure credits scheme for village youth

Summarised from an item entitled 'Village of the Year' in the London Daily Telegraph (December 9th 2000), monitored for the Global Ideas Bank by Yvonne Ackroyd.

The village of Mere, near Warminster in Wiltshire (population 2,000) is offering its youngsters leisure credits in return for community work in the village during the summer holidays, such as painting the clock tower or clearing the village stream. They can exchange the credits for more high-octane leisure activities, such as water-skiing, paintballing and snowboarding.

'Leisure credits in return for painting the clock tower or clearing the village stream'

Mere was also commended by the judges of the Daily Telegraph Village of the Year competition – in which it was a runner-up – for preserving its historical archives, caring for its environment and looking after its elderly.

New rules to build communities for the future

Summarised from information on the New Rules website.

A project run by the Institute for Local Self-Reliance hope to create a storehouse of rules and laws that could help build and maintain local communities and economies. The New Rules Project puts forward a set of new rules that builds community by encouraging and supporting human-scale politics and economics. The rules, in particular, call for:

• Decisions to be made by those who will feel the impact of those decisions
• Communities (and the households within them) to possess or own sufficient productive capacity to generate real wealth
• Communities to accept responsibility for the welfare of all their members and for the welfare of the generation that follows them

To this end, they have divided their suggested rules into ten sections: agriculture, electricity, environment, equity, finance, governance, information, retail, sports and taxation. Each section on the website contains rules relating to that particular topic, rules which "honour a sense of place and prize rootedness, continuity and stability as well as innovation and enterprise". Each topic sector also contains a list of policy tools for that particular area.

Institute for Social Inventions, £15 subs, £17 from abroad by credit card, tel London 020 8208 2853

'For people to view their communities as far more than just places of residence and retail'

The Institute for Local Self-Reliance, who run the project, are a non-profit organisation devoted to the case of what they call 'New Localism', whose three main principles are outlined above. Their aim is for people to view their communities and neighbourhoods as more than just places of residence, leisure and retail; to view them as areas that can nurture informed and active citizens with the skills and abilities to provide for, and govern, themselves. The Institute's belief is that it is localism that is progressive, not globalism, and that localism and smallness are not only more environmentally friendly and more democratic, but also more cost-effective and more profitable. As they put it, "The only thing that smallness lacks is power, the power to make the rules"; this project hopes to change that.

- *The New Rules website is at www.newrules.org*
- *For a further look at local issues, see the review of 'Localization – a Global Manifesto' in the International section of this book.*

ENVIRONMENT & ECOLOGY

Earth's natural resources will be exhausted by 2075

Summarised from an article by Nick Nuttall, entitled 'Planet will be a wasteland by 2075', in the London Times (October 20th 2000). Additional information from the World Wide Fund for Nature website (www.wwf.org).

'Two more planet Earth's would be needed today if everyone in the world were as wasteful as the so-called developed countries'

The world's natural resources are being exploited at such a rate that nothing may be left by the year 2075. *The Living Planet Report 2000* put together by the World Wide Fund for Nature (WWF) contained assessments of the planet's ecosystems, and each individual country's impact on the environment. Both measures found that the world's seas, forests and farmlands are being rapidly exhausted, and that there is simply not enough time or land (never mind inclination) to halt the process. Western European and Middle

20 Heber Road, London NW2 6AA, UK (rhino@dial.pipex.com), 2001, 300pp, ISBN 0 948826 58 4

Eastern countries are primarily held to blame, with the WWF report stating that two more planet Earth's would be needed today if everyone in the world were as wasteful as the so-called developed countries.

The impact of each country is measured by its 'ecological footprint', a measurement that estimates a population's consumption of food, materials and energy in terms of the area of biologically-productive land or sea required to produce those resources. Each country's footprint is made up of six components:

'The area of forest required to absorb the carbon dioxide emissions resulting from the country's energy consumption'

• The area of cropland needed to produce the crops which that country consumes.

• The area of grazing land required to produce the animal products consumed.

• The area of forest required to produce the amount of wood and paper used.

• The area of sea needed to produce the marine fish and seafood eaten.

• The area of land required for housing and infrastructure.

• The area of forest required to absorb the carbon dioxide emissions resulting from the country's energy consumption.

As people use resources from all over the world, and affect places faraway from them with their pollution, the ecological footprint is the sum of the areas above wherever they are on the planet.

'The United Arab Emirates is the most environmentally damaging country, followed by Singapore and the United States'

Under this analysis, the United Arab Emirates emerges as the most environmentally damaging country, followed by Singapore and the United States. As Francis Sullivan, director of conservation at the WWF, puts it: "The UAE has the biggest ecological footprint on the planet" due to its consumption of fish, timber and other natural resources, and because of its exporting of vast quantities of oil which contribute to global warming. These things, when allied to its small size, make it the world's most environmentally damaging country. And the rest of the developed world isn't far behind, to the extent that there may be nothing left to exploit by the end of this century.

• *For a downloadable copy of the Living Planet Report 2000, see http:// panda.org/livingplanet/lpr00/download.cfm*

101 solutions to global climate change

Stormy Weather: 101 Solutions to Global Climate Change *by Guy Dauncey and Patrick Mazza (published by New Society, 2001, ISBN: 0865714215; see www.newsociety.com). Reviewed by Stephanie Wienrich.*

Guy Dauncey and Patrick Mazza want to help us to become 'climate-smart' so that we can no longer say "we don't know what to do". They theorise that the more advanced human-equivalents on other planets in the universe have also had to "wean themselves off their mother planet's stored fossil fuels and learn to generate their own energy". Now it's our turn.

Of the 101 solutions in the book, here are ten that struck me as being particularly socially innovative. (Much of the advice is directed at North Americans, but could in theory be adapted for use by any nationalities.)

See your city as a whole

In the 1980s, the residents of Chattanooga, "the dirtiest city in America", were invited to imagine a future for their city. They named 40 goals and proposed 233 solutions.

> 'The residents were invited to imagine a future for their city. They named 40 goals and proposed 233 solutions'

20 years later the city has: a 22-mile riverside walk with playgrounds, performance spaces, fishing-piers and leaf-shaded walkways; a river from which you can eat the fish; a revitalised shopping district of converted warehouses; 3,500 units of inner city housing; a free electric shuttle bus; and a business that exports electric buses.

• *For a computer-based modelling tool for sustainable cities see www.envisiontools.com*

Dig up the concrete

Greening School Grounds, a Tree Canada project, aims to help students, teachers and parents plant trees and shrubs in schoolyards. The new landscapes absorb carbon dioxide, create shade and even help reduce bullying. In LA, there is a Cool Schools programme to plant 8,000 trees in schools.

• *See www.ladwp.com/coolschools for more information.*

20 Heber Road, London NW2 6AA, UK (rhino@dial.pipex.com), 2001, 300pp, ISBN 0 948826 58 4

Make car-free Sunday work

A car-free Sunday won't push cars out of the city for good, but will send out the message that cars are cooking the planet. Here's how to do it:
- Get support from the city council, the local media and local celebrities.
- Negotiate free or half-price rides on the buses.
- Organise street festivals, community walks and bicycle rides.
- Advertise the availability of bicycle trailers.
- Issue polite notices to local motorists.

'Organise train or bus rides to hiking areas outside the city'

- Organise train or bus rides to hiking areas outside the city [see www.DoBe.org for country walks accessible by train from London, UK].
- *See the websites of Car-Free Cities (www.carfree.com) and World Car-Free Day Consortium (www.ecoplan.org/carfreeday) for further information.*

Create a commotion

Make alliances with other likeminded groups. Form an affinity group – a self-sufficient support system of five to 15 people. Hold a non-violence training session. Stage an action: have a plan (and have some fun).
- *For more on affinity groups see: www.actupny.org/documents/CDdocuments/Affinity.html*

Adopt a politician

When you have found a potential political champion, arrange to meet him or her and start building a relationship. Ask "How can we help you?". That will shock them; most politicians never hear that question.

'Ask, "How can we help you?". That will shock them; most politicians never hear that question'

- *For inspiring stories about local groups influencing their politicians see http://results.action.org/shirley.html*

Educate the media

Most journalists are poorly informed about climate change. Arrange to meet them, send them stories they might find useful, and suggest they sign up for an environmental e-mail news service.

    • *Free e-mail resources include: The Daily Grist (www.earthday.net); Environmental News Network (www.enn.com) and Planet Ark (www.planetark.org).*

Introduce smart meters

A 'smart' electricity meter would give a coloured digital readout of power consumption for each room and even function in the house; switch off when power is expensive; receive messages from the utility company; and offer monthly carbon dioxide emission figures.

Buy climate-neutral gas

When customers in the UK buy their gas from Amerada using the Climate Care tariff, the company pays eight per cent of their tariff plus a £10 donation to Climate Care which invests the money in energy efficiency, renewable energy and tree-planting to offset the carbon dioxide released.

- *Amerada: www.amerada.co.uk*
- *Climate Care: www.co2.org*

Fly carbon-neutrally

Flying is responsible for six to ten per cent of the global warming problem, but air passengers can now pay for their flights to be carbon-neutral (CN). If they book through the US travel agency Triple E's 'Travel Cool' club, some of their travel dollars will be invested in environmental projects and technologies. Triple E is the first travel company to receive CN certification. To become certified as CN by the Climate Neutral Network a company must analyse its carbon emissions, plan to reduce these emissions, and buy 'carbon offsets' to cover the remaining emissions.

'Some of their travel dollars will be invested in environmental projects and technologies'

- *See www.climateneutral.com and www.TripleE.com*

Balance fiscal and environmental debt

The world's richest nations have accumulated an ecological debt of $13 trillion for their use of the global atmosphere. The world's poorest nations owe $376 billion. Can the two debts be balanced? The developed nations could account for their use of the atmosphere at a price between $10 to $50 per tonne of carbon dioxide ($200 to $1,000 per year for each US and Canadian citizen, levied via a carbon tax). This income could then be used to write off developing debt on the condition that the retained income was spent

20 Heber Road, London NW2 6AA, UK (rhino@dial.pipex.com), 2001, 300pp, ISBN 0 948826 58 4

on reducing poverty and greenhouse gas emissions.

• *See Drop the Debt (www.dropthedebt.org) and Jubilee 2000 (www.j2000usa.org and www.jubilee2000uk.org) for more on this subject.*

Hedgehogs used to protect strawberry crop from slugs

Summarised from an item on GreenGuide (online version), entitled 'Hedgehogs police Sainsbury's strawberries' (June 18th 2001) and from an article by Rachael Crofts, entitled 'Hungry hedgehogs keep strawberries on the menu', in PA News (July 3rd 2000).

50 hedgehogs have been employed by an organic farm in Herefordshire, UK, to prevent slugs from ruining their crop of organic strawberries. The hedgehogs were recruited from a local animal sanctuary to eat the slugs because no artificial chemicals or pesticides can be used in the growing of organic crops. This rule also caused the problem in the first place, because the matting brought in to prevent weed growth doubled as a warm and moist paradise for slugs. The subsequent slimy pest invasion prompted the introduction of the hedgehogs, who were deemed more suitable for the task than toads or birds (other renowned slug-munchers). The crop has thus been protected, while the hedgehogs have been feasting well away from the perils of traffic-filled roads.

• *Green Guide can be found at www.greenguideonline.com where you can also subscribe to a weekly e-mail of environmental news.*

Declare the 21st century a century of ecological restoration

Summarised from an item in Econews No. 101 of January 2001 (contact: Guy Dauncey, Econews, Sustainable Communities Consultancy, 395 Conway Rd, Victoria, BC, V8X 3X1, Canada (tel/fax Int.+1 250 8811304; e-mail: guydauncey@earthfuture.com; web: www.earthfuture.com))

Alan Watson Featherstone, of the conservation charity 'Trees for Life', has proposed that the United Nations should declare the 21st century a century of ecological restoration. In the terms of his proposal, every nation would be requested to redirect 10 per cent of their annual military budget to ecological restoration projects. Furthermore, an Earth Restoration Service would be created, enlisting volunteers from all over the world to restore and repair the environment.

'To restore the world's ailing ecologies, from the Mekong Delta in Vietnam to the Caledonian pine forest in Scotland'

The idea hopes to restore the world's ailing ecologies, from the Mekong Delta in Vietnam to the Caledonian pine forest in Scotland, and to put people back in touch with the world around them. In cleaning beaches or restoring tigers to their natural habitat in India, the project's founders hope that people will be reconnected with nature, place and life. And in a century prefigured by the failure of the world's politicians to agree any sort of consensus on the way forward, such a declaration could be just what the world needs.

• *The Restoring the Earth Project is run by Trees for Life, The Park, Findhorn Bay, Forres IV36 3TZ, Scotland (fax Int.+44 [0]1309 691155; e-mail: trees@findhorn.org; web: www.restore-earth.org).*

A pattern language for bioregional sustainability

Summarised from an e-mail by Tom Atlee (The Co-Intelligence Institute, Eugene, Oregon, (e-mail: cii@igc.org; web: www.co-intelligence.org).to the Global Ideas Bank.

The website www.conservationeconomy.net articulates a 'pattern language' for bioregional sustainability, which is architect and planner Christopher Alexander's term for a collection of architectural and planning elements that go to make a liveable place – from micro-factors to macro-factors – all interrelated in a coherent whole.

'A mini-encyclopedia of sustainability ideas and practices'

Stuart Cowan of EcoTrust has created a list of such modular factors applied to the issue of bioregional sustainability. His pattern language is a veritable mini-encyclopedia of sustainability ideas and practices, such as Awareness of Consumption and Its Effects, Beauty and Play, Community-Based Financial Institutions, Cyclical Patterns of Production and Consumption, Local Currencies and Trading Systems, Practical Skills in Support of Place, Regional Tax Revenue Sharing, Urban Growth Boundaries, Waste as a Resource, Wildlife Corridors, and dozens more.

20 Heber Road, London NW2 6AA, UK (rhino@dial.pipex.com), 2001, 300pp, ISBN 0 948826 58 4

Click on any item in the list and you get a succinct description of it and links to related elements in the pattern language. It is, itself, a web of life – a truly remarkable achievement.

A biodiversity census to create an inventory of all species

Summarised from an article by Beth Daley, entitled 'State plans a census with nature in mind'; in the Boston Globe (May 18th 2001; http://www.boston.com/ dailyglobe2), and from the Massachusetts State website (www.state.ma.us).

The state of Massachusetts is conducting its own census of biodiversity to create a database of known species in the state. The 'Biodiversity Days', held in June each year, have the dual aims of trying to track how species are progressing in the state, and of trying to reconnect the people of the state with the natural world and their own environment. As sightings of species are collected, state wildlife agencies then use the data to document their locations and to monitor habitat and health trends. Everything bigger than a millimetre is inventoried, and the database will eventually allow environmental officers to spot when a species is beginning to become endangered or even extinct.

'Over the years, seven animals native to the state have become extinct and many species of insects and flowers have disappeared'

Nearly 20,000 people are thought to have taken part in June 2001, with every piece of information being considered valuable. As Peter Alden, a biodiversity officer in Massachusetts' Executive Office of Environmental Affairs, says, "We're just trying to note these species' existence in towns. Endangered species were once common somewhere. We have lost a lot of things through the years and, if we know where they lived, maybe we could have managed them better". Indeed, in the last century or so, seven animals native to the state have become extinct, and many species of insects and flowers have similarly disappeared. This census of nature intends on never letting that happen again, and part of that process is to track the spread of unwanted species in the state as well. Powerful non-native plants can thus be prevented from overrunning native plant populations.

'Just getting 20,000 people to notice their environment is a big achievement'

The state's environmental officers are not expecting the schoolchildren and gardening fanatics to unearth new species, and most will only document well-known species. But the location and number of the species is just as important as logging which species are present. Furthermore, just getting 20,000 people to notice their natural surroundings and be aware of their environment is almost as big an achievement. Thus far, reports have come in of 541 field trips in 182 towns, involving everyone from schoolchildren to gardeners. Therefore, the census not only obtained valuable environmental information, but also encouraged people to get back into nature and rediscover their links with the outside world, and that is something else which we can little afford to allow to become extinct.

    • *For more information on Massachusetts' annual Biodiversity Days, call Peter Alden, Executive Office of Environmental Affairs, on Int.+1 617 626 1192, or check out the information on the web at www.state.ma.us/envir/ biodiversity.htm*

An organic public swimming pool

Summarised from an article by Guy Dauncey, in Econews no.99 of October 2000. Guy Dauncey, Econews, Sustainable Communities Consultancy, 395 Conway Road, Victoria, BC, V8X 3X1, Canada (tel/fax Int.+1 250 8811304; e-mail: guydauncey@earthfuture.com; web: www.earthfuture.com).

In the town of Biberstein in Switzerland, an organic public swimming pool has just been opened with no chlorine, no tiles in outrageous shades of blue and no ridiculous water slides. Its focus instead is on clear, clean water which brings simple joy back to the swimming experience.

'Dragonflies, reeds, water lilies, snails and frogs have all been introduced into the pool'

Added to this banning of artificiality, dragonflies, reeds, water lilies, snails and frogs have all been introduced into the pool. The old pool on the site was 25 by 12 metres, so two new ponds of the same size were added to aid the purification process. The new pool is, therefore, cleaner, purer, more natural and, the builders hope, more enjoyable. Nature, it could be said, has come back full force into the lives of swimmers in Biberstein.

20 Heber Road, London NW2 6AA, UK (rhino@dial.pipex.com), 2001, 300pp, ISBN 0 948826 58 4

Fish trained to respond to sounds are called back from the sea when they reach maturity

Summarised from an article by Nick Nuttall, entitled 'Sounds train fish to swim into net', in the London Times (October 10th 2000), and from information from the archives of Cyber Britain magazine (www.britain.or.kr).

A researcher has trained fish to swim into nets by using sounds, just as a sheepdog reacts to a farmer's whistle. It is believed that this could lead to more environmentally-friendly fish-farming methods, and also be used to replenish overfished (and understocked) seas. If fish can be trained to come towards sounds, then fish-farmers could produce young fish in tanks on their farms and then release them into the sea to feed and mature in their natural habitat. A few years later, the sound to which that fish group have been specifically attuned could be played from a 'station' on the shore, attracting them back to a boat or farm. As well as allowing the seas to be replenished, this system would also prevent the problems of disease and pollution that can be caused by overcrowded fish farm cages.

'Different fish species respond to different sounds with different frequencies'

Jonathan Lovell, of Plymouth University's Institute of Marine Studies, used to be the captain of a fishing boat before becoming involved in the field on a more academic level. His experiments have involved different species of fish, including cod, carp and sea bass; different species respond to different sounds with different frequencies. Mr Lovell claims that the fish have learned to link the sounds with a food reward, not unlike Pavlovian responses shown in other animals. He also claims to have demonstrated, over the space of a number of months, that the memory of the fish is far from short-term. In experiments thus far, the fish have remembered sounds for at least four months. Like dolphins and whales, fish have particular physiological adaptations that enable them to hear sounds from many miles away, making them especially suited to this system.

In the future, farmers could lay claim to the fish they reared that are then let out into the sea, perhaps even marking those that respond to their particular call signs. This would perhaps improve possibilities of conservation, because fish farmers would have more of a vested interest in what happens to the stocks in their neighbouring oceans. To test the system to the full, Mr Lovell is planning to release 10,000 young bass off Plymouth and then try to call them

Institute for Social Inventions, £15 subs, £17 from abroad by credit card, tel London 020 8208 2853

back. If that succeeds, music could soon be playing underwater all around the coast of Britain.

• *Jonathan Lovell can be contacted at Plymouth University's Institute of Marine Studies, Drake Circus, Plymouth, UK, PL4 8AA (e-mail: j.lovell@plymouth.ac.uk).*

Community orchards for nutrition, education and relaxation

Summarised from an article by Lynne Greenwood, entitled 'In apple pie order', in the Daily Telegraph (November 25th 2000), monitored for the Global Ideas Bank by Yvonne Ackroyd, and from information sent to the Institute by Common Ground who publish The Common Ground Book of Orchards: Community, Conservation and Culture *(ISBN 1 870364 21 X; 224pp; £18.95).*

In a world increasingly divorced from nature, and one increasingly worried by the industrialisation of food production, community orchards could prove a suitably natural and organic idea. As well as providing fruit for sale or consumption, they can also act as wildlife havens, places to play and relax, and as a sort of outdoor village hall for local festivities. They may also help to generate interest in horticulture, ensuring skills and knowledge are passed between generations. In these ways, a community orchard can be a communal asset, a focal point for the village or parish, and that is why the Common Ground charity have been promoting them for the past decade.

The idea for such an orchard is that openness and accessibility should be at the core of its planning: the primary purpose is not intended to be the production of fruit, but the enjoyment of the place itself. They can be owned or leased for the community by a local group, a parish council or by a local authority. Local people are encouraged to take part in the gardening and nurturing of the trees, and can then share in the harvest or profit from fruit sales. It is often the case that local people eat or cook with the fruit themselves, or distribute it locally, but in years where there is surplus, sales can provide funds to be ploughed back into the orchard.

> 'Community orchards could help with the new government initiative to provide every child aged between four and six with a piece of fruit on school days'

And it should not be thought that orchards are limited to the countryside: the book insists that "they can work in housing estates, industrial estates,

20 Heber Road, London NW2 6AA, UK (rhino@dial.pipex.com), 2001, 300pp, ISBN 0 948826 58 4

hospitals and schools", and backs up this claim with examples from around the country. An old brickworks in Walbottle on the banks of the River Tyne near Newcastle has become the site of an orchard that was planted in 1996. Villagers now receive crab apples and Victoria plums, and there is promise of more, with a couple of apple trees having self-seeded in the brickworks itself. Schools near Kentish Town in London and Stirling in Scotland have also been improving their horticultural skills on orchards, with fruit being given away to local projects or providing a healthy alternative at lunch times. With the new government initiative to provide every child aged between four and six with a piece of fruit on school days by 2004, such an orchard can link in nutritionally, as well as educationally, in British schools.

In their new book, Common Ground advise those trying to save old orchards, or plant new ones, that active local support is crucial, as is expert advice on which fruits and which varieties are most suited to each particular area. But a community orchard can be combined with other schemes to make them even more viable. Orchards around the country are used as caravan and camping parks or as nature reserves, as well as being a resource for local schools and residents. Ultimately, though, the orchard should provide its own reward. Although there is little instant gratification, a number of years nurturing and caring could result in great pride in the fruits of a community's labour, both literally and metaphorically.

• *For more information on community orchards, contact Common Ground, PO Box 25309, London NW5 1ZA, UK, or see their website at www.commonground.org.uk*

Plant fruit trees alongside roads

Daniel Davis

Adapted from a submission to the Global Ideas Bank. Daniel Davis writes that he is "at present a desk clerk in Kentucky".

I would like to see all countries that are spending money to beautify roadways starting to plant fruit trees alongside the road, on government land, instead of shrubs and flowers.

'Fruit-bearing trees would truly help people in need of food'

A cherry or apple tree or many other kinds of fruit-bearing tree would truly help people in need of food. The world might have less hungry people.

• *Daniel Davis (e-mail: davisdaniel@hotmail.com).*

Restful tunes yield more milk from cows

Summarised from an article by Jeevan Vasagar, entitled 'Music hath charms to boost milk yield', in the Guardian (June 27th 2001).

A pair of Leicester researchers have discovered how to increase cows' milk yield naturally: by pacifying them with slow music. The phenomenally successful Anchor butter adverts which depicted a field of dancing 'happy cows' may just have been on to something. When the Hostein Fresians were played relaxing tunes, such as Beethoven's 'Pastoral Symphony' or REM's 'Everybody Hurts', their milk yield increased by 0.73 litres per cow per day. Lecturer Adrian North and researcher Liam MacKenzie installed a sound system in the cows' sheds and played them music for 12 hours a day; they found the cows to be remarkably responsive. When subjected to more energetic songs, however, such as The Wonderstuff's 'Size of a Cow' or Jamiroquai's 'Space Cowboy', the cows produced less milk than normal.

'Any means of humanely increasing production is to be welcomed'

The researchers now intend to carry out similar experiments with chickens, to see whether musical hutches will increase their egg-laying capabilities. Again, though the research might seem frivolous, any means of increasing production humanely could be crucial to farmers, particularly organic ones.

Leaf recognition software to identify plants

Summarised from an idea submitted to the Idea A Day website (www.idea-a-day.com) by Davey Moore.

Davey Moore's suggestion is that a software program be developed that can recognise types of plants from the shape of its leaves.

'Tell the user what the plant is and how to care for it'

This could mean, for example, that a leaf from a plant could be scanned into a computer and compared with thousands of plant types on the web. Such an encyclopaedia would not only tell the user what the plant is, but also how to

20 Heber Road, London NW2 6AA, UK (rhino@dial.pipex.com), 2001, 300pp, ISBN 0 948826 58 4

care for it and other information of interest. Eventually, with advancement in technologies, hand-held scanners could be used to scan the leaves without removing them from the plant or tree in question.

There could even come a time when children on a school trip could scan a leaf with a hand-held scanner, then transmit that information to a PalmPilot or hand-held PC with the leaf recognition software. In seconds, they could know not only what the plant is, but also further information on where it grows, whether it is deciduous or evergreen, and what size it could eventually become.

Increase your ecoemotion IQ

Dr Michael Cohen

Adapted from a submission to the Global Ideas Bank and from Dr Cohen's web site (www.ecopsych.com). Dr Cohen writes that he "lives on San Juan Island in Washington State, USA, where he directs Applied Ecopsychology degree programs for several universities".

'We will not fight to save what we do not love'

We cannot win this battle to save species and environments without forging an emotional bond between ourselves and nature as well – for we will not fight to save what we do not love.

Stephen Jay Gould

Research at my Institute of Global Education shows that, using a nature reconnecting process, even a child can safely build, and teach others to build, the emotional bond with nature described above by best selling author, Dr Stephen Jay Gould, of Harvard.

The Institute's readily available education and counselling process trains and pays people to build connective bonds with nature independently, or in conjunction with others. Through this process, natural systems and people help each other recover from contemporary society's abusiveness by transforming it into supportive relationships.

The Institute of Global Education's Project NatureConnect's web page ('Wellness for person, planet and spirit') offers, inter alia, books, courses by e-mail, low cost distance learning degree programmes, internships, post doctoral training and research discussion groups, workshops, careers and therapies.

'As a child, I felt more alive, free and happier in a natural area. More intelligent, too'

As a child, instinctively, like most children, I felt more alive, free and happier in a natural area than indoors. More intelligent, too.

With my friends, I grew up and was educated in the indoor box world of contemporary society. It detached our psyche from genuine contact with its biological origins in nature's joy, wisdom and balance. To fill this void we psychologically attached to society's ways, including the destructive trespasses of nature and people by our scientific, economic and spiritual dogma.

The box-world assured me that people only felt and related better in nature because in nature they escaped from reality. Reality was the challenges of home, work, and school, escaping to nature was 'recreation'.

35 years of counselling and educational research in natural areas taught me a different story, one of re-creation. I lived in settings similar to the *Survivor* TV series except that our goal was not to competitively scheme to win a million dollars. Rather it was to sustainably live in balance with people and the environment. I explored and discovered 'webstrings', how to think and relate in ways that free our psyche from the grip of the indoor world's invasiveness and discontents.

'A nature-connected psychological science that restores people to their fullness, their natural integrity and deeper ideals'

I have founded and packaged a nature-connected psychological science that restores people to their fullness, their natural integrity and deeper ideals. Through the internationally recognised Natural Systems Thinking Process, people and natural systems co-create and grow into balance. They let the unifying strands of the web of life help them rejuvenate the sensory truths, ideals and loves we are born with as part of the global life community.

Anybody can use and teach the Process as a hobby or professionally. It is a hands-on learning tool that enables you to let conscious sensory contact with nature help you get your thinking to incorporate the intelligence and balance of the web of life. Through nature-connected psychological activities, courses and degree programmes, people master how to relate in co-operative unity, just as nature works.

'I continue to sleep outdoors throughout the seasons'

In 1998, I celebrated my 50th year as an outdoor educator, counsellor and

20 Heber Road, London NW2 6AA, UK (rhino@dial.pipex.com), 2001, 300pp, ISBN 0 948826 58 4

traditional folk singer, musician and dancer. I celebrated by doing exactly the same thing I did the previous year and for 49 years before that, for I still do what I like to do best. I use my science, education, counselling and musical expertise to catalyse responsible, enjoyable relationships with the nature in people and places. I continue to sleep outdoors throughout the seasons.

'Earth acts homeostatically, like a living organism'

In 1965, a transformational experience in a freak thunderstorm on the Colorado River in Grand Canyon National Park added new dimensions to my thinking. The profound geological effects of that storm on the landscape convinced me that Earth acted homeostatically, like a living organism, and that acts of nature and humanity could be rationally explained from this point of view. Most of my work since then has come out of that realisation.

• *The Institute of Global Education, Box 1605, Friday Harbor, WA 98250, USA (tel Int.+1 360 378 6313; e-mail: nature@pacificrim.net; web: www.ecopsych.com).*

Focused industrial development to help save rainforests

Summarised from an article by Fred Pearce, entitled 'Going, going ...', in New Scientist (June 10th 2000; New Scientist subs £97 or $140, tel 44 [0]1622 778000).

A more realistic and pragmatic approach to saving what is left of the world's rainforests could involve actually encouraging the development of land. Rainforest conservation could be boosted by some forms of development because these then replace logging as a source of income. Such development would include, for example, mining, oil drilling and some heavy industry.

'Oil exports can increase the value of local currencies to the extent that timber exports become economically unviable'

Oil exports have the effect of increasing the value of local currencies to the extent that timber exports become economically unviable. The increase in income from such activity also allows a country to import food, rather than needing land to grow food on.

This difference becomes clear in a comparison of the neighbouring countries of Cameroon and Gabon. In Cameroon, forests are chopped down to make money from timber and to clear land for farming. In Gabon, where their exports are dominated by oil, the amount of deforestation is considerably smaller. Added to this, farmers who lose business are then moving to jobs on oil rigs or in the cities rather than resorting to logging.

> **'Some Kenyan farmers have realised that trees are actually more profitable than crops like maize, and have started growing them on their farms'**

Elsewhere in Africa, farmers are starting to grow trees precisely to harvest them for wood, bark and fruit. In Kenya, farmers have realised that trees are actually more profitable than crops like maize, so they have started growing them on their farms. This has resulted in an increase in tree cover in some regions, rather than a process of deforestation.

There is no doubt that these are small movements against a massive deforesting flow in the other direction, but such development schemes may help to save at least part of the rainforests around the world.

The lesson would seem to be that centralised conservation from governments is not helpful, and that more is achieved through giving incentives and rights to those who live and work in the forests. Intelligent development and focused industry might just prevent the rate of deforestation becoming any more severe.

Make industries drink their effluent discharges

Ian Gascoigne

Adapted from a submission to the Global Ideas Bank.

Every commercial, industrial and agricultural organisation should be allowed to discharge effluent into all rivers and water courses with one condition only. That condition would be that they take their drinking water out of the same river or water course from downstream of the discharge, and use it without treatment as drinking water for all employees. This would have to take place by law, irrespective of the physical location of the company's site in relation to the river.

- *Ian Gascoigne (ian.gascoigne@bradford.gov.uk).*

20 Heber Road, London NW2 6AA, UK (rhino@dial.pipex.com), 2001, 300pp, ISBN 0 948826 58 4

A label for food from well-treated animals

Bierbooms Guido

From a submission to the Global Ideas Bank.

Introduce a label for food coming from animals which have been bred and treated according to animal-friendly and ecological standards. These standards would be set by an independent committee and controlled by dedicated inspectors. Standards should include enough living space and no long transportations.

> 'Standards should include enough living space and no long transportations'

Promote the label and have retail distributors participate in the costs (not unlike other green quality labels).

This should substantially contribute to the quality of life on our planet, be it in the first instance animal life – but also then, indirectly, human life.

• *Bierbooms Guido (e-mail: Guido.Bierbooms@belgacom.be).*

Repairing coral reef systems with eco-friendly concrete balls

Summarised from an item by Michael Menduno, entitled 'Reefer Madness', in Wired magazine (September 1998), monitored for the Global Ideas Bank by Roger Knights. Additional updated information from the Reefball website (www.reefball.org).

The Reef Ball Foundation in Georgia, USA, hopes to repair coral reef with patented 'Reef Balls' made of eco-friendly concrete which are designed to mimic natural reef systems. These can be towed behind any size of boat, and then be sunk to create habitats for fish and other marine species.

The destruction of coral reefs around the world is occurring at such a rate that there are estimated to be almost 30,000 square miles of dead reefs around the world, and the number is rising all the time. The Reef Ball Foundation's aim is to help restore this ocean ecosystem. It also works with schools and communities on educational projects, as well as with governments and eco-charities internationally.

'Each one is three-by-four feet and looks like a piece of Emmenthal cheese made of stone'

Over 200 projects have been running worldwide, from a Boy Scout programme in Florida to a marine turtle sanctuary in Malaysia. And the new Reef Balls are at the centre of the restoration process. Each one is three-by-four feet and looks rather like a piece of Emmenthal cheese made of stone. They can have algae or other plant material attached to them, or can have living coral reef planted in them to stimulate growth. Gradually, sponges, crab and shrimp will also be attracted back to their replacement habitat.

Todd Barber, the chairman of the foundation (and its associated company that makes the balls), intends to sink over one million of the concrete balls into the ocean near the Philippines where some of the most serious damage to the reefs has occurred. It is action on this scale that is now necessary, and sinking concrete balls could , he believes, save the 'rainforests of the oceans' before it is too late.

'The person's ashes are mixed into a specially designed artificial reef unit'

In a similar vein, a company called Eternal Reefs is now offering individuals the chance to contribute cremated remains to a personalised 'Memorial Reef'. The person's ashes are mixed into a specially designed artificial reef unit which then goes on to form part of the reef restoration project. Eternal Reefs' founder Don Brawley says that, "A Memorial Reef becomes an idyllic, eco-friendly resting place, a physical legacy where the remains of one's existence are also part catalyst for a new cycle of life."

• *The Reef Ball Foundation, 603 River Overlook Road, Woodstock, GA 30188, USA (tel: Int.+1 770-752-0202; fax: Int.+1 770-360-1328; web: www.reefball.org; e-mail: kkirbo@hotmail.com).*

• *Eternal Reefs (web: www.artificialreefs.org/Articles). There is more material on Eternal Reefs in the death section of the Global Ideas Bank.*

Ice Guard – allows gases to escape from ponds in winter

John Myall

Adapted from a submission to the Global Ideas Bank

Ice Guard is a device that keeps a hole in ice to allow gases to escape from

20 Heber Road, London NW2 6AA, UK (rhino@dial.pipex.com), 2001, 300pp, ISBN 0 948826 58 4

garden ponds. It is also a frog house. It has won a wildlife trust award.

Manufactured from highly compacted polystyrene, incorporating a substantial weighting mechanism for stability, Ice Guard is a hollow device which sits on your pond's surface with its lower, tube-like part seated permanently below the surface. The insulating properties of the polystyrene keep the warmer water, beneath the ice, above freezing temperature inside the device, maintaining a permanent route for noxious gases to escape to the atmosphere.

Prolonged periods of hot, dry weather can also have a detrimental effect on your pond life, thickening the water's surface tension, making it difficult for gases to escape. In these circumstances, Ice Guard effectively reduces surface tension, helping to keep your pond's environment clear and healthy.

'Ice Guard provides frogs with a ready-made home which they keenly inhabit'

During trials, we found that frogs were particularly drawn to the device, setting up colonies inside it, where they flourished all year round. Ice Guard provides frogs with a ready-made home, which they keenly inhabit.

If you do not want frogs to colonise your pond, a net placed over the bottom of Ice Guard will solve your problem.

• *John Myall (e-mail: johnmyall@greenideasltd.co.uk; web: www.greenideasltd.co.uk).*

Is being pro-only-native trees akin to being anti-immigration?

Summarised from an article by Peter Warshall, entitled 'Green Nazis?', in Whole Earth magazine (Spring 2001 issue; for subscription details, see www.wholeearth.com).

The environmental movement is always portrayed as somewhat holier-than-thou, basking snugly in the knowledge that they are on the right side of the moral argument. But there have been suggestions lately that some restorationists – environmentalists who wish to restore and protect native species in a particular country or area – are fostering anti-immigration feelings.

After all, under some circumstances, they do recommend ridding their homeland of, for instance, alien, invasive trees or preventing a non-native from entering the country. As Michael Pollan, a gardener writing in the New York Times, puts it: "It's hard to believe that there is nothing more than scientific concern about invasive species behind the current fashion for natural gardening and native plants in America – not when our national politics are rife with anxieties about immigration and isolationist sentiment."

No one is suggesting that environmentalists are actually fascists, but their lobbying power and influence has increased exponentially in recent years, and they were never elected in any democratic way. This feeling has led to some locals in places like Montana, where logging and mining used to be secure jobs-for-life, boycotting stores that sell green and organic goods.

> 'The restorationists argue that they are trying to protect minorities in the plant world, not target them'

The restorationists argue, with some justification, that they are trying to protect minorities, not target them. They would compare native species under threat to the Jews and gypsies under the Nazis: minorities who are increasingly weak in the face of a homogenized landscape. It is they who are trying to keep multiculturalism amongst nature alive and well, although insisting that the natural habitat of a location relies on interdependent native species if it is to be restored to its former glory.

Nevertheless, care needs to be taken in how things are phrased, and how situations are handled. Wishing to restore native trees, or to protect a country's diverse landscape, need not be couched in inflammatory terms. Just as we are more vigilant about genetic modification and the bioengineered plants taking over areas of our countryside, we should also be vigilant in the other direction; making sure that the debate doesn't swing too far to the extreme either way.

SCIENCE, TECHNOLOGY AND ENERGY

Boycott to support Internet-based Public Library of Science

Summarised from an article entitled 'Scientists threaten journal protest' by Mark Ward on BBC News Online (April 26th 2001; on the web at: http://news.bbc.co.uk/hi/english/sci/tech/newsid_1296000/1296750.stm); monitored for the Global Ideas Bank by the Arlington Institute's FuturEdition.

As of September 2001, over 17,000 scientists, including some Nobel

20 Heber Road, London NW2 6AA, UK (rhino@dial.pipex.com), 2001, 300pp, ISBN 0 948826 58 4

Laureates, are boycotting scientific journals (refusing to send in papers or to renew subscriptions) unless these journals make old research papers available for free – so that these papers can form part of a massive Internet-based Public Library of Science.

'The amount of scientific literature in genetics alone doubles every 10 years'

Michael Ashburner, a geneticist at Cambridge University, UK, said that the online Public Library of Science was essential if scientists were to keep up with developments in their field – the amount of scientific literature in genetics alone doubles every 10 years, and scientists needed sophisticated databases that could search the full text of papers to aid their work. The Public Library of Science could act like the GenBank repository which makes DNA sequence information freely available.

The Public Library of Science group is asking scientific journals to make the papers they publish freely available in the library six months after they have first been printed. The Proceedings of the National Academy of Sciences and the British Medical Journal and five other journals have already signed up to the project, declaring themselves willing to put papers into the library.

'A compromise – a searchable version of a paper leading back to the website of the journal'

The journal Science has said it is willing to support a compromise – to put a searchable version of a paper into the library, but to have the links to copies leading back to the website of the journal that originally published it.

International space agency to co-ordinate all spacecraft movements

Summarised from a letter from Robert Thurman, entitled 'Making space a safer place', to the New Scientist (January 13th 2001; New Scientist subs £97 or $140, tel 44 [0]1622 778000).

As space traffic continues to increase, the chances of a collision increase proportionately, as does the possibility of a piece of hardware falling from the skies on to an inhabited part of Earth. The recent concerns over the disintegration of the Mir space station and it hitting its splash zone in the ocean have only heightened anxiety. Robert Thurman, of Nerrina, Victoria, therefore suggests that an international space agency be created to "oversee the exploration and development of space." All countries would be required to lodge a bond with the agency every time they intend to launch a spacecraft, and the agency would administer the bond, ensuring the spacecraft in question safely reaches the end of its working life.

'An international space agency could be responsible for making sure planned trajectories do not intersect'

Such an agency could be responsible for various duties, such as making sure planned trajectories do not intersect, or certifying the geostationary positions for satellites so there is no disagreement over rights. Most importantly, though, the bond system would mean the agency would ensure that every spacecraft is, as Thurman puts it, "safely retrieved, refitted or sent into solar orbit rather than spiralling down to Earth." Only then could the fears of being struck by falling space debris truly be allayed.

Moving the Earth to solve global warming

Summarised from an article by Robin McKie, entitled 'Getting too hot down here? So move the Earth', in the Observer (June 17th 2001).

As scientists and politicians struggle to decide the best way to solve the global warming problem, a group of American space engineers and astronomers have come up with what may be the most radical solution of all: moving the Earth. Their concept is to direct a few comets at Earth which will then change its orbit. When that happens, our planet will be moved into a cooler, and therefore safer, part of the solar system. The NASA engineers say it could add something like six billion years to the possible lifetime of the Earth and its inhabitants.

'The comet would pass by the Earth closely enough for some of its gravitational energy to transfer to our world'

The technology involved would be similar to that proposed by those looking into the possibilities of deflecting asteroids bound for collision with Earth. Thus, a series of small explosions or chemical rockets attached to the comet would alter its course. The comet would then pass by the Earth closely

20 Heber Road, London NW2 6AA, UK (rhino@dial.pipex.com), 2001, 300pp, ISBN 0 948826 58 4

enough for some of its gravitational energy to transfer to our world. This, in turn, would increase the Earth's speed of orbiting and move us to a higher orbit away from the sun. When that has happened, the plan would be to direct the comet so it passed closely by Jupiter or Saturn, picking up more gravitational energy to transfer to Earth and as such repeating the process. One of the three scientists involved, Don Korycansky, describes it as "the astronomical equivalent of transferring bank payments from one account to another".

There are possibly worrying side-effects to the plan, though. A miscalculation in directing the comet could result in it hitting the Earth with catastrophic consequences. Added to that, the plan could result in the Moon being stripped away from the Earth, which could result in a destabilisation of the Earth's poles and a far more devastating effect on our climate than any amount of global warming could ever produce. More research and testing could make clear how viable the plan actually is. But, as the procrastination continues about what should be done *on* Earth, it might well be time to look at what can be done above and around our planet to alleviate the climate problems we face.

Usable electricity from discarded car batteries

Summarised from an article by Mark Freeman, entitled 'Dying batteries give new energy', in the Seattle Times (January 27th 2001), monitored for the Global Ideas Bank by Roger Knights.

Church Watson, an Oregon businessman, has started using leftover power from discarded batteries to provide electricity in his workplace.

He had come to the conclusion that there had to be a better way of using this unwanted energy – so instead of just discharging the batteries before disposal, he created a system which meant he could use the energy to power his lights and tools. By connecting the batteries to an inverter, he converted the electricity to the appropriate voltage to power his soldering iron, his lamp, his electric screwdriver and a heater in his workshop. Soon, he hopes to expand the system to run his overhead lights in his storeroom as well and he is making further improvements all the time.

> ## 'The average used car-battery, for example, has enough energy left in it to power four or five electrical tools for a day'

The batteries that people throw away tend to be from cars, wheelchairs, computers and other electrical machinery, and while they can no longer power those vehicles or appliances, they do still have energy in them. In financial terms the savings are paltry (half a dollar a day) but Watson finds satisfaction in the fact that the average used car-battery, for example, has enough energy left in it to power four or five electrical tools for a day, even though it contains insufficient power to start a car engine.

Making Media Labs from trash – cost-free computers and software

Summarised from an item from the Communities Online discussion network (CONet – e-mail conet@ukco.org.uk to subscribe), and from the Access Space website of the Redundant Technology Initiative.

Although the Internet has opened up a myriad of possibilities to people across the world, it does have one major drawback: online access costs. But a group of artists in Sheffield, calling themselves the Redundant Technology Initiative, have created a media lab with scavenged computers and open source software.

They have managed to create web pages, process images, publicise creative projects, set up networks and much more, relying particularly on Linux as their free operating system. They are currently running an exhibition with a video wall (which was cost-free due to their methods), and they run a drop-in lab in Sheffield which allows access to creative technology for people in the area.

They find that as more people upgrade their computers, so the 'trash' is upgraded as well.

'You don't need a capital budget – you just need a small group of committed people prepared to learn new skills'

Now the Redundant Technology Initiative are looking for partners who want to set up labs nationwide, offering web space and help in learning how to scrounge and use free software as they did. As their founder James Wallbank puts it, "What we've shown is that you simply don't need a capital budget to get involved with digital media – you just need a small group of committed people prepared to learn new skills"; and now they hope to help others use the knowledge and expertise they've gained.

• *Redundant Technology Initiative, Access Space, 1 Sidney Street, Sheffield S1 4RG (tel. 0114 2495522; fax 0114 2495533; e-mail: rti@lowtech.org; web: www.lowtech.org).*

20 Heber Road, London NW2 6AA, UK (rhino@dial.pipex.com), 2001, 300pp, ISBN 0 948826 58 4

In a fast society slow emotions become extinct

Adapted from an e-mail sent to the Global Ideas Bank by Sushil Yadav.

Today's world runs at high speed: messages are delivered instantly across the world by e-mail; passenger jet planes fill the sky; constantly changing visual images bombard us every day on television, on computers and outside the cars speeding along the road. We live in a fast society and, as a result, we are losing the capacity to feel slow emotions. That is the premise of a new theory propounded by Sushil Yadav from India.

Sushil Yadav argues that fast visuals and words that are prevalent in a large society can cause slow emotions (by which he means pain, remorse, empathy, etc) to wither and become extinct. He believes that the increase of rapid visual images and words in the last hundred years has made the brain less capable of focusing on the feelings associated with slowness such as tragedy, pain and suffering. In this way, the industrialisation and globalisation of the world can be linked to an increasing 'unfeelingness' in humans around the world, which could help to explain the way animals and the environment are being treated.

'Emotion can intensify only when the visual and verbal processing associated with the emotion slows down'

Sushil Yadav believes there is a link between visual and verbal speed (in memory, perception and imagery) and the biochemical state of the brain and the body. Following on from this, he states that "emotion can intensify and sustain itself only when the visual and verbal processing associated with the emotion slows down".

As evidence for his theory, he points to films in which tragic moments are often slowed down – indeed the most intense moments are almost static or stationary. He also believes that a fast-thinking society is a non-feeling one, with the important emotions of empathy and suffering overruled by equations, accounts or business plans. Thus, "in a fast society slow emotions become extinct. In a thinking (predominantly scientific and industrial) society, emotion itself becomes extinct".

Yadav seeks neuroscientists who might be prepared to help test his hypotheses.

• *Sushil Yadav (e-mail: mpyadav@bol.net.in; web: www.netshooter.com/ emotion).*

Give workers half of savings on energy bills

Summarised and adapted from an idea sent to the Global Ideas Bank by Larry Baum.

Larry Baum suggests that, to conserve electricity, companies should give their workers half of the money saved as compared to last year's energy bill as a bonus. This would encourage workers to turn off lights, air conditioning and equipment either when these things are not being used, or during breaks and on leaving at the end of the day. The company would make energy savings, the workers would get a bonus, and the environment would benefit from less energy wastage. If every company in a region, or even a country, applied the same rule, the impact could be huge.

• *Larry Baum runs the Idea Explore website which contains many social and technological inventions (http://ideaexplore.net).*

Amazonian tribes gain plant knowledge through hallucinogenics

Jeremy Narby

Jeremy Narby, PhD, grew up in Canada and Switzerland, studied history at the University of Canterbury, and received his doctorate in anthropology from Stanford University. The material of this article comes from his book The Cosmic Serpent: DNA and the Origins of Knowledge *(Tarcher/Putnam, 1998). The article originally appeared in Noetic Sciences Review (Vol. 48, Summer 1999, pages 16-21), and is reprinted here by kind permission of both the author and the magazine.*

The Cosmic Serpent: DNA and the Origins of Knowledge

The first time an Ashaninca man told me that he had learned the medicinal properties of plants by drinking a hallucinogenic brew, I thought he was joking. We were in the forest squatting next to a bush whose leaves, he claimed, could cure the bite of a deadly snake. "One learns these things by drinking ayahuasca," he said. But he was not smiling.

It was early 1985, in the community of Quirishari in the Peruvian Amazon's

20 Heber Road, London NW2 6AA, UK (rhino@dial.pipex.com), 2001, 300pp, ISBN 0 948826 58 4

Pichis Valley. I was 25 years old and starting a two-year period of field-work to obtain a doctorate in anthropology from Stanford University. My training had led me to expect that people would tell tall stories. I thought my job as an anthropologist was to discover what they really thought, like some kind of private detective.

During my research on Ashaninca ecology, people in Quirishari regularly mentioned the hallucinatory world of ayahuasqueros, or shamans. In conversations about plants, animals, land, or the forest, they would refer to ayahuasqueros as the source of knowledge. Each time, I would ask myself what they really meant when they said this.

'The Amazonians insisted that their extensive botanical knowledge came from plant-induced hallucinations'

My fieldwork concerned Ashaninca resource use – with particular emphasis on their rational and pragmatic techniques. To emphasize the hallucinatory origin of Ashaninca ecological knowledge would have been counterproductive to the main argument underlying my research. Nevertheless, the enigma remained: These extremely practical and frank people, living almost autonomously in the Amazonian forest, insisted that their extensive botanical knowledge came from plant-induced hallucinations. How could this be true?

The enigma was all the more intriguing because the botanical knowledge of indigenous Amazonians has long astonished scientists. The chemical composition of ayahuasca is a case in point. Amazonian shamans have been preparing ayahuasca for millennia. The brew is a necessary combination of two plants, which must be boiled together for hours. The first contains a hallucinogenic substance, dimethyltryptamine, which also seems to be secreted by the human brain; but this hallucinogen has no effect when swallowed, because a stomach enzyme called monoamine oxidase blocks it. The second plant, however, contains several substances that inactivate this precise stomach enzyme, allowing the hallucinogen to reach the brain.

So here are people without electron microscopes who choose, among some 80,000 Amazonian plant species, the leaves of a bush containing a hallucinogenic brain hormone, which they combine with a vine containing substances that inactivate an enzyme of the digestive tract, which would otherwise block the hallucinogenic effect. And they do this to modify their consciousness.

It is as if they knew about the molecular properties of plants and the art of combining them, and when one asks them how they know these things, they say their knowledge comes directly from hallucinogenic plants.

I had not come to Quirishari to study this issue, which for me relates to indigenous mythology. I even considered the study of mythology to be a useless and "reactionary" pastime. My focus as an anthropologist was Ashaninca resource development. I was trying to demonstrate that true development consisted first in recognizing the territorial rights of indigenous people. My point of view was materialist and political, rather than mystical – yet I found myself quite impressed with the pragmatism of the Quirishari.

This is a people who teach by example, rather than by explanation. Parents encourage their children to accompany them in their work. The phrase "leave Daddy alone because he's working" is unknown. People are suspicious of abstract concepts. When an idea seems really bad, they will say dismissively, "Es pura teoría" ("That's pure theory"). The two key words that cropped up over and over in conversations were práctica and táctica, 'practice' and 'tactics' –no doubt because they are requirements for living in the rainforest.

'Their empirical knowledge was undeniable, but their explanations of it were unbelievable'

After about a year in Quirishari, I had come to see that my hosts' practical sense was much more reliable in their environment than my academically informed understanding of reality. Their empirical knowledge was undeniable, but their explanations concerning the origin of their knowledge were unbelievable to me. My attitude was ambivalent. On the one hand, I wanted to understand what they thought – for instance, about the reality of 'spirits' –but on the other, I couldn't take seriously what they said because I did not believe it.

On leaving Quirishari, I knew I had not solved the enigma of the hallucinatory origin of Ashaninca ecological knowledge. I left with the strange feeling that the problem had more to do with my incapacity to understand what people had said, rather than the inadequacy of their explanations. They had always used such simple words.

In June 1992, I went to Rio to attend the world conference on development and environment. At the 'Earth Summit', as it was known, everybody was talking about the ecological knowledge of indigenous people, but certainly no one was talking about the hallucinatory origin of some of it, as claimed by the indigenous people themselves.

Colleagues might ask, "You mean Indians claim they get molecularly verifiable information from their hallucinations? You don't take them literally, do you?" What could one answer? There is nothing one can say without contradicting two fundamental principles of Western knowledge.

First, hallucinations cannot be the source of real information, because to consider them as such is the definition of psychosis. Western knowledge considers hallucinations to be at best illusions, at worst morbid phenomena.

Second, plants do not communicate like human beings. Scientific theories of communication consider that only human beings use abstract symbols like

20 Heber Road, London NW2 6AA, UK (rhino@dial.pipex.com), 2001, 300pp, ISBN 0 948826 58 4

words and pictures and that plants do not relay information in the form of mental images. For science, the human brain is the source of hallucinations, which psychoactive plants merely trigger by way of the hallucinogenic molecules they contain.

'Their hallucinatory knowledge has been confirmed and used by the pharmaceutical industry'

It was in Rio that I realized the extent of the dilemma posed by the hallucinatory knowledge of indigenous people. On the one hand, its results are empirically confirmed and used by the pharmaceutical industry; on the other hand, its origin cannot be discussed scientifically because it contradicts the axioms of Western knowledge.

When I understood that the enigma of plant communication was a blind spot for science, I felt the call to conduct an in-depth investigation of the subject. Furthermore, I had been carrying the mystery of plant communication around since my stay with the Ashaninca, and I knew that explorations of contradictions in science often yield fruitful results. It seemed to me that the establishment of a serious dialogue with indigenous people on ecology and botany required that this question be addressed.

I had myself ingested ayahuasca in Quirishari, an experience that brought me face to face with an irrational and subjective territory that was terrifying, yet filled with information. In the months afterwards, I thought quite a lot about what my main Ashaninca consultant, Carlos Perez Shuma, had said. What if it were true that nature speaks in signs and that the secret to understanding its language consists in noticing similarities in shape or in form? What if I took him literally?

I liked this idea and decided to read the anthropological texts on shamanism, paying attention not only to their content but to their style. I taped a note on the wall of my office: "Look at the FORM."

One thing became clear as I thought back to my stay in Quirishari. Every time I had doubted one of my consultants' explanations, my understanding of the Ashaninca view of reality had seized up; conversely, on the rare occasions when I had managed to silence my doubts, my understanding of local reality had been enhanced – as if there were times when one had to believe in order to see, rather than the other way around.

It had become clear to me that ayahuasqueros were somehow gaining access in their visions to verifiable information about plant properties. Therefore, I reasoned, the enigma of hallucinatory knowledge could be reduced to one question: Was this information coming from inside the human brain, as the scientific point of view would have it, or from the outside world of plants, as shamans claimed?

Both of these perspectives seemed to present advantages and drawbacks.

On the one hand, the similarity between the molecular profiles of the natural hallucinogens and of serotonin seemed well and truly to indicate that these substances work like keys fitting into the same lock inside the brain. However, I could not agree with the scientific position according to which hallucinations are merely discharges of images stocked in compartments of the subconscious memory. I was convinced that the enormous fluorescent snakes that I had seen thanks to ayahuasca did not correspond in any way to anything that I could have dreamed of even in my most extreme nightmares.

'The speed and coherence of some of the hallucinations exceeded the best rock videos'

Furthermore, the speed and coherence of some of the hallucinatory images exceeded by many degrees the best rock videos, and I knew that I could not possibly have filmed them.

On the other hand, I was finding it increasingly easy to suspend disbelief and consider the indigenous point of view as potentially correct. After all, there were all kinds of gaps and contradictions in the scientific knowledge of hallucinogens, which had at first seemed so reliable: Scientists do not know how these substances affect our consciousness, nor have they studied true hallucinogens in any detail. It no longer seemed unreasonable to me to consider that the information about the molecular content of plants could truly come from the plants themselves, just as ayahuasqueros claimed. However, I failed to see how this could work concretely.

Maybe I would find the answer by looking at both perspectives simultaneously, one eye on science and the other on shamanism. The solution would therefore consist in posing the question differently: It was not a matter of asking whether the source of hallucinations is internal or external, but of considering that it might be both at the same time. I could not see how this idea would work in practice, but I liked it because it reconciled two points of view that were apparently divergent.

My research revealed that in the early 1960s, anthropologist Michael Harner had gone to the Peruvian Amazon to study the culture of the Conibo Indians. After a year or so he had made little headway in understanding their religious system when the Conibo told him that if he really wanted to learn, he had to drink ayahuasca. Harner accepted, not without fear, because the people had warned him that the experience was terrifying. The following evening, under the strict supervision of his indigenous friends, he drank the equivalent of a third of a bottle. After several minutes he found himself falling into a world of true hallucinations.

20 Heber Road, London NW2 6AA, UK (rhino@dial.pipex.com), 2001, 300pp, ISBN 0 948826 58 4

'His visions emanated from giant reptilian creatures'

He saw that his visions emanated from "giant reptilian creatures" resting at the lowest depths of his brain. These creatures began projecting scenes in front of his eyes. "First they showed me the planet Earth as it was eons ago, before there was any life on it. I saw an ocean, barren land, and a bright blue sky. Then black specks dropped from the sky by the hundreds and landed in front of me on the barren landscape. I could see the 'specks' were actually large, shiny, black creatures with stubby pterodactyl-like wings and huge whale-like bodies ... They explained to me in a kind of thought language that they were fleeing from something out in space. They had come to the planet Earth to escape their enemy. The creatures then showed me how they had created life on the planet in order to hide within the multitudinous forms and thus disguise their presence. Before me, the magnificence of plant and animal creation and speciation – hundreds of millions of years of activity – took place on a scale and with a vividness impossible to describe. I learned that the dragon-like creatures were thus inside all forms of life, including man."

At this point in his account, Harner writes in a footnote at the bottom of the page: "In retrospect one could say they were almost like DNA, although at that time, 1961, I knew nothing of DNA."

I had not paid attention to this footnote previously. There was indeed DNA inside the human brain, as well as in the outside world of plants, given that the molecule of life containing genetic information is the same for all species. DNA could thus be considered a source of information that is both external and internal – in other words, precisely what I had been trying to imagine.

I plunged back into Harner's book, but found no further mention of DNA. However, a few pages on, Harner notes that 'dragon' and 'serpent' are synonymous. This made me think that the double helix of DNA resembled, in its form, two entwined serpents.

'A human brain with a snake lodged between the two hemispheres'

The reptilian creatures that Harner had seen in his brain reminded me of something, but I could not say what. After rummaging around my office for a while, I put my hand on an article called 'Brain and Mind in Desana Shamanism' by Gerardo Reichel-Dolmatoff. Paging through it, I was stopped by a Desana drawing of a human brain with a snake lodged between the two hemispheres.

Several pages further into the article, I came upon a second drawing, this time with two snakes. According to Reichel-Dolmatoff, within the fissure "two intertwined snakes are lying ... In Desana shamanism these two serpents symbolize a female and male principle, a mother and a father image, water and land ...; in brief, they represent a concept of binary opposition which has to be overcome in order to achieve individual awareness and integration. The snakes are imagined as spiralling rhythmically in a swaying motion from one side to another."

'Their ancestors arrived in canoes shaped like huge serpents'

Concerning the Desanas' main cosmological beliefs, Reichel-Dolmatoff writes: "The Desana say that in the beginning of time their ancestors arrived in canoes shaped like huge serpents."

I was astonished by the similarities between Harner's account, based on his hallucinogenic experience with the Conibo Indians in the Peruvian Amazon, and the shamanic and mythological concepts of an ayahuasca-using people living a thousand miles away in the Colombian Amazon. In both cases there were reptiles in the brain and serpent-shaped boats of cosmic origin that were vessels of life at the beginning of time. Pure coincidence?

To find out, I picked up a book about a third ayahuasca-using people, entitled (in French) *Vision, Knowledge, Power: Shamanism Among the Yagua in the North-East of Peru*. In this study by Jean-Pierre Chaumeil (to my mind, one of the most rigorous on the subject), I found a "celestial serpent" in a drawing of the universe by a Yagua shaman. Then, a few pages away, another shaman is quoted as saying: "At the very beginning, before the birth of the earth, this earth here, our most distant ancestors lived on another earth ..." Chaumeil adds that the Yagua consider that all living beings were created by twins, who are "the two central characters in Yagua cosmogonic thought."

These correspondences seemed very strange, and I did not know what to make of them. Or rather, I could see an easy way of interpreting them, but it contradicted my understanding of reality: A Western anthropologist like Harner drinks a strong dose of ayahuasca with one people and gains access, in the middle of the 20th century, to a world that informs the "mythological" concepts of other peoples and allows them to communicate with life-creating spirits of cosmic origin possibly linked to DNA. This seemed highly improbable to me, if not impossible. Still, I had decided to follow my approach through to its logical conclusion. So I casually pencilled in the margin of Chaumeil's text: "twins = DNA?"

These indirect and analogical connections between DNA and the hallucinatory and mythological spheres seemed amusing to me, or at most intriguing. Nevertheless, I started thinking that I had perhaps found with DNA the scientific concept on which to focus one eye, while focusing the other on the shamanism of Amazonian ayahuasqueros.

20 Heber Road, London NW2 6AA, UK (rhino@dial.pipex.com), 2001, 300pp, ISBN 0 948826 58 4

'DNA might be the concept that would best translate what the ayahuasqueros were talking about'

About this time, as I continued looking out for new connections between shamanism and DNA, I received a letter from a friend who suggested that shamanism was perhaps "untranslatable into our logic for lack of corresponding concepts." I understood what he meant, and I was trying to see precisely if DNA, without being exactly equivalent, might be the concept that would best translate what ayahuasqueros were talking about.

As I browsed over the writings of authorities on mythology, I discovered with surprise that the theme of twin creator beings of celestial origin was extremely common in South America, and indeed throughout the world. The story that the Ashaninca tell about Avíreri and his sister, who created life by transformation, was just one among hundreds of variants on the theme of the 'divine twins'.

Another example is the Aztecs' plumed serpent, Quetzalcoatl, who symbolizes the 'sacred energy of life', and his twin brother Tezcatlipoca, both of whom are children of the cosmic serpent Coatlicue.

When I read the following passage from Claude Lévi-Strauss' latest book, I jumped: "In Aztec, the word coatl means both 'serpent' and 'twin.' The name Quetzalcoatl can thus be interpreted either as 'Plumed serpent' or 'Magnificent twin.'"

A twin serpent, of cosmic origin, symbolizing the sacred energy of life? Among the Aztecs? I wondered what all these twin beings in the creation myths of indigenous people could possibly mean. I was trying to keep one eye on DNA and the other on shamanism to discover the common ground between the two. I reviewed the correspondences that I had found so far. Ruminating over this mental block, I recalled Carlos Perez Shuma's challenge: "Look at the FORM."

I had looked up DNA in several encyclopedias and had noted in passing that the shape of the double helix was most often described as a ladder, or a twisted rope ladder, or a spiral staircase. It was during the following split second, asking myself whether there were any ladders in shamanism, that the revelation occurred: "THE LADDERS! The shamans' ladders, 'symbols of the profession' according to Métraux, present in shamanic themes around the world according to Eliade!"

'The symbolism of the ladder necessarily implies communication between sky and earth'

I rushed back to my office and plunged into Mircea Eliade's book

Shamanism: Archaic Techniques of Ecstasy and discovered that there were "countless examples" of shamanic ladders on all five continents, here a "spiral ladder," there a "stairway" or "braided ropes." In Australia, Tibet, Nepal, ancient Egypt, Africa, North and South America, "the symbolism of the rope, like that of the ladder, necessarily implies communication between sky and earth. It is by means of a rope or a ladder (as, too, by a vine, a bridge, a chain of arnyaw, etc) that the gods descend to earth and men go up to the sky."

Eliade even cites an example from the Old Testament, where Jacob dreams of a ladder reaching up to heaven, "with the angels of God ascending and descending on it." According to Eliade, the shamanic ladder is the earliest version of the idea of an axis of the world, which connects the different levels of the cosmos, and is found in numerous creation myths in the form of a tree.

Until then, I had considered Eliade's work with suspicion, but suddenly I viewed it in a new light. I started flipping through his other writings in my possession and discovered: cosmic serpents. This time it was Australian Aborigines who considered that the creation of life was the work of a "cosmic personage related to universal fecundity, the Rainbow Snake," whose powers were symbolized by quartz crystals.

How could it be that Australian Aborigines, separated from the rest of humanity for 40,000 years, tell the same story about the creation of life by a cosmic serpent associated with a quartz crystal as is told by ayahuasca-drinking Amazonians? The connections that I was beginning to perceive were blowing away the scope of my investigation. How could cosmic serpents from Australia possibly help my analysis of the uses of hallucinogens in Western Amazonia?

I tried answering my own question: One, Western culture has cut itself off from the serpent/life principle, in other words DNA, since it adopted an exclusively rational point of view. Two, the peoples who practice what we call 'shamanism' communicate with DNA. Three, paradoxically, the part of humanity that cut itself off from the serpent managed to discover its material existence in a laboratory some 3,000 years later.

'In their visions, shamans manage to take their consciousness down to the molecular level'

People use different techniques in different places to gain access to knowledge of the vital principle. In their visions shamans manage to take their consciousness down to the molecular level.

This is how they learn to combine brain hormones with monoamine oxidase inhibitors, or how they discover 40 different sources of muscle paralyzers, whereas science has only been able to imitate their molecules. When they say their knowledge comes from beings they see in their hallucinations, their words mean exactly what they say.

According to the shamans of the entire world, one establishes communica-

20 Heber Road, London NW2 6AA, UK (rhino@dial.pipex.com), 2001, 300pp, ISBN 0 948826 58 4

tion with spirits via music. For the ayahuasqueros, it is almost inconceivable to enter the world of spirits and remain silent. Angelika Gebhart-Sayer discusses the "visual music" projected by the spirits in front of the shaman's eyes: It is made up of three-dimensional images that coalesce into sound and that the shaman imitates by emitting corresponding melodies. I should check whether DNA emits sound or not.

It seemed that no one had noticed the possible links between the 'myths' of 'primitive peoples' and molecular biology. No one had seen that the double helix had symbolized the life principle for thousands of years around the world. On the contrary; everything was upside down. It was said that hallucinations could in no way constitute a source of knowledge, that Indians had found their useful molecules by chance experimentation, and that their 'myths' were precisely myths, bearing no relationship to the real knowledge discovered in laboratories.

At this point, I remembered that Michael Harner had said that this information was reserved for the dead and the dying. Suddenly, I was overcome with fear and felt the urge to share these ideas with someone else. I picked up the phone and called an old friend, who is also a writer. I quickly took him through the correspondences I had found during the day: the twins, the cosmic serpents, Eliade's ladders. Then I added: "There is a last correlation that is slightly less clear than the others. The spirits one sees in hallucinations are three-dimensional, sound-emitting images, and they speak a language made of three-dimensional, sound-emitting images. In other words, they are made of their own language, like DNA."

There was a long silence on the other end of the line.

Then my friend said, "Yes, and like DNA they replicate themselves to relay their information." I jotted this down, and it was later in reviewing my notes on the relationship between the hallucinatory spirits made of language and DNA that I remembered the first verse of the first chapter of the Gospel according to John: "In the beginning was the logos" – the word, the verb, the language.

That night I had a hard time falling asleep.

'DNA is the source of their knowledge, which can only be attained in non-rational states of consciousness'

My investigation had led me to formulate the following working hypothesis: in their visions, shamans take their consciousness down to the molecular level and gain access to information related to DNA, which they call 'animate essences' or 'spirits'. This is where they see double helixes, twisted ladders, and chromosome shapes. This is how shamanic cultures have known for millennia that the vital principle is the same for all living beings and is shaped like two entwined serpents (or a vine, a rope, a ladder ...). DNA is the source of their astonishing botanical and medicinal knowledge, which can be attained only in defocalized and 'nonrational' states of consciousness, though its results are empirically verifiable. The myths of these cultures are filled with biological imagery. And the shamans' metaphoric explanations correspond quite precisely to the descriptions that biologists are starting to provide.

Like the axis mundi of shamanic traditions, DNA has the form of a twisted ladder (or a vine ...); according to my hypothesis, DNA was, like the axis mundi, the source of shamanic knowledge and visions. To be sure of this I needed to understand how DNA could transmit visual information. I knew that it emitted photons, which are electromagnetic waves, and I remembered what Carlos Perez Shuma had told me when he compared the spirits to radio waves: "Once you turn on the radio, you can pick them up. It's like that with souls; with ayahuasca ... you can see them and hear them". So I looked into the literature on photons of biological origin, or 'biophotons'.

In the early 1980s, thanks to the development of a sophisticated measurement device, a team of scientists demonstrated that the cells of all living beings emit photons at a rate of up to approximately 100 units per second and per square centimeter of surface area. They also showed that DNA was the source of this photon emission.

During my readings, I learned with astonishment that the wavelength at which DNA emits these photons corresponds exactly to the narrow band of visible light. Yet this did not constitute proof that the light emitted by DNA was what shamans saw in their visions. Furthermore, there was a fundamental aspect of this photon emission that I could not grasp. According to the researchers who measured it, its weakness is such that it corresponds "to the intensity of a candle at a distance of about 10 kilometers," but it has "a surprisingly high degree of coherence, as compared to that of technical fields (laser)."

How could an ultra-weak signal be highly coherent? How could a distant candle be compared to a laser?

I came to understand that in a coherent source of light, the quantity of photons emitted may vary, but the emission intervals remain constant. DNA emits photons with such regularity that researchers compare the phenomenon to an "ultra-weak laser." I could understand that much, but still could not see what it implied for my investigation.

I turned to my scientific journalist friend, who explained it immediately: "A coherent source of light, like a laser, gives the sensation of bright colours, a luminescence, and an impression of holographic depth."

My friend's explanation provided me with an essential element. The detailed descriptions of ayahuasca-based hallucinatory experiences invariably mention bright colour, and, according to the authors of the dimethyltryp-

20 Heber Road, London NW2 6AA, UK (rhino@dial.pipex.com), 2001, 300pp, ISBN 0 948826 58 4

tamine study: "Subjects described the colours as brighter, more intense, and deeply saturated than those seen in normal awareness or dreams: It was the blue of a desert sky, but on another planet. The colours were ten to 100 times more saturated."

It was almost too good to be true. DNA's highly coherent photon emission accounted for the luminescence of hallucinatory images, as well as their three-dimensional, or holographic, aspect.

On the basis of this connection, I could now conceive of a neurological mechanism for my hypothesis. The molecules of nicotine or dimethyltryptamine, contained in ayahuasca, activate their respective receptors, which set off a cascade of electrochemical reactions inside the neurons, leading to the stimulation of DNA and, more particularly, to its emission of visible waves, which shamans perceive as 'hallucinations'.

'The source of knowledge: DNA, emitting photons like an aquatic dragon spitting fire'

There, I thought, is the source of knowledge: DNA, living in water and emitting photons, like an aquatic dragon spitting fire.

Am I wrong in linking DNA to these cosmic serpents from around the world, these sky-ropes and axis mundi? Some of my colleagues would undoubtedly say yes. They would remind me that 19th century anthropologists had compared cultures and elaborated theories on the basis of the similarities they found. When they discovered, for instance, that bagpipes were played not only in Scotland, but in Arabia and the Ukraine, they established false connections between these cultures. Then they realized that people could do similar things for different reasons.

Since then, anthropology has backed away from grand generalizations, denounced "abuses of the comparative method," and locked itself into specificity bordering on myopia. Yet by shunning comparisons between cultures, one ends up masking true connections and fragmenting reality a little more, without even realizing it.

Is the cosmic serpent of the Shipibo-Conibo, the Aztecs, the Australian Aborigines, and the Ancient Egyptians the same? No, will reply the anthropologists who insist on cultural specificity; but it is time to turn their critique on its head. Why insist on taking reality apart, but never try putting it back together again?

According to my hypothesis, shamans take their consciousness down to the molecular level and gain access to biomolecular information. But what actually goes on in the brain/mind of an ayahuasquero when this occurs? What is the nature of a shaman's communication with the animate essences of nature? The clear answer is that more research is needed in consciousness, shamanism, molecular biology, and their interrelatedness.

• *The Noetic Sciences Review, in which this article first appeared, is the magazine of the Institute of Noetic Sciences, a non-profit organisation that conducts and sponsors research into the workings and powers of the mind. For more information, see www.noetic.org*

TRANSPORT

Fit car exhausts the far side from pedestrians

Mayer Hillman

Mayer Hillman, Senior Fellow Emeritus, Policy Studies Institute, supplies a regular 'Hillman's Musings' column to the Global Ideas Bank.

A review of successive governments' policies directly or indirectly affecting the attractions of walking as a means of transport would be likely to conclude that there must have been a malign and ingenious spirit masterminding a strategy to make it an unpleasant and unsafe way of getting about in daily life.

One has only to note the doubling of motor traffic over the last 25 years and the considerable increase in the performance of vehicles in terms of their speed and acceleration. The outcome of these apparent manifestations of economic success is that pedestrians are now more vulnerable than they were a generation ago, their relatively low average speed has been lowered still further when road crossing is involved, and they have to exercise more vigilance to reduce the risk of their involvement in what are euphemistically termed 'accidents'.

'Toxic fumes are expelled at low level in the direction of small children in pushchairs'

The positioning of exhaust pipes at the rear of vehicles can be cited as a particularly effective means of reducing the attractions of walking. Anyone whether in a vehicle or on foot can carry out an observational survey of the current situation by a simple count. It will reveal that the great majority – between 80 per cent and 90 per cent – are located on the *left-hand* side. As a consequence, the toxic fumes are expelled at low level in the direction most damaging to the health of pedestrians, especially small children, those in pushchairs, and cyclists – not to mention diminishing other qualitative aspects of the local environment. The fumes also remain suspended for some time

20 Heber Road, London NW2 6AA, UK (rhino@dial.pipex.com), 2001, 300pp, ISBN 0 948826 58 4

before settling, thereby increasing the period of exposure to them.

'Requiring manufacturers to fit exhaust pipes on the right-hand side of all new vehicles for the UK market'

Two suggestions can be put forward to remedy this unfortunate outcome. First, and obviously, legislation could easily be passed through Parliament requiring manufacturers to fit exhaust pipes on the *right-hand* side of all new vehicles for the UK market. This should pose no problem for sales in countries in which vehicles are driven on the right: after all, vehicles for use here have their steering wheels on the right side – and for use on the Continent on the left side.

Second, albeit more contentiously, a strong case could be made for legislation requiring exhaust pipes to be fitted at the roof level of vehicles. This would have the advantage of ensuring that the fumes were dispersed more efficiently than releasing them at low level. At the same time, it would alert road users to the immediate toxicity of the air they were breathing and enable them better to avoid inhalation of the fumes. As they would be more visible, the general public would be more aware of this health hazard which in turn could lead to more political pressure for stricter regulations on the composition of the fumes.

• *Mayer Hillman, The Coach House, 7a Netherhall Gardens, London NW3 5RN, UK (tel/fax Int.+44 [0]20 7794 9661).*

Car seats for cats and dogs

Krystal Koszyk

From a submission to the Global Ideas Bank.
My idea is to have a car seat for cats and dogs.

'They should have carriers with restraints on them'

Since many people travel these days with their pets along with them, they should have carriers with restraints on them. A seat belt could go through their cage just like child car seats, which would be far preferable to just putting them in a cage and letting them tumble around.

• *Krystal Koszyk (bkoszyk@altavista.com).*

Vehicles with front braking lights

Simon Martin

From a submission to the Global Ideas Bank.

A law should be introduced that would require vehicles to have red braking lights on the *front*, not just on the back.

As a pedestrian, I am often involved in a potentially lethal guessing game: is the car coming towards me going to stop? Has the driver seen me? Is the driver coming straight on but has forgotten to switch off the indicator? This is no fun as a driver, either.

• *Simon Martin (otherwise@talk21.com).*

Coloured numberplates to reduce city centre pollution

Summarised from a letter by A. Edward Gottesman to the London Times (August 29th 2000).

To reduce urban traffic congestion and pollution, only vehicles with a distinctive coloured numberplate (say, green) should be allowed inside certain postal districts in city centres.

The annual urban tax disc would cost three times as much as that for cars not allowed into the centre, but would be available to anyone. Foreign visitors could rent city-qualified vehicles or buy a temporary plate.

Vehicle Incident Recorder to be mounted in all vehicles

Kris Hansen

Adapted from a submission to the Global Ideas Bank. Kris Hansen is a software developer and system integrator specialising in workflow applications and enterprise communication.

I propose that a Vehicle Incident Recorder be mounted in all vehicles. This would consist of a computer-controlled system with a central processing unit, connections into a vehicle's electronic systems and a single fish lens camera mounted in the ceiling of the cab.

The information storage area would be sealed, secured and virtually indestructible. A Three I/O ports would be available for the reading of VIR

20 Heber Road, London NW2 6AA, UK (rhino@dial.pipex.com), 2001, 300pp, ISBN 0 948826 58 4

data. The VIR would provide the following:

'A recording of the vehicle's speed, direction, temperature and state at the moment of impact'

- A recording of the vehicle's speed, direction, temperature and state at the moment of impact, collision or alarm.
- A recording of passenger trauma during the incident.
- A recording of surrounding activities during the incident.

Motor vehicle accidents are one of the top ten causes of death in most countries. It is my hope that lives could be saved with a system such as this.

Information, including video footage of the accident would be available for download by paramedics for quick assessment of injuries and more effective treatment.

The camera would also capture video footage of any vehicle break-ins or thefts. This footage could be gathered by police and used to identify suspects and understand break-in methods.

Overall, this system could help the automotive industry to create safer vehicles and more effective safety devices.

- *Kris Hansen (e-mail: krish@perlharbor.org).*

Green Speed stickers (55mph urban roads, 20mph residential areas)

Ronald Sharp

Adapted from a submission to the Global Ideas Bank by Ronald Sharp, who writes that he "set up Last Laugh *as a think sink: a small think tank where good ideas go down the drain for the lack of a good plug".*

My proposal is for a '20>55>>' sticker to be placed prominently on the rear of your car to indicate to the car behind that you are a socially and environmentally responsible driver who knows that about 55mph is the most efficient speed on inter urban roads and that about 20mph is a reasonable speed in residential areas.

'The reduction in emissions and consumption would be about 25 per cent'

The reduction in emissions and consumption when reducing the average trunk road speed from 70 to 55 would be about 25 per cent. The reduction in both deaths and the severity of accidents at lower urban and inter urban speeds would also be very considerable.

Crucially, these speeds also seem to be the speeds where alternatives to the internal combustion engine become viable. They are also slow enough for alternative means of transport to become competitive; the bus and coach outside town and the bus and bike in town.

It seems that it will only be when traffic speeds are reduced voluntarily that governments may even consider the reduction in the official speed limits which will consolidate the virtuous circle started off by voluntary action.

The Green Speed sticker is a necessary accessory as protection for the driver who wants to keep to a responsible speed on roads that are full of drivers who want to race at or above the official speed limit. They may back off or have a pang of conscience once the sticker has become instantly recognisable.

'Green Speed is necessary if we are going to fulfil Kyoto commitments with the current generation of vehicles'

Green Speed is absolutely necessary if we are going to fulfil Kyoto commitments with the current generation of vehicles.

• *Ronald Sharp (e-mail: lastlaugh@rippington.nildram.co.uk).*

Ten ideas to solve Britain's transport crisis

Summarised from a paper by Mark Perryman, entitled 'A Back of the Bus Ticket Answer to the Transport Crisis', from the website www.signsofthetimes.org.uk . This item was monitored for the Global Ideas Bank by Matthew Mezey.

Mark Perryman has come up with ten simple ideas which could solve many of our transport problems in the UK. They are as follows:

• the **abolition of VAT on bicycles**, to stop the government penalising cycling instead of encouraging it.

• the creation of a **government transport factory** which would make bicycles and offer them at special prices to employers buying in batches. Money could also be offered to employers willing to provide shower facilities and cycle parking.

• the **widening of pavements**, in order to both narrow the roads and to introduce a cycle lane on the pavements.

• the **sponsorship of New Year's Eve transport** (buses, tubes) as

20 Heber Road, London NW2 6AA, UK (rhino@dial.pipex.com), 2001, 300pp, ISBN 0 948826 58 4

successfully took place at the Millennium celebrations in London; other days of free travel could also be instituted.

• the introduction of **automatic life bans** for anyone causing death or serious injury by dangerous or reckless driving.

• the introduction of legislation to enforce a **no-drink limit** for drivers, rather than the 'one or two pints is OK' system which we have at present.

• the **testing of all drivers every five years**, without exception.

• the formation of a **national transport bank** which offers interest-free loans to enable people to buy season tickets, and the introduction of further incentives such as half-fares if passengers book early.

• the **reintroduction of bus conductors**, and the positioning of buses at the centre of the road (with stops as mini-islands) to reinforce the fact that the car should not rule the road – and nor should the parked car obstruct buses time and time again.

• the creation of an all-encompassing **transport website** (see another idea below – 'Smart urban transport website')

• *For more information, events and other papers, Signs of the Times can be contacted via their website at www.signsofthetimes.org.uk (e-mail: info@signsofthetimes.org.uk; tel Int.+44 [0]20 8257 1440).*

Buses automatically broadcasting name of next stop

Aaron Campbell

From a submission to the Global Ideas Bank.

In many major cities, drivers of local buses seem to be unable to announce an upcoming stop with any sort of coherency. Often, they don't announce the next stop at all. Passengers (especially those new to that route) often miss their stop and carry that bad vibe around all day.

'Passengers (especially those new to that route) often miss their stop'

A solution to this problem would be to install transmitters on the roofs of bus stop booths that alert buses nearby of the name of the upcoming stop, then the bus' public address system would broadcast that name in a coherent (and audible) way.

A pleasant and consistent voice announcing the next stop would help people on their way, and they wouldn't have to pester the driver as to his or her last mumbling. This would prove particularly helpful to occasional visitors and tourists.

• *Aaron Campbell (aaroncampbell@netscape.net)*

Encourage the use of public transport with one-day parking charges

Philip L. Winters

Summarised from a submission to the Global Ideas Bank.

Our idea would be to charge a much lower parking rate (eg $20 per month) but make this 'monthly' parking rate payable on only one day and assign the days per month to various subsets of the workforce. For example, in a 100-person office working 20 days per month, five people (Group A) would pay $20 on the first working day of the month but 95 would continue to have free parking. On the second day of the month, another five people (Group B) would pay $20 but Group A and the other 90 people would park free. The idea is that some or all of these people might alter their travel behaviour for one day (eg telecommute, ride the bus, carpool, schedule offsite business, etc) to avoid a steep one-day rate of $20. The pain is shared by all but not all on the same day.

'The pain is shared by all but not all on the same day'

Traffic congestion, and its associated environmental and quality of life impacts, is a severe problem in many urban and suburban areas. Research has shown that removing the parking subsidy and/or changing the price of parking contributes to how commuters choose to travel to and from work (usually the most congested part of the day).

According to the US Department of Transportation (http://www.fta.dot.gov/library/planning/tdmstatus/FTAPRKNG.HTM):

"In suburban settings, both public and private employers have reduced solo driving through a combination of pricing strategies and alternative mode programs such as carpool and transit encouragements". Cases summarised in the literature illustrate the possible range of reduction in solo driving:

• 12 per cent reduction in the case of the Nuclear Regulatory Commission compared to before pricing (though the 42 per cent solo share is about 40 per cent below solo shares of other employers in the area)

20 Heber Road, London NW2 6AA, UK (rhino@dial.pipex.com), 2001, 300pp, ISBN 0 948826 58 4

- 17 per cent less for Bellevue City Hall compared to before pricing
- 25 per cent less for CH2MHill compared to before pricing
- 25 per cent decline in the case of Twentieth Century Corporation
- 40 per cent lesser proportion of solo drivers at Pacific Northwest Bell compared to other employers in the area.

"In an urban but not downtown setting, Commuter Computer outside the Los Angeles central business district dropped the 'drive alone' share from 42 per cent to eight per cent by eliminating free parking." Clearly, increased parking rates decidedly influence trip making and parking behaviour.

The introduction of parking pricing in the suburbs (where parking is free or very cheap) is extremely difficult. As one local company put it: "It would take $100 per month for people to change modes! We can't raise our rates from $0 to $100!!" Nevertheless, parking pricing could play an important role in the changing of transport attitudes, and that is worth paying for.

- *Idea developed by Philip L. Winters and Francis Cleland, Center for Urban Transportation Research, University of South Florida, 4202 E. Fowler Ave., CUT 100, Tampa, FL 33620, USA.*

Smart urban transport website

Summarised from a submission by Robert Alcock to the Global Ideas Bank.

I've spent time in cities dominated by private automobiles (LA) and cities where public transportation works acceptably (SF, London, Dublin, Bilbao). For quality of life, I would choose the second group every time. Unfortunately no matter whether you're using trains, buses, trams or funiculars, urban transport systems are generally incomprehensible, unreliable, disjointed, unresponsive, and, in a word, stupid. What if every city had an independent website devoted to making public transport more intelligent?

Features would include:

- One-stop timetable consultation, with timetables for all the modes of transport linked to a database of postal addresses. Put in where you are and where you want to go, and you'll be told the easiest route, along with directions for getting to and from the bus/train stops at either end.
- Fully integrated information for disabled users
- Statistics on the reliability of different routes, to be able to calculate the likely delay on any route
- Information about special conditions due to repairs, weather, strikes, etc
- A message board for travellers
- Organising public transport users to lobby for improvements. This would include: submitting and voting on suggestions for improvements, polls on the best and worst services in areas (punctuality, cleanliness etc), results of polls

sent to those in charge of public transport and replies posted, and links to other organisations working to improve public transport

'The website should be independent to avoid information being provided in a piecemeal way that reflects organisational divisions'

I'd emphasise the independent or at least autonomous nature of the proposed website, because otherwise you would tend to get the information provided, but in a piecemeal way that reflects organisational divisions between transport modes and companies, and without effective feedback mechanisms (since companies/governments aren't very keen on funding people to put pressure on them to improve their services!)

For instance, in Bilbao (where I live) the city government are starting to do this, with interactive maps of the city bus services available in public information kiosks. They are also installing a tracking system for the buses (so they know where they really are, instead of where they should be!) But that's only one out of the six transport systems in this city of just one million people (metro, tram, two local bus companies plus national, at least three train systems...) And naturally the systems for feedback are next to useless.

A private company should build a generic system that could be adapted to fit any city. The large number of potential users would provide advertising revenue to fund the operation of the system. Although many companies are working on different applications of intelligent technology for urban transport, I think the key to smarter transport is putting all the information together in one easily accessible site.

An allowance for people who live and work in the same neighbourhood

Adapted from a submission to the Global Ideas Bank by Greet Gosseye.

The government could give allowances to people who both live and work in the same neighbourhood. Although life is much more expensive in big cities, people who both live and work locally do not get any refund for our transport although they contribute in a positive way to the solution of traffic jams.

Furthermore, in order to get to work without spending hours behind some delivery lorry or refuse lorry, it should be prohibited to deliver or collect in the

20 Heber Road, London NW2 6AA, UK (rhino@dial.pipex.com), 2001, 300pp, ISBN 0 948826 58 4

centre of the city between 7am and 9am. Lorries tend to park in the middle of the road and to block all the traffic. My suggestion could make it possible for employees to get to work in time without being stressed or irritated.

• *Greet Gosseye (e-mail: greetgosseye@yahoo.com).*

Remote diagnostic technology for air passengers

Summarised from an article by Bob Brewin, entitled 'Airline readies telemedicine tools', in Computerworld (4th December 2000), monitored for the Global Ideas Bank by Roger Knights.

In a move that could radically improve healthcare on aeroplanes and save money on costly emergency landings, a British company has designed and produced a remote diagnostic system that allows doctors on the ground to monitor the vital signs of the ill passenger.

'Electrocardiogram information, blood pressure figures, temperature and other vital signs are sent to a centre on the ground'

The Tempus 2000, designed by Remote Diagnostic Technologies, sends electrocardiogram information, blood pressure figures (via a wrist cuff), temperature (via an ear probe) and other vital signs (such as respiration rates and blood oxygen levels) down to a centre on the ground. The computers at the centre, MedAire's MedLink facility at Good Samaritan Hospital in Phoenix, receive the information via a built-in modem connected to a seat-back satellite phone on the plane. The doctors on the ground can then decide on a course of action.

The unit also includes a hands-free voice communication system, so the patient can answer the doctor's questions as if he or she were in a hospital. It can also transmit pictures of the patient to medical centres if necessary. Many cardiac problems are not serious enough to warrant a plane making an emergency landing at the closest airport, and avoiding such standard procedures could save airlines millions of pounds a year.

But if a doctor does consider the patient's condition to be serious enough to necessitate an emergency landing, the company who make the Tempus have a database of 5,000 hospitals worldwide (correlated to airports) in order to determine the closest airport with the best medical facilities to treat the passenger.

As a result of the Tempus 2000 system's capabilities, Virgin Atlantic is installing them on all its planes. And the device could set a new trend for improved healthcare on planes, particularly when one considers that, in some years, heart attacks in the air are more numerous than deaths or injuries by crashes.

Biodiesel fuel made from recycled cooking oil

Summarised from an article by Jane Kay, entitled 'Biodiesel revolution in San Francisco', in the San Francisco Chronicle (May 23rd 2001) and from an article entitled 'Diesel fuel made from recycled cooking oil on sale in Nevada' in the Las Vegas Sun.

Biodiesel fuel, made from recycled cooking oils, has gone on sale in a number of petrol stations across the US. It reduces emissions, recycles unwanted restaurant waste, and requires no alterations to any diesel-engined vehicles built after 1986. Diesel fuel is known to be particularly smelly and polluting, so the introduction of such an alternative is all the more welcome. The new yellow fuel gives off less thick, pungent fumes with a slight smell of french fries, and although it doesn't reduce nitrogen oxides, it does substantially reduce carbon emissions.

'Already, recycling trucks, school buses and the Department of Energy's own vehicle fleet are using the fuel'

One gas station in San Francisco is selling fuel that is 100 per cent biodiesel made from soybean oil, a by-product of food processing. Already, recycling trucks, school buses and the Department of Energy's own vehicle fleet are using the fuel, and many other environmentally-minded people are expected to join them. Biodiesel is more expensive, and it does reduce fuel economy slightly, but the costs are coming down year on year and the economy can be improved by adding a small amount of petroleum diesel to the mix. A station in Nevada has pre-empted this problem by selling a fuel which is 20 per cent biodiesel and 80 per cent petroleum diesel. This reduces the price and the economy problems, although the environmental benefits are obviously reduced to some extent as well. Nevertheless, it does point a way forward for the future. As Jim Brandmueller, administrator of the Nevada State Energy Office, says, "By taking our waste cooking oil and turning it into biodiesel, we are not only cleaning up the air at a reasonable price, but also creating jobs."

20 Heber Road, London NW2 6AA, UK (rhino@dial.pipex.com), 2001, 300pp, ISBN 0 948826 58 4

'Instead of mining in the Arctic National Wildlife Refuge, we can mine the nation's supplies of restaurant grease'

Sales of the fuel are expected to grow massively in the next few years. 6.7 million gallons of biodiesel were sold in 2000, but that is estimated to reach 20 million gallons in 2001, and the Department of Energy aims to replace ten to 20 per cent of petroleum diesel with biodiesel in the next 20 years. As Teri Shore of environmental campaigners Bluewater Network puts it, "We've got to break our nation's dependence on foreign oil. We can use the vast source of soybeans and other fuel crops grown right here in the United States, and instead of mining in the Arctic National Wildlife Refuge, we can mine the nation's supplies of restaurant grease." Perhaps George W Bush will be funded by the biodiesel companies in the future.

• *See www.biodiesel.org for more information.*

Traffic signals tell pedestrians how long they have to cross

Summarised from an article by Peyton Whitely, entitled 'New signals that count', in the Seattle Times (May 29th 2001), and from an item on the Lake County, Illinois website (www.co.lake.il.us/press/hd_cntdwn.htm). The former was monitored for the Global Ideas Bank by Roger Knights.

Cities in America are starting to install new traffic signals that tell pedestrians how long they have to cross a street. It is hoped that this will increase safety for pedestrians and drivers, and also improve pedestrian traffic flow in busy areas. The signals display a countdown of the time remaining until the intersection should be clear, and they inform pedestrians when it is safe to begin to cross. Pedestrians therefore also know how much time is remaining before the lights change.

'With seven seconds to go the green 'WALK' signal changes to a flashing red hand'

The council or transport division can set the time for each signal at any particular crossing, and the timer counts down at one-second intervals. A signal in Seattle at Ninth Avenue and Olive Way, for example, starts at 35 seconds and counts down to zero. When it reaches seven seconds to go, the green 'WALK' signal changes to a flashing red hand, warning the pedestrians that the lights are about to change. The new signals cost little more than present traffic signals, but they could help improve road safety: as easy as 1-2-3.

COMMUNICATIONS
Top ten 21st century futures

These (naively?) optimistic futures are summarised from 'Futurist Update' for June 2001, e-mailed to the Global Ideas Bank by its publishers, the World Future Society.

Earl C. Joseph, chairman of the World Future Society's conference in Minneapolis held in July 2001, offers his list of the top emerging futures transforming society in a recent issue of the Minnesota Futurists' newsletter:

(1) E-Cybernation: computers, TV, newspapers, and other media merge, along with their content – entertainment, news, training, etc.

(2) Bio-Age: biotechnology transforms medicine, eliminating many human ills.

(3) Personal robot slaves: sentient but obedient robots will become affordable and commonplace.

(4) Intelligent things: computer chips will be embedded in all of our stuff – and in ourselves.

(5) Exploiting outer space: exploration of our neighbouring planets will lead to settling, mining, and manufacturing.

(6) Quantum, nanotech, and holodeck computer ages: computers are destined to become a billion times more capable than today's systems.

(7) Interactive TV sitcoms: the entertainment industry will continue to be a key driver of technological advances.

(8) Nonlethal weapons: public safety will increase thanks to advances in humane crime fighting and weapons technologies.

(9) Redesigned humans: bioengineering will merge with computing to create healthier, wiser people.

(10) Doubling of human lifespans: reversing the physical and mental processes of aging may soon be within our reach.

• *For more forecasts from the Minnesota Futurists see www.mnfuturists.org/futuring.htm*

• *The World Future Society, (7910 Woodmont Avenue, Suite 450, Bethesda, MD 20814, USA;tel Int.+1 301 656-8274; e-mail: info@wfs.org; web: http://www.wfs.org) is a non-profit, non-partisan scientific and educational association with some 30,000 members worldwide. Its mission is to help individuals and*

20 Heber Road, London NW2 6AA, UK (rhino@dial.pipex.com), 2001, 300pp, ISBN 0 948826 58 4

organizations identify and understand key trends and to create their preferred futures. Membership to the Society, including a subscription to the Futurist magazine and numerous other benefits, is $39 per year.

Bored and lonely parrots taught to surf the web

Summarised from an article by Graham Lawton, entitled 'Give that bird a mouse', in the New Scientist (July 8th 2000; New Scientist subs £97 or $140, tel Int.+44 [0]1622 778000) and from the 'Interpet Explorer' website (www.media.mit.edu/~benres/parrot/index.html).

At the Massachusetts Institute for Technology (MIT) Media Lab, Professor Irene Pepperberg and colleagues are trying to teach a parrot to surf the net. They believe that by enabling parrots to use the Internet they could potentially liberate thousands of caged parrots all over the world from a life of bored loneliness. Furthermore, the research could provide interesting information about parrot behaviour and recognition skills.

'Parrots may learn to augment face-to-face social interaction with online communities and relationships'

Parrots are naturally sociable in the wild, living in flocks and becoming anxious if separated from their fellow birds. They also crave attention, and a bored and understimulated parrot can become depressed and withdrawn or, in the worst cases, violent towards its owner. The MIT researchers therefore suggest that "intrinsically social, intelligent animals such as parrots – if given appropriate tools – may, like humans, learn to augment face-to-face social interaction with online communities and relationships."

With this in mind, the researchers are teaching their African grey parrot named Arthur to use a simple browser. After that, they may investigate the possibilities of a video link-up to other parrots, and possibly even videoconferencing. If that proves successful, then parrot chat rooms on the web could not be too far away, allowing lonely parrots all over the world to socialise and interact with each other. As Arthur's supervisor Ben Resner puts it, "If parrots like it and owners want it, the service providers would be moronic not to do it. Parrots could be really heavy users." And after the parrots are online, the team hope to do the same with dogs.

An Internet service linking you to your home e-mail provider anywhere in the world

Summarised from an article by Ben Hammersley in the London Times (27th November 2000) and from the Twigger website (www.twigger.co.uk).

One of the downsides to travelling abroad is that you cannot use your home e-mail address, necessitating the opening of a web-based e-mail account (such as hotmail or yahoo) to remain in constant contact. This annoyance can now be avoided by a new Internet service called 'Twigger' which allows the user to keep only one e-mail address at all times and in all locations. It works by giving you access to your home country provider (which you select on twigger's website), and then all you need is your normal username and password.

As well as being free, the Twigger service also allows you to view attachments before downloading them to your PC, meaning large, corrupt and uninteresting attachments can be removed in advance. And in allowing access from any PC in the world, there need not be any trepidation about facing a teeming inbox on your return.

- *For more information or to find out how to use the service, see the website www.twigger.co.uk for British users, or www.twigger.com for the rest of the world.*

Website where IT support technicians bid for your custom

Summarised from an article by Sami Lais, entitled 'Site lets service vendors bid to help you', in Computer World (January 24th 2000; p.58)

A website based in Silicon Valley is providing a round-the-clock online resource for IT services and support in which support technicians submit bids to customers looking for help. Users with computer problems go to ePeople.com and either search its online knowledge banks, e-mail questions to the site or request live interactive support.

'Customers not only get a range of bids, but can also check the ratings of bidders'

Customers not only get a range of bids for IT technical support but can also check the ratings of bidders. The site then charges a fee for every bid

20 Heber Road, London NW2 6AA, UK (rhino@dial.pipex.com), 2001, 300pp, ISBN 0 948826 58 4

transaction. Not all technicians charge a fee for their services, though. As an ePeople spokeswoman points out, "There are people in the Internet community who do this just for fun." As a result, the costs of such interactive technical support could be substantially lower than they might be elsewhere. This could prove particularly attractive, for example, to small businesses with limited finances. Meanwhile, the e-mail support and the access to the knowledge banks are free to all.

• *For more information check out the ePeople website (previously known as NoWonder.com) at www.epeople.com*

A billion online radio stations

Summarised from an article entitled 'The numbness is just a bonus' by Mike Vago in the Stranger (1535 11th Ave 3rd Fl, Seattle, WA 98122, USA; September '99), from 'The world streaming in' by Bill McKibben in The Atlantic Monthly (July 2000), and from an article by Anita Hamilton, entitled 'World Wide Radio', in Time magazine (October 9th 2000), all monitored for the Global Ideas Bank by Roger Knights.

You can go to a site on the Internet called www.comfm.fr and choose to listen to any of about 4,000 radio stations around the world, selected by place or by theme (eg Tamil love songs, underground love songs, easy listening love songs, etc). Unrestricted by the physical realities of the radio dial, there's enough room for a billion stations online.

Mike Vago says that it's fairly easy and cheap to set up a web-only radio station: "Armed only with my beat-up Mac Performa, some audio equipment, some free software and a sizable record collection, I started broadcasting as InvisibleRadio.com". Vago had already launched a college station, so he knew how to sound good on air and how to get record labels to send him new releases, and he also knew how to put together a good-looking web page.

His winning concept was to "play good bands that people know and like, that sound good on the radio, but that aren't big enough to get played on the 'Radio'. Little by little, people started to listen. His audience is now big enough that he can hope for income from advertisements being sufficient one day to mean he can do this full-time.

'Several radios designed specifically for the Internet are now in production or are available'

Several radios designed specifically for the Internet (and its many stations) are now in production, although prices are still quite high. Two of the better known ones are Sonicbox, which can also be downloaded free of charge, and

Kerbango which will need broadband connection to work. Other sites worth checking out are www.realguide.real.com/tuner and http://www.radio.yack.com which both have extensive guides to Internet radio stations by genre. Another site which acts as something of an online radio community is www.Live365.com . With an Internet connection in place, there's no need to stick to you regional and national stations – there's a whole world of listening out there.

 • *Ira Glass has produced a comic book for novice radio producers entitled 'Radio – an illustrated guide' (See www.thislife.org). Two useful shareware programs are, for Macs, Sound Studio, and, for others, CoolEdit 2000.*

 • *An online manual for starting up your own web radio station can be found at http://wdvl.Internet.com/Multimedia/WebRadio/index.html . It contains details of legal requirements, the types of equipment needed, and the different levels of technology worth investigating.*

Lock up mobile phone in glove compartment while driving

Summarised from a letter from Ned Tolbert, of Sacramento, California, to Newsweek (June 4th 2001). This item was monitored for the Global Ideas Bank by Roger Knights.

Ned Tolbert suggests that to avoid drivers instinctively diving for their phone when it rings, people should lock their phone in the glove compartment. Several recent crashes have been caused by people looking away from the road to pick up their phone and then losing control for a vital few seconds. With the phone locked up in the glove compartment, the ignition key is needed to get to the phone. Thus, if the driver is expecting an important call (or needs to make one), he or she is forced to pull over, stop the car and then use the phone.

'Even hands-free sets can prove distracting to the driver'

A simpler alternative, of course, is to simply switch the phone off, diverting callers to voicemail. But if someone is expecting a crucial call that needs to be responded to fairly instantly, this glove compartment idea could prove more appropriate. The Department of Transport in the UK insist that 'the driver *must* have proper control of the vehicle at all times', and that even hands-free sets can distract the driver. The use of hand-held mobile phones while driving is illegal, and the courts can then disqualify the driver, or even imprison them

20 Heber Road, London NW2 6AA, UK (rhino@dial.pipex.com), 2001, 300pp, ISBN 0 948826 58 4

for up to two years (depending on the severity of the offence). To avoid an accident, disqualification or even imprisonment, putting the phone in the glove compartment seems a small, effective measure to take.

• *To see the UK Department of the Environment, Transport and the Regions' report on mobile phones and driving, see www.detr.gov.uk/campaigns/mobile*

The Interplanetary Internet

Summarised from an article by Ben Hammersley, entitled 'Ready to reach for the stars', in the London Times (March 26th 2001; Interface section).

The Internet revolution that has spread like technological wildfire across the world in the last decade may not just stop at terrestrial domination. Vint Cerf, the man who co-invented the TCP/IP system which allows the Internet to work, is now looking into the possibilities of an interplanetary Internet.

'Every probe will have the ability to send and receive Internet data, without necessarily going via Earth'

Up to now, NASA has had no standard procedures for outer space communication, and Cerf thinks it is time that they did. His vision is of a future where every satellite, space station and explorer probe will have the ability to send and receive Internet data, without necessarily going via Earth.

Not only would Earth to space communication be made much simpler, but satellites could 'speak' to each other, perhaps engendering some sort of traffic system which needed no administering from Earth.

For now, Cerf is just aiming to extend the Internet's many advantages to outer space, with Earth to space communication at the heart of that project. For example, NASA staff on Earth could communicate much more easily and reliably with a probe looking at Jupiter if the messages were travelling on an Internet system: from Earth to satellite to space station to a satellite near Jupiter and down to the probe itself. Simpler, quicker and probably cheaper than a massive radio dish or having hundreds of transmitters on every planet.

'If one device were to fail, contact back to Earth would still be possible via another route'

Furthermore, with each new space satellite or station launched with Internet capabilities, the possible routes for messages to travel increases, simultaneously increasing the power and dependability of such an interplanetary Internet. If one device were to fail, contact back to Earth would still be possible via another route within the solar system. The more Internet-enabled things that are launched into space, the better the system becomes. As space traffic continues to increase, and with orbiting debris from previous missions a growing problem, a system by which the space vehicles can communicate with each other whilst navigating could be both useful and crucial to future exploration.

International Internet-Free Day

The next International Internet-Free Day will be Sunday 27 January 2002.
The background to Internet-Free Day is as follows:

www.DoBe.org, the new non-profit website for participatory events in every city in the world, promotes the last Sunday of January (eg January 27th 2002) as International Internet-Free Day, a day for doing and being out in the real world.

DoBe.org proposes:

(1) A Dice Sunday, as in a watered-down version of Luke Reinhart's Diceman novel. You write down half a dozen unusual or creative or challenging real world things your small group could do on the day, number these options from 1 to 6, then throw the dice, accepting a commitment to do whichever option the dice chooses.

(2) The DoBe.org London website contains a number of more sober examples of the kind of real world activities small groups could organise, ranging from country walks and dancing to writing groups and discussion salons – ie any group activity that involves more than just passively consuming, watching or listening.

(3) Have a real chat instead of a virtual chat room. Interact in real time with real live people! Be your own Home Page.

(4) By all means use e-mail and the Internet in advance to arrange real world participatory events for January 27th 2002 but then turn off the computer for that   day.

And if you need fellow participants for the events you come up with, you can advertise them for free in advance on DoBe.org. Afterwards, please send DoBe an e-mail describing how the day went for you – such stories will be an encouragement for Do Be day participants in future years.

'It's a matter of reclaiming the web, using it for a different message'

20 Heber Road, London NW2 6AA, UK (rhino@dial.pipex.com), 2001, 300pp, ISBN 0 948826 58 4

"It's not hypocritical to be using a website to tempt people away from the web," say the DoBe.org crew, "It's a matter of reclaiming the web, using it for a different message. The Internet did not start off as a vehicle for social isolation and damaged eyesight. That is what big business has done with it. It began as a medium for communication between researchers, a quick and simple way of exchanging information.

"But it's so easy nowadays to get addicted to a half life in a virtual world, and to lose touch with your family, friends and neighbours. Yet we're creatures evolved from a tribal past and an annual Internet-Free Day on the fourth Sunday in January is a recognition of our need for contacts out in the real world. E-mail and the Internet are just not enough."

DoBe.org's slogan for the day is:

"Log Out! Get Out! Get a Life! The real world needs you!"

• *For more on the international aspects of the day, see www.internet-free-day.org*

• *For a London event that took place on the first International Internet-Free Day in 2001 see the epic parks walk discussion salon at: http://www.dobe.org/ events/641.html (in the London 'Social' category)*

Let bureaucrats know how it feels with a form of your own

Summarised from no.89 in '101 Things to Do 'til the Revolution' by Claire Wolfe, monitored for the Global Ideas Bank by Roger Knights.

In response to bureaucrats' intrusive requests for personal information, Claire Wolfe and Charles Curley suggest you hand them a copy of a 'Bureaucracy Encounter Form' to give them a taste of their own paperwork. The form would request certain information for personal records, ask that the form be filled out in triplicate and request that the bureaucrat in question should fill out a separate form for each request that they themselves have made. A note to the effect that this is all in order to better facilitate the bureaucrat's request is also advised. And, in the spirit of bureaucratic red tape, there is no limit on how many times you can use the form.

A sample form could be as below:

Date:

Location:

Your name:

Agency(ies) you represent:

Your business address:

City and county:

Post code:

Telephone number:

Your annual salary:

Your supervisor's name:

Supervisor's telephone number:

Describe your request in detail: (leave two lines at least here)

Are you required to make this request?

If so, what person or agency required it of you?

Please state what statute, and what section and/or subsection of that statute authorises you to make this request:

Please state what law or part of the constitution authorises you to make this request:

Have you filled out a form for me like this in the past?

When? Exact dates:

What will be done with the information you receive from me?

Is this part of a criminal investigation?

Will this become part of a criminal investigation?

I swear (or affirm) under penalty of perjury that the foregoing is true and correct.

Signature:

This is just an example, though, and imagination and creativity would be encouraged in order to give the 'Bureaucracy Encounter Form' your own personal touch. Not so much fighting fire with fire as tying the bureaucrats up in their own particular brand of red tape.

Nifty neologisms

From an e-mail circular monitored for the Global Ideas Bank by Karen McCosker. For more on neologisms see Heenan's Universal Dictionary (on the web at: www.heenan.net/words/index.html).

* **Arachnoleptic fit** (n.) The frantic dance performed just after you've accidentally walked through a spider web.

* **Beelzebug** (n.) Satan in the form of a mosquito that gets into your bedroom at three in the morning and cannot be cast out.

* **Bozone** (n.) The substance surrounding stupid people that stops bright ideas from penetrating. The bozone layer, unfortunately, shows little sign of breaking down in the near future.

* **Cashtration** (n.) The act of buying a house, which renders the subject financially impotent for an indefinite period.

20 Heber Road, London NW2 6AA, UK (rhino@dial.pipex.com), 2001, 300pp, ISBN 0 948826 58 4

• **Caterpallor** (n.) The color you turn after finding half a grub in the fruit you're eating.

• **Decaflon** (n.) The gruelling event of getting through the day consuming only things that are good for you.

• **Dopelar effect** (n.) The tendency of stupid ideas to seem smarter when you come at them rapidly.

• **Extraterrestaurant** (n.) An eating place where you feel you've been abducted and experimented upon. Also known as an E-T-ry.

• **Faunacated** (adj.) How wildlife ends up when its environment is destroyed. Hence faunacatering (v.), which has made a meal of many species.

• **Foreploy** (n.) Any misrepresentation or outright lie about yourself that leads to sex.

• **Grantartica** (n.) The cold, isolated place where art companies dwell without funding.

• **Hemaglobe** (n.) The bloody state of the world.

• **Intaxication** (n.) Euphoria at getting a tax refund, which lasts until you realize it was your money to start with.

• **Kinstirpation** (n.) A painful inability to move relatives who come to visit.

• **Lullabuoy** (n.) An idea that keeps floating into your head and prevents you from drifting off to sleep.

Silent gestures that add depth to conversations

Adapted from an e-mail sent to the Global Ideas Bank by Tom Atlee, The Co-Intelligence Institute, Eugene, Oregon, USA (e-mail: cii@igc.org; web: www.co-intelligence.org).

The summarised piece below details certain 'gestures of conversational presence', gestures which can be used by two people or more to convey their state of mind and heart during a conversation. This conversational innovation can, says Tom Atlee, "make a big difference in how a conversation feels and progresses". The ideas is that as the gestures are used more and more, they become a natural part of conversations, as and when they are needed.

Gestures of Conversational Presence
Rosa Zubizarreta and Michael Bridge

When Michael and I first met, we discovered that we shared a passion for exploring how the use of language affects our consciousness, not just as individuals but also in terms of group dynamics. For the last few years, we have been exploring a simple method of hand gestures as a way to deepen and transform communication. While the gestures are very simple, their use implies a profound shift in the habitual attitudes towards speech that we carry as members of our 'modern', 'civilised' culture. We have found that the gestures offer an alternative to the unconscious patterns of domination and alienation that tend to permeate verbal communication. They serve to strengthen our inner voice, and help us regain a sense of the sacred in our communication with one another.

'Equalising power between those who are more verbal and those who are less so'

In one-on-one or small group settings, the gestures can serve to alter the pace and rhythm of conversation, thus equalising power between those who are more verbal and those who are less so. Instead of focusing on what any one person has to say, our attention expands to include the quality of what is taking place between us.

In larger groups, the gestures can be used as a simple feedback system for the speakers when incorporated as an enhancement to the existing conversational arrangement. Or, more radically, they can be used as part of a movement towards group mind – that state of synergy where our individual creativity and our collective process are experienced as profoundly interdependent.

Here are some of the gestures, to get you started in your own explorations. Note: as with any living language, there can be multiple shades of meaning, depending upon the context.

Offering Presence. Palms together, in the traditional gesture of prayer. Can be used as a non-verbal greeting, in order to frame our verbal communication within a larger context. This gesture is also used to convey the message that "I have full attention to offer", especially in response to the next gesture, 'The Stirring'.

'We view this sign as a way of honouring what is taking place inside one's self'

The Stirring. Hands clasped, two index fingers pointing upward. Can be used to signal that 'there is something stirring within'. We tend to view this sign as a way of acknowledging and honouring what is taking place inside one's self, rather than as a request for permission to speak. (The latter perspective tends to reinforce the paradigm where the listener is giving away their power.) At the same time, a speaker who observes someone else making this sign may choose to respond by offering their attention, either immediately or at the next opportune moment.

Retreat. Hands fully clasped. Used to signal that one's attention is

20 Heber Road, London NW2 6AA, UK (rhino@dial.pipex.com), 2001, 300pp, ISBN 0 948826 58 4

withdrawing or becoming unavailable. The speaker may continue to speak if he or she so wishes, but the listener shall not be held accountable for not hearing any of it.

Pause. Hands clasped, pinkies pointing upwards. Used to request a pause, or to signal a brief interruption. For example, it can be used by a listener as a substitute for: "I'm really interested in what you are saying right now, and I need to take a break to use the toilet." It could also mean that I am requesting a pause to process, and/or inviting you to take a breath.

Alternatively, this sign might be used by a speaker to signal, "I see that something is stirring within you, and I am just about to reach the end of my train of thought."

Requesting Another's Voice. Hands clasped, index and middle fingers of both hands pointing towards another person. Can be used as a substitute for: "It seems John hasn't said anything in a while. I wonder if he has something that he'd like to share." Or, if we see someone making the 'Retreat' sign, we might use the 'Requesting' sign to inquire about what is happening with them.

'The use of the signs reminds us of the dimension of wonder in every meeting'

For us, the use of the signs reminds us of the dimension of wonder in every meeting. We find the use of creative ritual in communication helpful for developing greater balance between words and silence.

In closing, we'd like to emphasise that we welcome your collaboration in this shared endeavour, and we'd love to hear any stories about your experiences using these or your own signs to deepen communication.

Copyright © 2000 Rosa Zubizarreta and Michael Bridge. The full version can be obtained by e-mailing the authors at: rosalegria@igc.org

Silent brainstorming

Dr K. R. S. Murthy

Adapted from a submission to the Global Ideas Bank. Dr Murthy adds: "This technique is applicable to any topic of your choice and to any forum, including web-based applications."

Have you attended any brainstorming sessions in your life? The sessions are normally run by a facilitator, who introduces the purpose of the session to the participants, explains the ground rules and coordinates the process. A note taker or scribe may be used to document all the ideas generated in the session. Generally, the session is open to any ideas. The all-important guideline is that no idea is too simple, stupid or wild.

'The power of silence as a supplement to the communication-oriented parts of the session'

I am presenting a new approach to the brainstorming process, and also indicate some potential variations to the approach. At present, I have termed it 'Silent Brainstorming' or 'Mind Conferencing', even though the process is not completely silent. My approach makes efficient use of silence and communication interleaved in the brainstorming session – particularly of the power of silence as a supplement to the communication-oriented parts of the session.

First idea generation session

The session would start with a facilitator detailing the process steps used for the particular session. The session is conducted in a normal fashion with the participants speaking out their ideas in a round robin or random fashion for some duration. The facilitator can choose any format for this session. There are numerous brainstorming session techniques and format in use. It is a good idea to pick one comfortable for the facilitator and the participants.

Invoking the Silent Brainstorming session

The facilitator or one of the assistants rings a bell. The guidelines of the silent brainstorming process would require the participants to stop talking and quickly get to the silent part of the session. In the silent mode the participants are asked to come up with more ideas, but not to voice them. They write out the ideas.

'Participants guess the ideas that they imagine the others may be getting'

In addition, the participants have to start guessing the ideas that they imagine the others may be getting and writing. They may guess the ideas of their colleagues by name one at a time. For example, if the participants are A, B, C, D, E, F and G, then A would not only write his/her idea, but also guess what B, C, D, E, F, and G may have as their ideas. A would do this in a deep thinking process, based on the way others answered during the speaking part of the session.

Presentation session

In this session, each of them reads their own ideas, and also their best guesses

20 Heber Road, London NW2 6AA, UK (rhino@dial.pipex.com), 2001, 300pp, ISBN 0 948826 58 4

of the ideas for others. The others simply listen in silence.

Discussion session

The presentations are followed by a detailed discussion session. In this session, the participants may discuss why and how they guessed other's ideas. Each participant can also comment on the guesses of the other participants, and validate or clarify. Notes can be taken of the highlights and conclusions resulting from discussion.

Continuing silent and speaking sessions

The successive sessions would repeat the session sequence already used. However, in the second and in any subsequent silent sessions, the participants are required to improve their guesses. In these silent sessions each one will also be thinking into deeper levels of others' thinking. For example, the following increasing complexities of thinking would result:

- B would be thinking of his/her own ideas
- B would also be thinking of what A, C, D, E, F and G are thinking
- B would also be thinking of what A is thinking of B, C, D, E, F and G.

'The number of ideas generated would be many times more than normal'

The number of ideas generated would be many times more than done in any other more normal brainstorming technique. Regular teams can be formed to practice this technique. True diversity in gender, age, ethnic background, educational levels, race, and personality types will ensure a team that is fertile in ideas.

- *Dr K. R. S. Murthy, CEO, Virtual Think Tank, Silicon Valley, California, USA (tel Int.+1 408 219 2236; e-mail: geniuspoet@hotvoice.com; web: http:// members.fortunecity.com/geniuspoet/genius/index.html).*

A cultural rosary for remembering insights and information

Summarised from a document by Anthony Judge, entitled 'Designing cultural rosaries to sustain associations within the pattern that connects'; on the Union of International Associations website (http://www.uia.org/uiadocs/cultrose.htm).

A 'cultural rosary' could be used as a mnemonic device for remembering insights or information important to an individual person. Just as religions use beads to remember the order of prayers or mantras, so a cultural rosary could be used as a device for jogging the memory and connecting or ordering information. Varying the size, colour, number and divisions of the beads allows for a wide variety of options in how things can be ordered, grouped and remembered. Insights in a person's life could be recalled instantly, and connections between those insights would begin to emerge.

'Rosaries could take the place of an instruction manual or be used as a revision aid for students'

Suggestions for a cultural rosary include one that has the 30 articles of the Universal Declaration of Human Rights. When placed next to each other in the form of beads, the little explored connections and associations between the articles will also become more apparent. Other more prosaic rosaries could take the place of an instruction manual for basic computer working methods, or even be used as an aid for revision for students. The beads could even become a sort of low-tech personal organiser, with each bead signifying a type of meeting or a particular person, with the beads grouped into days of the week.

* *For more ideas concerning rosaries and beads, see 'Wearable story beads' at http://ic.www.media.mit.edu/StoryBeads/thesispropfinalweb.htm*
* *or 'A History of Prayer Beads' at http://www.beadshows.com/ibs/articles/prayer.html*

ARTS & LIFESTYLE

A restaurant in complete darkness to educate about blindness

Summarised from an article by Stephen Moss, entitled 'Blind Date', in the Guardian (December 8th 2000) and from an article by Allan Hall, entitled 'Taste of luxury in the first hotel for disabled', in the Financial Times (December 8th 2000).

Finding work if you are blind is never an easy matter, particularly when the vast majority of the world has no idea what it is like to be unable to see. These two issues were at the forefront of Jorge Spielmann's mind when he set up the Blind Cow restaurant in Zurich. It is a restaurant staffed with blind waiters and where everybody eats in complete darkness, in order to provide work for blind people and to give sighted people a sort of brief 'blind' experience. As Adrian

20 Heber Road, London NW2 6AA, UK (rhino@dial.pipex.com), 2001, 300pp, ISBN 0 948826 58 4

Schaffner, the restaurant's (sighted) manager, explains, "We hope to make people more sensitive to the problems of the blind. It's a new experience for diners: you take one sense away, so you have to use all the others much more."

The Blindekuh (Blind Cow) is named after the Swiss equivalent of the party game blind man's buff, and it has its own rules which must be followed. Bags and coats are left in lockers for safety reasons, and the eaters are led to their seats by placing their hands on the shoulders of a waiter or waitress. The room does not allow even the merest chink of light, ensuring that no ghostly figures or shapes can be made out in the gloom. Waiters then take orders by memorising them, and eating can soon commence.

'The emphasis is on what you say and what you know rather than what you are wearing or how you look'

Apart from it being a totally new eating experience, it is also a new social experience for sighted customers. Conversation without gesture, facial expression and eye contact puts the emphasis on what you say and what you know rather than on what you are wearing or how you look. Schaffner puts it more bluntly: "If you don't talk, you don't exist." There is undoubtedly a liberating element to the experience as well, with no-one knowing if you're downing your wine glass every three seconds or gnawing on a chicken leg bone with your hands. Whether not seeing your food makes you savour the food more is debatable, but the mixture of blind eating and blind education is an excellent one. And the public agrees – the restaurant is taking bookings six months ahead, and restaurateurs from America, Ireland and Britain have already expressed an interest in franchising the idea.

Restaurant critics to include decibel ratings in reviews

Summarised from a letter from Alison Munro to the London Times (July 6th 2000).

Restaurant critics should include a note on the average decibel levels in a restaurant in their review. A note on the presence and type of background music could also be helpful in enabling the discerning diner to make a more informed choice of the suitable eaterie for them.

Restaurants have long been judged on the standard of food, the service, and the amount of cigarette smoke (or lack of therein), but quietness is now a priority for the frequent restaurant diner.

Institute for Social Inventions, £15 subs, £17 from abroad by credit card, tel London 020 8208 2853

An outdoor piano for parks, mountains, estates etc.

Summarised from a letter to the Institute from Keith Lawton B.Sc. in January 2001. Additional information from an article by Conrad Gorinsky, entitled 'New sound of the forest', in the Guardian (November 22nd 2000).

Mr Lawton's idea is for an outdoor piano to be placed in various locations around the country: parks, remote areas, inner cities etc. The piano would be vandal-proof, weatherproof, and fixed by concrete to its chosen spot. He then imagines, for example, a group of walkers coming across a piano in a remote mountain area, or youngsters learning the piano on an inner-city estate. And, if need be, the pianos could be funded by a coin-operation system, with a pound coin unlocking the keyboard (or connecting the circuit if a battery-driven electric piano was used). Music could both echo off the hillsides and enrich walks through the park, with an outdoor piano providing the means.

'The piano was pulled on a sled, taken in a canoe, and still managed to arrive almost in tune'

And if this idea seems implausible, a recent expedition led by Colonel John Blashford-Snell should be brought to attention. He led an expedition in the autumn of 2000 which delivered an 800lb grand piano to a remote Amazonian tribe in Guyana. The piano was pulled on a sled, taken in a canoe, and still managed to arrive almost in tune – and it is now a fixture in the villagers' church. Onlookers were said to be deeply moved by the intuitive playing of the members of the tribe which resonated powerfully with the majestic rainforest background – a brand new sound introduced to a new location by an outdoor piano.

• *Keith Lawton ,170 York Street, Cambridge, CB1 2PY, UK.*

Special cinema screenings for mothers with babies

Summarised from an article by Clare Longrigg, entitled 'The crying game', in the Evening Standard (July 28th 2000), which was monitored for the Global Ideas Bank by Yvonne Ackroyd.

For those film buffs who demand complete silence in the cinema, please look away now. A far worse noise than popcorn-crunching or stray phone-calls

20 Heber Road, London NW2 6AA, UK (rhino@dial.pipex.com), 2001, 300pp, ISBN 0 948826 58 4

can now be heard at the Clapham Picture House in south London: babies. The cinema has just brought in weekly screenings specifically for mothers and babies, endeavouring to fill a niche in the market and provide a service to those mothers wishing to escape home imprisonment.

The idea was devised by staff at the cinema after mothers with prams kept protesting at being debarred from 18 certificate films. So now the ushers double as pram parking attendants, aisles are for rocking and burping, and the toilet's primary use is as a nappy-changing facility. Those who wish to munch popcorn and use their phone can probably do so with barely an eyebrow raised.

A ten-factor way of rating novels

Nicholas Albery

I find that when I read a novel I enjoy it well enough at the time but then at the end I put it aside and don't consider how it worked its magic or how good it was compared to other books I've read. Or I can get carried away by a particular aspect of it, and not be consciously aware of all its other facets.

The rating scheme I have now drafted helps me to see how a particular book works from ten different angles, so I can build up a much broader view. And I end up with a percentage rating that allows me to compare it to other books I have read; or to other people's ratings of the same book.

So where I used to say to myself: 'Yes I enjoyed that, but how much and why?', now I have pointers to answers.

In case others would like to adapt this rating scheme for their own use, adding other aspects that are important for them, here's a tentative attempt – using for test purposes the book *When I lived in Modern Times* by Linda Grant (Granta Books, London) – so the marks out of ten given after each question relate to this book:

Rate each answer out of ten (except the last one, which is out of 100):

(1) To what extent is how the plot develops consistent and believable? 4
(2) Is it a page turner, keeping me gripped? 6
(3) How much do I feel I'm there, inside the book? 6
(4) How rich are the descriptive passages? 3
(5) To what extent does it have socially or historically interesting aspects? 10
(6) To what extent does it have a sense of mystical or philosophical depths? 3
(7) How sensuous is the writing? 1
(8) How much was I able to empathise with the characters? 4
(9) To what extent does the author show a sense of humour? 3
(10) To what extent can I envisage re-reading this book ever? 3
(11) Overall, how would I rate this book (out of 100)? 40

Institute for Social Inventions, £15 subs, £17 from abroad by credit card, tel London 020 8208 2853

These add up to a maximum possible total of 200. Divide your total by two for your percentage rating. So Linda Grant's book rates 41.5% for me. How was it for you?

• *Please send feedback and suggested improvements to The Institute for Social Inventions, 20 Heber Road, London NW2 6AA, UK (tel Int.+44 [0]20 8208 2853; fax Int.+44 [0]20 8452 6434; e-mail: rhino@dial.pipex.com; web: www.globalideasbank.org).*

Creative ideas for making poetry more widely available

Dr. K. R. S. Murthy

These ideas have been extracted and adapted from a submission to the Global Ideas Bank. See also Dr Murthy's item in the Communications section on silent brainstorming.

The following are some of my brainstormed ideas for making poetry more widely available.

• Poetry on bills, cheques, notepads, napkins, receipts and fortune cookies.
• Poetry on invoices and billboards, in rock carvings and as graffiti.
• Poetry readings while people are waiting for flights or eating in airport restaurants.
• Poetry readings on planes in flight.
• Poetry on toilet paper.
• Slow dose poetry – only one line, stanza or word per day, hour, week; sent on the Internet, read on television or in other poetry reading forums

• *Dr K. R. S. Murthy, CEO, Virtual Think Tank, Silicon Valley, California (tel 408 219 2236; e-mail: geniuspoet@hotvoice.com; web: http:// poets_2001.tripod.com/Poets/ and also: http://members.fortunecity.com/ geniuspoet/genius/index.html).*

Print-on-demand breathes new life into out-of-print books

Summarised from an article by Hillel Italie, entitled 'New service gives new life to out-of-print books', in the Seattle Times, and from information on the www.Backinprint.com website. This item was monitored for the Global Ideas Bank by Roger Knights.

The Authors Guild in America has started a programme under which

20 Heber Road, London NW2 6AA, UK (rhino@dial.pipex.com), 2001, 300pp, ISBN 0 948826 58 4

authors can reissue their out-of-print books on the internet and in stores. The system allows the authors to either sell off spare or leftover copies of their books, or sell new editions printed on demand. The technology of 'print-on-demand' allows a book to be printed, assembled and bound within minutes, and also helps solve the problem of returns and warehouse storage. With books printed on demand, there is no danger of unsold books being returned, and there is no possibility of a slow-selling book having to be stored in a warehouse at the cost of the publisher. This makes it the perfect system for more obscure or slow-selling books that may have fallen out-of-print for those very reasons.

To facilitate the process, the guild set up an online store (www.Backinprint.com) with a full catalogue of all the titles presently available. The site points out that many of the copies on the sale often come directly from the authors themselves, and many are therefore rare signed copies with an extra cachet to them. The system is also helping the Authors' Guild to support its members, because ten per cent of all profits go back to the guild, a non-profit organisation.

'With today's technology, there is no reason why a book should ever go out of print again'

The titles being brought back to life include books by established authors like Lawrence Block and Thornton Wilder as well as those whose work is less well known. The authors are understandably pleased at the development, with Block saying, for example, "I'm delighted. I always get questions about [such books] at signings, from people wondering if [they're] going to be available again". With today's technology, there is now no reason why a book should ever go out of print again. A copy of the manuscript, including the original cover and artwork, can be kept as a computer file, and the book can be printed on demand if someone requests it. It's a strike back for the small author, and those books that are no less important for having a small or limited audience.

• *For more information, or to order out-of-print books, see www.backinprint.com*

Museums let visitors behind the scenes to see full collections

Summarised from an article by Andrew Curry, entitled 'Out of storage, and into the light of day', in US News & World Report (April 30th 2001), monitored for the Global Ideas Bank by Roger Knights.

Museums are letting visitors wander around their attics and back rooms in an effort to get more of their items out on display. At present, some museums are only able to show one per cent (or less) of their collections. So, rather than rely on big exhibitions to attract visitors, some museums have started to allow people to conduct their own investigation in their attics and stores. Such schemes allow the public to see how important the collections are in addressing issues of science and history up to the present day, and they also encourage visitors to take a more active role in shaping their own museum experience.

'The visitors can sense for themselves what a valuable resource these collections are for research'

Chicago's Field Museum offers behind-the-scenes tours to members, allowing them to experience what professional scientists do. At the Smithsonian's Naturalist Centre in Virginia, meanwhile, officials have re-placed curated displays with cabinets full of the thousands of items that have been going unseen, from shark teeth to stuffed polar bears. It has over 124 million natural history specimens, which are continuously maintained, and these are an incredibly valuable resource for those studying everything from taxonomy to biodiversity.

In Britain's Natural History Museum, plans are afoot to open a new centre that will put almost 80 per cent of the museum's collection on display. It is part of a drive to allow the public to see what museums actually do – that they are far more than just a storage and display facility. It is also a case of giving the visitor more credit, believing that they do not have to be led by storyboards through a nice, neat display but can come up with their own questions and investigations. As Stephen Asma, an expert on natural history museums, points out, "To let people experience what research scientists are really doing treats the visitor with more respect".

INTERNATIONAL

Giving bikes needing repair to developing countries

Summarised from the Re-Cycle website (www.re-cycle.org).

While Merlin Matthews was studying at the London School of Economics (LSE), he acquired the nickname Dr Bike, fixing bikes and running repair

20 Heber Road, London NW2 6AA, UK (rhino@dial.pipex.com), 2001, 300pp, ISBN 0 948826 58 4

workshops in exchange for beers on Friday evenings. In due course he was approached by Jo Dufort for advice about starting up a bike factory in Haiti, as she had seen the need for cheap, pollution free transport for the masses. Merlin was eager to get involved, aware that there were large numbers of bikes being thrown away which could be fixed.

He aimed to set up this project on his own and envisaged establishing a 'process' in the UK, then spending most of his time in Haiti running the workshop. Over time, he realised that he would be of more use to the Haitians and people in other countries if he spent most of the time in the UK, fund-raising and facilitating the collection and shipping of bikes. Since then, Re-Cycle has linked up with three US organisations – ITDP, Bikes Not Bombs and the International Bicycle Fund – teaching local people the skills of how to repair and maintain bikes to improve their lives in a sustainable manner.

'Re-cycle celebrated having shipped over 3,000 bicycles to five countries'

This year, Re-Cycle celebrated having shipped over 3,000 bicycles to five countries, amongst them Sierra Leone, Zambia, and Nigeria, and their efforts will be assisted in the future by Royal Mail's agreement to donate some 4,000 old bikes from their considerable fleet every year.

• *For details of the other organisations doing similar work to Re-Cycle, some of whom are mentioned above, see: www.re-cycle.org/Links/Our_Partners/ our_partners.html*

• *Re-Cycle, 60 High St, West Mersea, Essex CO5 8JE, UK (tel Int. 44 [0]1206 382207; mobile 0797 073 1530; e-mail: info@re-cycle.org*

The Free and Independent Republic of Frestonia

Submitted by Nicholas Albery, erstwhile Frestonia's Minister of State for the Environment.

The Free and Independent Republic of Frestonia was founded on October 27th 1977. The residents in Freston Road, Notting Dale, London W11, threatened with eviction to make way for a giant factory estate, held a referendum. There was a 95% majority in favour of independence from Great Britain and a 73% majority in favour of joining the Common Market. An application for membership, complete with coat of arms, was sent to the United Nations, along with its warning that a peace-keeping force might be required.

There were 120 residents in Frestonia living in about 30 houses on one acre of land. Everyone who wanted to take part became a minister, but there was no prime minister. The Minister of State for Education was a two-year-old, Francesco Bogina-Bramley, and the Minister of State for Foreign Affairs was a dwarf, the actor David Rappaport-Bramley (who wore a T-shirt saying 'Small is Beautiful'). The nation's motto on its coat of arms was 'Nos sumus una familia', 'We are one family' and everyone adopted the surname 'Bramley' (just in case the Greater London Council (GLC) were to succeed in evicting us, they might have to rehouse us together, as one family).

The media descended on Frestonia from around the world. The Daily Mail printed a leader column and a report 'from our Foreign Correspondent in Frestonia'. Japanese TV filmed New Zealand TV filming nothing much going on in our uneventful communal garden. Coachloads of young tourists, mainly from Denmark, arrived, and were shown round the borders in ten minutes or so, receiving their Frestonian passport stamps and leaving, rather dissatisfied.

A National Film Theatre of Frestonia opened in the People's Hall, with the first showing being 'Passport to Pimlico' and films by the Sex Pistols. The National Theatre of Frestonia opened with the international premiere of 'The Immortalist' by Heathcote Williams, preceded by no less than three national anthems. (The London Evening Standard had urged their readers to submit suitable anthems to us.) Frestonia applied to join the International Postal Union and printed its own postage stamps, with replies to our letters coming in from around the world.

It all worked like a dream. The Greater London Council (GLC), who previously had refused to deal with us, now told the media that they would negotiate with us "in New York or wherever" and their Tory leader, Sir Horace Cutler, sent us a letter saying "If you did not exist it would be necessary to invent you". We replied "Since we do exist, why is it necessary to destroy us?". Sir Geoffrey Howe MP wrote to us that as one who has "a childhood enthusiasm for the Napoleon of Notting Hill Gate", he could hardly fail to be moved by our plight.

'We were transformed in the GLC's eyes from a bunch of squatters, hobos and drug addicts into an international incident'

We were suddenly transformed in the GLC's eyes from a bunch of squatters, hobos and drug addicts into an international incident that was providing them with an opportunity to show how enlightened they were and threatening them with the prospect of negative media coverage if they carried on with their plans to evict us.

A public enquiry was ordered. The GLC had their QC, and I represented

Frestonia as the Minister of State for the Environment. We proposed that Frestonia become a mixed used site for houses and craft workshops. We won the enquiry.

Frestonia was eventually rebuilt to our design with several millions of pounds of foreign aid from Great Britain, channelled via the Notting Hill Housing Trust to our own co-operative. We used the superb Pattern Language book on timeless architecture, by Christopher Alexander (published by OUP), which is as simple as painting by numbers, to vote as a co-op on the various architectural patterns we wanted incorporated in our new development.

Today, I am immensely proud of the development that was built, complete with its overhanging roofs, enclosed communal gardens and decorated brickwork. Recently, there was a great party in a marquee in the communal garden to mark the 21st anniversary of independence. The spirit is still strong.

Frestonia goes to show that with imagination and humour you can run rings round the establishment.

Localization – A Global Manifesto

A review of 'Localization – A Global Manifesto *by Colin Hines (Earthscan Books, ISBN 1-85383-612-5, 190pp, £10.99). Reviewed by Nick Temple.*

This book aims to promote and debate what the author calls 'a move away from acquiescence to the new theology of globalization' towards a replacement system of localization. This localization would involve the protection, encouragement and rebuilding of local economies as a viable alternative to globalization's profit-led free trade system. Colin Hines believes that the inevitability of globalization (world free-trade capitalism) should be challenged and resisted. This could be said of many activists and authors, though: where he goes further is to suggest actual economic initiatives and policies which could engender localisation as an alternative.

'Long-distance trade should only be for acquiring what cannot be provided in the place where people live'

The concept put forward in the book is that long-distance trade should only be for acquiring what cannot be provided within the place where people live. To reinforce this, preference would have to be given to local goods and suppliers in a way that benefits workers, the local community and the environment. But Hines is more persuasive than those who call for simple outright protectionism, pointing out that internal competition would be both necessary and healthy within a country's economy, and thus admitting that capitalism's market forces have proved successful within countries, if not between them.

There are problems with this ambitious, polemical manifesto, and Hines recognises this in his appendix called 'Answers to Some Criticisms of the 'Protect the Local, Globally' Form of Localization'. While there is something slightly smug about predicting what the reader's questions and problems with his manifesto might be, the answers given are mostly as persuasive as the manifesto itself. Two problems were swiftly and partially dealt with, though: the tendency to nationalism, and the commercial power of the Internet.

In response to the former problem of localization pandering to right-wing nationalism, Hines points out that fascism is on the rise in free market countries in Europe, and that the by-products of globalization (public sector job losses, expenditure cut-backs etc) lead to an insecurity which fosters the rise of this neo-fascism and right-wing nationalism. This may be true enough, and localization may indeed provide the 'hope and security' which Hines believes it will, but a protectionist blocking of imports (however selective) surely runs alongside a blocking of immigration. If people become more prosperous by preventing others' goods from entering, are they likely to welcome immigrants into the country with open arms?

'It is crucial that there be no impediments to the international flow of new information and relevant technology'

Furthermore, the author does seem to have missed out the Internet altogether (neither 'Internet' nor 'worldwide web' are even in the index) which seems odd in a discussion of globalization. He does write that 'although there would be constraints on long-distance trade of goods and services, it is crucial that there be no impediments to the international flow of new information and relevant technology where it contributes to the localization end goals'. But what of the information that doesn't contribute to those goals – how would that be stopped from entering a particular country? And how would Internet trade be regulated under his quasi-protectionist rules?

These issues aside, though, the book is an inspiring one for all those who recognize the importance of local cultures and societies. It is a passionate, ambitious effort to truly confront the problems that globalization has fostered: that means actual financial alternatives, not just criticism of the status quo. And it is for this reason that Hines is more persuasive, for the reader is swayed by his figures and economics as much as his polemics.

• *Localization – a Global Manifesto is available from Earthscan Books who also publish many other titles dealing with the environment and ecology. Contact*

20 Heber Road, London NW2 6AA, UK (rhino@dial.pipex.com), 2001, 300pp, ISBN 0 948826 58 4

them at Earthscan Publications Ltd, 120 Pentonville Road, London, N1 9JN, UK (web: www.earthscan.co.uk; e-mail: earthinfo@earthscan.co.uk).

Property rights of the poor must be better protected

Summarised from a review by Peter Coy, entitled 'Why the world's poor stay that way', in Business Week magazine (November 13th 2000) and from publicity material for The Mystery of Capital *by Hernando de Soto (published by Basic Books). Both items were monitored for the Global Ideas Bank by Roger Knights.*

A new book by Hernando de Soto, *The Mystery of Capital,* claims to have solved the largest remaining mystery of capitalism: the persistence of poverty amid plenty, or the failure of some countries to build and sustain a capitalist economy. He highlights the failure of legal systems in many third world and developing countries to recognise and respect the property of the poor.

'In Peru, it used to take 728 separate steps for a squatter to obtain legal rights to his or her home'

Bureaucratic red tape prevents property being recorded, and then it cannot be borrowed against, with the result that a huge amount of capital just lies there dormant and unused. In Peru, for example, it used to take 728 separate steps for a squatter to obtain legal rights to his or her home. In Haiti, it takes two years of bureaucracy to lease some land for five years. Is it any wonder that entrepreneurs and those wishing to own homes go elsewhere outside their homeland?

'De Soto estimates this dead capital owned by poorer people worldwide to be $9 trillion'

De Soto stresses this need for a clear legal concept of private property at the heart of a capitalist economy, and blames lawyers for not allowing changes to happen. He argues that, if the legal system were reformed in these countries, the 'dead capital' of unofficially owned property could become a starting point for growth and a way out of poverty. De Soto estimates this dead capital owned by poorer people worldwide to be $9 trillion and he emphasises the huge potential for change. Simplifying the legal recognition of property, the regulation on businesses, and the bureaucracy surrounding capital and its movement, could make a massive difference to these countries' economies.

Institute for Social Inventions, £15 subs, £17 from abroad by credit card, tel London 020 8208 2853

What de Soto fails to recognise, so his critics say, is that there are other factors that play a significant role in such economic failures – political pressures, flawed macroeconomic policies, and exploitative corporate strategies can all have a hindering impact on a nation's economy; and he dismisses out of hand the possibility of culture playing a role in capitalist systems failing (pointing out, for instance, that Protestants don't have a monopoly on the work ethic). But does not culture play a part in how the bureaucracy has come about, or the lack of will to change it even when its flaws are obvious? If there is no will for change amongst the political and the elite, does that not affect the way the economy can progress? That this book is valuable in its highlighting of certain crucial issues is incontestable – but its conclusions should be seen as part of a wider solution, not the answer to every developing country's prayers.

But Brian Bollen, reviewing *The Mystery of Capital* on Amazon.co.uk, sums up the book's importance as follows: "A great deal of the power of legal property comes from the accountability it creates, from the constraints it imposes, the rules it spawns and the sanctions it can apply. The lack of legal property thus explains why citizens in developing and former communist nations cannot make profitable contracts with strangers, cannot obtain credit, insurance or utilities services. Because they have no property to lose, they are only taken seriously as contracting parties by their immediate family and neighbours.

'People with nothing to lose are trapped in the grubby basement of the pre-capitalist word'

"To put it another way, while most western homeowners dream about paying off their mortgage, their counterparts in the less developed countries could transform their existence if they could only access such sums. 'People with nothing to lose are trapped in the grubby basement of the pre-capitalist word.' This is the nub of *The Mystery of Capital*. Read just that one sentence and you catch a glimpse of the reason why, as the author puts it, four-fifths of humanity lack the ability to turn dead assets into live capital."

Satellite phones for disaster victims

Summarised from an item by Veronique Mistiaen in the London Guardian (August 30th 2000).

Telecoms San Frontieres (TSF), a French organisation, establishes satellite

20 Heber Road, London NW2 6AA, UK (rhino@dial.pipex.com), 2001, 300pp, ISBN 0 948826 58 4

communications in disaster areas, using about 20 laptop-sized Inmarsat satellite phones. TSF President Jean-Francois Cazenave says they helped save 14 lives when Turkey was hit by an earthquake in 1999: "All the terrestrial networks were destroyed, but instead of having to drive 20km to find an acoustic drill or some other piece of equipment, we could use our satellite phones. We saw that for people directly affected by disasters, the need for communication was almost as vital as food."

'The satellite phones helped save 14 lives when Turkey was hit by an earthquake in 1999'

About half TSF's phones are used by Kosovar refugees, who have made over 130,000 calls in just one year – to contact their families, ask for aid, receive documents and find lost relatives.

Reviving traditional medicine in Ladakh

Summarised from information distributed by the Rolex Awards for Enterprise in October 2000.

Laurent Pordié, a French anthropologist and ethno-pharmacologist, is attempting to reintroduce traditional Amchi medicine to the region of Ladakh in northern India. Such a reinstatement of Amchi skills should not only revive and perpetuate the tradition but also, in doing so, improve the healthcare in one of the world's least hospitable environments.

In the past, the local doctors known as Amchis provided their skills free of charge to their village in return for having their farming chores done. With the other villagers doing their communal duties of raising livestock, ploughing and harvesting, the Amchis were allowed to concentrate on consultations, treatment and gathering medicinal minerals and plants.

'The Amchi medical system is based on a strong sense of community, which is now declining'

But in the last twenty years, things have dramatically changed. Increasing social mobility has eroded the rural communities, with people being much less likely to remain in the village they were born in. Allied to this, market forces have to some extent replaced the barter systems of before. The Amchi medical tradition has also been undermined by government initiatives to introduce conventional Western medicine to these impoverished areas. Their intent may have been worthy, but the result has been a marginalisation of the holistic skills upon which such communities used to depend. As a result, the traditional Amchi skills have begun to disappear. As Laurent Pordié himself says, "Modernisation has brought a sense of individualism and a breakdown in the traditional system of help between families in the villages. The Amchi medical system is suffering because it is based on a strong sense of community, which is now declining."

That some action is needed now is unquestionable. Ladakh can be one of the coldest places on earth, with temperatures sometimes as low as -40ºC in winter, and its communities are often as isolated as they are impoverished. The government initiatives have failed to provide an adequate substitute for the traditional system, with drugs too expensive, knowledge scarce, and hospitals and clinics being few and far between. With the Amchis no longer passing their skills from father to son, Ladakhis have neither the traditional nor the Western medical systems to rely on. The standard of health in the region has suffered as a consequence, with the region having the highest infant mortality rate in India.

Pordié's aims, therefore, are threefold: to educate individuals from Amchi families, and new students, in the traditional system; to set up banks of medicinal drugs accessible to all on a fee-paying basis; and to develop Amchi projects in alliance with government organisations.

The education programme was officially launched in November 1999, and 13 people were taken on after an entrance exam (including four women and six students with no prior knowledge of the traditional techniques). Assuming all goes well, they should qualify with diplomas in April 2002.

'Villagers will either pay for their medicinal 'withdrawals' or will barter goods and labour'

The medicine banks were needed because it is no longer possible for Amchis to take the sole responsibility for the gathering of medicinal plants and minerals, because they now have to take care of their own farming tasks. With the system of medicine banks in each village, the villagers will be able to choose to either pay for their medicinal 'withdrawals' or to barter goods and labour in the traditional way. Pordié set up a pilot project in a part of Ladakh, Senghi-La, in August 1998, and six medicine banks are now up and running there. His eventual aim is to set up enough banks to supply the whole of Ladakh.

Pordié hopes to further improve the lot of the Amchi doctors by getting the new diplomas accredited and recognised by central government, and by producing a journal to bring the 400-odd practising Amchis together into some sort of professional network. He also plans to run 10- or 15-day seminars to hone the skills of those existing Amchi doctors, in collaboration with the

20 Heber Road, London NW2 6AA, UK (rhino@dial.pipex.com), 2001, 300pp, ISBN 0 948826 58 4

Tibetan Medical and Astrological Institute. It should also be stated that, although Amchi practitioners do use basic instruments, they normally leave major surgery to Western physicians. They view illness as being caused by an imbalance of bodily or mental states coming from climate, diet, behaviour or the influence of demons. As a result, it is possible for the two systems to work in tandem with each other.

Perhaps most importantly of all, the local people have responded with enthusiasm to Pordié's efforts, and his work is supported by most of the existing Amchi doctors. Many observers expect the project to have a significant impact on both the healthcare of the Ladakhis and on the preservation of their culture. Furthermore, as their presence is essential for the cohesiveness and mental well-being of their communities, the revival of Amchi medicine could repair and strengthen the very fabric of life in these isolated mountain villages.

• *Dr Laurent Pordié can be contacted at NOMAD Health & Education, 24 chemin du Roussimort, 31270 Frouzins, France (e-mail: nomadplant@hotmail.com).*

• *Laurent Pordié was a Laureate in the Rolex Awards for Enterprise 2000. For more information about the awards, write to Rolex Awards Secretariat, PO Box 1311, 1211 Geneva 26, Switzerland, or see the website: www.rolexawards.com*

Volunteers bring computer skills into the developing world

Summarised from an article by Maria Trombly, entitled 'Volunteer brings computers to the Bedouin', in Computerworld (16th October 2000), which was monitored for the Global Ideas Bank by Roger Knights.

In an effort to close the technological divide between the developed world and Third World countries, the United Nations Information Technology Services (UNITeS) has been sending out IT experts to countries from Benin to Tanzania. One such operative, Sean Osner, recently set up a community centre in a Bedouin village with ten Intel 486 computers and five Pentium III's. And while it might seem that a nomadic shepherd would have no need for the Internet, it can help locals get better education and medical care. It may help with business too; as Osner points out, "One of the things we designed the community centre for was to help the local women find markets in other parts of the world for their products. That would keep those traditions alive in their community."

'The UNITeS programme aims to help businesses in developing countries exploit the opportunities afforded by the Internet'

The UNITeS program, with volunteers co-ordinated by United Nations Volunteers (UNV), aims to play a key role in helping businesses in developing countries exploit the opportunities afforded by the Internet, but it is also aimed at teaching people how to use computers not just at putting computer systems in place. This could also help reduce the shortage of IT-skilled people in such countries, which is a major hurdle to their involvement in the digital revolution. And the demand is undoubtedly there; in a recent visit to Zagazig in Egypt, Osner was faced with 4000 people, all waiting for a chance to use one of four computer terminals. Those who did get the chance learned how to do word processing, to e-mail, to search the Internet, and to set up their own e-commerce sites. But, as Osner says, "There is an overwhelming demand that we can't possibly fill."

Up to October 2000, 23 volunteers had gone on assignments in countries including Burundi, Ecuador and India. More are planned, and funding from computer companies eager to exploit an untapped market will help the scheme to widen its reach.

• *For more information, see the UNITeS website (www.unites.org).*

WAR & PEACE

Virtual peacekeeping by webcam

Summarised from an article in Boardwatch Magazine, entitled 'Virtual Peacekeeping', by Doug Mohney (March 2000; p.116)

In order to fully use the capabilities of Internet video technology, it has been suggested that virtual peacekeeping could be put in place with cameras and monitoring rooms taking the place of armed forces. Whereas traditional peacekeeping has tended to have a token neutral force placed between the two warring parties as a symbolic buffer, virtual peacekeeping would use sealed remote transmitting cameras powered by solar cells to monitor a demilitarized zone.

The transmissions from such cameras would be encrypted and checked and monitored to prevent spoofing or interference. The video could be transmitted anywhere it was desired, from a newsroom to a UN monitoring centre. If anyone or anything wandered into the demilitarized zone, people would

20 Heber Road, London NW2 6AA, UK (rhino@dial.pipex.com), 2001, 300pp, ISBN 0 948826 58 4

know instantly and be able to respond appropriately. Destroying the cameras or tampering with them would also be considered a hostile action, just as any sort of attack on a traditional peacekeeping force would be.

Clearly, there are difficulties with this idea, with most people being far happier doing harm to inanimate equipment than to actual human beings. Furthermore, some of the areas where the technology would be required would be extremely remote, making the employment and upkeep of any such equipment a severe problem. Nevertheless, it may not be long before we see protest groups and campaigning minorities utilising such technology to highlight their selected concerns, thus putting a check on any authorities thinking of clamping down on such activities. Virtual peacekeeping might not be far behind.

Solve the dispute over Jerusalem by declaring God sovereign

Summarised from an article by Karin Laub, entitled 'A solution for Jerusalem: put God in charge', in the Seattle Times (31st August 2000), monitored for the Global Ideas Bank by Roger Knights.

The solution to one of the thorniest political and religious problems that exists today, who should have sovereignty over Jerusalem, could be a simple one: put God in charge. This proposal has the potential to provide common ground for both sides to at least begin to talk about how the city can be shared. The idea could also help defuse the explosive cocktail of emotions which are associated with the city.

Both Yasser Arafat and successive Israeli leaders have demanded full sovereignty over what they see as traditionally Arab and Jewish parts of the city. At the heart of the dispute is Temple Mount which is not only a sacred site to Jews, but is also home to Islam's third-holiest shrine. The raised area, in the centre of Jerusalem's Old City, is also the site of two major mosques which were, in turn, built on the site of ancient Jewish temples.

'Both sides could give ground without being labelled a traitor to their people'

If God were to be declared sovereign, both leaders could conceivably give ground without necessarily being labelled a traitor to their people. Only if the two leaders can save face can negotiations possibly succeed, and putting God in charge could allow them to do exactly that.

Institute for Social Inventions, £15 subs, £17 from abroad by credit card, tel London 020 8208 2853

Jerusalem, breakthrough without agreement?

Guido Enthoven

History is repeating itself. There is fighting between Jews and Palestinians again. The recent negotiations between Barak, Arafat and Clinton have scarcely produced any result. The most important point at dispute continues to be the status and future of Jerusalem. As the centre for different world religions, Jerusalem has a long history of conflict. On the one hand, Jerusalem – and particularly the Old City and the Temple Mount – is of great symbolic value in religious terms. On the other hand, there are also specific, practical differences of opinion on the day-to-day control, administration and planning of the various parts of the wider city. Long-term peace between Israel and the Palestinians cannot be achieved unless a solution is found to the Jerusalem question. But no solution seems to be in prospect at present. Past history, the mutually exclusive claims, the distrust between the parties and the geopolitical aspects make this issue one of today's most complex challenges.

'There have been long periods of peace-making and compromise in Jerusalem's history'

And yet there have been long periods of peace-making and compromise in Jerusalem's history. It has demonstrably been possible to achieve peaceful coexistence at certain periods. Some view the present explosion of violence as the long-drawn-out, painful birthpangs of a new era (eg R. Suudi). The following article explores some lines of thought which may offer (the prospect of) a way out of the spiral of violence. They are building blocks, partly inspired by the past and partly linking to modern developments, which deserve further analysis and elaboration.

1. No agreement, but two unilateral declarations of intent. At present, both parties claim full sovereignty over major parts of Jerusalem. These claims are mutually exclusive and cannot be reconciled in an agreement. However there is the opportunity for two unilateral declarations of intent to be made. Here, both parties claim full sovereignty over the city, but at the same time, for the sake of peace and as an expression of their genuine desire for peace, both parties are prepared under certain preconditions to transfer specific parts of that sovereignty temporarily to another party for limited periods. The other party might be the UN, but possibly also the opposite side. The preconditions may relate to full and undisturbed access to religious sites, public order, planning etc. The benefit of a construction of this kind involving two unilateral declarations of intent is that the extremists on both sides have the

20 Heber Road, London NW2 6AA, UK (rhino@dial.pipex.com), 2001, 300pp, ISBN 0 948826 58 4

wind taken out of their sails in principle, while in practice it becomes possible to 'collapse' the two intents for the purposes of day-to-day administration.

2. Purification and repentance. All the major world religions have concepts of sin, repentance, forgiveness and purification. If there is anything required in fundamental terms in the conflict between Israel and the Palestinians, it lies in this area. So much suffering has been inflicted, there has been so much fighting and killing and so much senseless violence that it is difficult to imagine long-term peace without considering this aspect. Recognition and repentance could relate to the events of the past 70 years: the Holocaust (international affirmation of repentance), the settlement by Jews in the Holy Land and the proclamation of the state of Israel, the attacks by the neighbouring Arab countries, the occupation of the West Bank, Gaza and Golan, the terrorist attacks and murders in Munich, Sabra and Shatila and in all the other places, the Intifada and its suppression. Reconciliation is often only possible through the recognition of the suffering that has been caused to the other party. If the two leaders, Barak and Arafat, were to make a public acknowledgement of the pain and loss suffered by the other party, that could provide a major impulse for the peace process. In addition, consideration might be given to a broader 'repentance movement', a 'recognition register', or a Truth Commission as in South Africa – a purification ritual to wash away, at least to some extent, the unspeakable suffering inflicted on each side in the past.

'Small steps forward may be taken on both sides. These could build on cautious experiments to increase mutual understanding'

3. Experiments. Small steps forward may be taken on both sides. These could build on cautious experiments (eg Neve Shalom) to increase mutual understanding. An educational project in which the various backgrounds to the conflict are outlined by both Jewish and Palestinian teachers. Mixed bus trips to both Jewish and Palestinian settlements and villages, with personal background stories. Neighbourhood projects at the micro level, with joint agreements on the management and maintenance of a street. Small steps as cautious experiments in peaceful coexistence.

4. International Internet initiative. Modern information technology and communications offer new possibilities to involve people from different countries in thinking about the Jerusalem question. Arabs, American Jews, experts and the general public can all participate. This could for instance take shape along three lines. Firstly, a virtual forum could be created for the expression and sharing of emotions (suffering, horror, j'accuse, compassion). Secondly, there could be an exploration of the issue on the Internet, an "Internet advisory council" in which opinions on current dilemmas are probed. Finally, it might be possible to set up a virtual think tank focussing on the development of policy options for current dilemmas. A definite link with current negotiations and the current situation would be desirable in that case. The approach is to develop 'variations on an agreement'.

'A concrete proposal would be for a consultative referendum among Jews and Palestinians in 2001'

5. Fluid division of Jerusalem. Until now, any division of Jerusalem has been envisioned as resulting in a western part (Israel) and an eastern part (Palestine). It is worthwhile considering other possibilities for a division. On the one hand, there is the possibility of a 'trusted third party' such as the United Nations. This is in line with current practice at the micro level. In the Middle Ages, the various Christian churches (Catholic, Greek Orthodox, Syrian Orthodox) were in conflict over the control of the Church of the Holy Sepulchre in Jerusalem. Finally, an independent party – a leading Muslim family (!) – was chosen, and remains the keyholder of the church to this day. Part of the city could also come under joint administration by Jews and Palestinians. A concrete proposal would be for a consultative referendum among Jews and Palestinians in 2001. The percentages of the vote could form the basis for the division of the city into four types of administration: 1) Jewish, 2) Palestinian, 3) UN, and 4) joint administration. The last category is perhaps the most interesting one; if that form of administration functions properly, the area coming under joint administration could be expanded in the course of time.

Some initiatives for new perspectives on the Jerusalem question have been outlined above. These are irreconcilable with the present spiral of violence and the associated enmity between the parties, and so the first priority is to work on ways to end the violence. At the same time, there must be a desperate search for ways to arrive at long-term peace; building blocks for a new Jerusalem.

• *The author is the director of the Institute for Social Innovation in Holland. The article is based on a discussion/brainstorming meeting on this subject held in Leiden on 7 November 2000.*

• *Guido Enthoven, Instituut voor Maatschappelijke Innovatie, Rapenburg 8-10, 2311 EV Leiden, Holland (tel Int.+31 71 5127707; fax Int.+31 71 5661945, e-mail: imi@xs4all.nl).*

20 Heber Road, London NW2 6AA, UK (rhino@dial.pipex.com), 2001, 300pp, ISBN 0 948826 58 4

Transform the Korean demilitarized zone into a wildlife sanctuary

Summarised from an article and interview by Josie Glausiusz, entitled 'Healer of a divided land', in Discover magazine (November 2000), monitored for the Global Ideas Bank by Roger Knights.

One of the more uplifting events of the year 2000 was the reconciliation between North and South Korea, although the accord remains an inevitably fragile one. A Korean-born entomologist, Ke Chung Kim, has proposed the creation of a peace park and wildlife preserve to transform the huge demilitarized zone between the two countries. He believes that this would cement the new relationship between the two countries, by providing a fitting joint memorial to the dead and in giving both countries a chance to work together in creation rather than destruction.

'In the 47 years since the end of the Korean war, the demilitarized zone has become a sanctuary for birds, mammals, fish and plants that have been wiped out elsewhere'

In the 47 years since the end of the Korean war, the demilitarized zone has become a sanctuary for birds, mammals, fish and plants that have been wiped out elsewhere. The growth in South Korea's population (it has doubled in the last 30 years) has led to increased pollution and the destruction of habitats, while massive deforestation in North Korea has caused flooding and soil erosion. The zone could restore some much-needed ecological balance in the area.

The potential of such a sanctuary has been revealed by an area of the zone in which 1,200 different species of flowers, 83 species of fish (18 unique to that area), and two of the world's most endangered birds, the red-crowned and white-naped crane, can all be found. And that is without mentioning the rare species of black bear, musk deer, leopards and even tigers. A preserved piece of land created by war could therefore be used for the peaceful protection of rare native species and habitats, and for the peaceful reconciliation of the two Koreas: an idea that, if fulfilled, could blend political and ecological harmony together.

• *Ke Chung Kim, Professor of Entomology, Penn State University, Massachusetts, USA.*

Use pigs to root for land mines

Brian Cady

Adapted from a submission to the Global Ideas Bank. Brian Cady says of himself that he "intends to bring economically and environmentally sustainable chestnut orcharding to North America's Northeast in such a way as to create lasting opportunity for those most without it". What follows is a more radical idea of his.

Penning hogs in mine fields could protect human life. They would tend to dig up the mines as they rooted about.

Shields for the pigs and training might protect them. These might cover the top and front of the head and the back of the pig.

'Training could teach pigs to safely excavate mines'

Pigs are reputed to be smarter than dogs, and training could teach them to safely excavate and gather land mines, or to drop them into buried explosion-proof pits.

• *Brian Cady (e-mail: bcady@equinox.shaysnet.com).*

Bribe war-torn communities to be peaceful

Aaron Campbell

Adapted from a submission to the Global Ideas Bank.

I think we should flat-out bribe people not to wage war. Offer grants to communities in war-torn areas to keep their homes and people non-violent. Track the progress of these communities in relation to their neighbours and see who prospers with peace. Make the incentive real, and pay half up-front and the rest after a year of (perhaps relative) non-violence.

'Pay half up-front and the rest after a year of non-violence'

Money often speaks louder than bombs. After calculating how much damage is done by war, one could easily see that if only one per cent of the money was spent on making peace, it would be quite well-spent. Ben & Jerry's promotes the one per cent for peace plan.

• *Aaron Campbell (e-mail: aaroncampbell@netscape.net).*

20 Heber Road, London NW2 6AA, UK (rhino@dial.pipex.com), 2001, 300pp, ISBN 0 948826 58 4

A television show for currently non-violent terrorists

Thomas Edward Sheridan

Adapted from a submission to the Global Ideas Bank.

Produce a television show, with an accompanying website, in which representatives from recognised and newer, as yet, unrecognised terrorists groups compete in 'capture-the-flag' and 'paint-ball' type war game competitions with the prizes being 15 minutes, etc, of public broadcasting television time (and/or web page space) to spout their manifestos and rants.

'This allows the terrorists to get what they really want – a mass audience'

This allows the terrorist game to be stripped of real world violence and the terrorists get what they really want – a mass audience. They can use their terrorist skills to win the competitions.

All entrants will get to have up to 100 words for a statement on their cause. They must be representatives (or convicted, currently jailed terrorists) of a bonafide, labelled terrorist group who have *not* claimed any violent acts within six months prior to the show. Also, the show's guidelines will be drawn up by a group of international law enforcers and terrorist prisoners.

This show will move the terrorist game into a non-violent arena and challenge these 'true believers' to use their brains instead of violence to capture an audience. All or some of the money generated from the shows will go to a fund for victims of terrorist attacks.

Terrorists would thus be encouraged to conduct their operations with non-lethal weapons and explosives and there would also be a place for the police and terrorists to communicate.

• *Thomas Edward Sheridan (e-mail: vendabard@hotmail.com).*

Digital photos of refugee children to reunite them with families

Summarised from an article by Marie de la Soudière, entitled 'Face Value', in Wired magazine (January 1999), monitored for the Global Ideas Bank by Roger Knights.

Though the threat of a major global war has receded in recent years, local and civil wars continue to proliferate exponentially around the world, and the number of refugees caused by those conflicts is escalating at a similarly speedy rate. Many are unaccompanied children, who are quickly labelled orphans, and their plight is perhaps more acute than that of any other age group.

In several recent conflicts, though, systematic tracing using photographs has proved very successful in finding parents and relatives of these 'orphans'. The International Rescue Committee uses a number of techniques to try and reconnect separated families, but has found photo tracing to be the most effective. Colour photos of children are placed on huge notice boards in refugee camps and villages, while a database is built up of the location and, if possible, the name of each child. The process of reuniting the families can then begin.

'The photo-displays invariably attract a large crowd, which multiplies the chances of someone recognising a particular child'

The system works primarily because the photo-displays invariably attract a large crowd, which multiplies the chances of someone recognising a particular child; if it is not a parent who recognises their child, it could be a neighbour or a distant cousin. In Zaire in 1995, in the midst of the fallout from the Rwandan conflicts, 10,000 children were photographed, and 3,500 were reunited with their families. The International Rescue Committee believes it could have done more, though, and more quickly, if it had not had to send photos abroad to be developed.

'Photos of children taken at one camp on a digital camera could be instantly transmitted to other camps'

So they are looking into the possibilities of using digital cameras in the future, with a colour printer on hand if necessary. The use of such technologies could also lead to the transmitting of photos and data on the Internet. Photos of children taken at one camp on a digital camera could be instantly transmitted to other camps in the region and printed out for people to see, thus speeding up the process before any enforced repatriation takes place and the chance of reunification is lost.

• *The website of the International Rescue Committee is www.intrescom.org*

20 Heber Road, London NW2 6AA, UK (rhino@dial.pipex.com), 2001, 300pp, ISBN 0 948826 58 4

POLITICS

Case for the UK to leave the EU, in 60 simple points

As regular readers will know, the Institute for Social Inventions, which founded the Global Ideas Bank, has a bias towards the human scale, believing that as long as people feel disempowered and alienated at the local level, with their lives and futures not theirs to control, our social, ecological and political problems will remain insoluble. Just as the planet needs ecological diversity, so we need a diverse, multi-cellular, power-dispersed political ecology of small communities and small nations – a world in which any small nation becoming aggressive or cancerously expansive could be cut down to size by a grouping of its neighbours. To try to create Europe as yet another centralist superpower throwing its weight around is simply not what the future needs, in an age of the breakdown of empires. The following is an innovative presentation of the case against the EU, adapted from a memorandum to opinion formers from Lord Pearson of Rannoch, Member, Lords Select Committee on the European Communities, 1992-96 (July 2000). For the full paper, including appendix and references, approach Lord Pearson of Rannoch (House of Lords, London SW1, UK).

'Most people also assume that the EU will safeguard peace in Europe, whereas it may have the reverse effect'

It is widely feared that the United Kingdom has become too insignificant to prosper outside the European Union, (which we haven't – see points 56-57). We are told that we must therefore be 'at the heart of Europe', and lead it into the paths of righteousness, (which we can't – see points 8-11). Most people also assume that the EU will safeguard peace in Europe, (whereas it may have the reverse effect, see point 28). Then all our leading politicians and media say that the advantages of being in the EU are so obvious and overwhelming that they refuse even to discuss what life may be like outside it.

So, in an attempt to encourage national debate on this greatest issue of our time, herewith some of the case for the UK to leave the EU, in 60 simple points.

History – How did we stray into this quicksand?

(1) The post-war ideas which inspired European integration are now obsolete. These were largely (a) to resist the growing menace of the Soviet Union, and

(b) to stop Germany going to war again. (See point 28.)

(2) During the 1960s and 1970s Britain had two other reasons for wanting to join what was then the European Common Market. These were (a) to emulate Germany's industrial success and (b) as a hedge against our far left taking power. These aims are now also redundant.

'The ever closer union of the peoples of Europe'

(3) The 1957 Treaty Establishing the European Community ('The Treaty of Rome') set up the Common Market. From the start, this had as its goal "the ever closer union of the peoples of Europe". The other signatories have always understood this to mean the gradual creation of an EU megastate. Only British Governments, both Labour and Conservative, have consistently fudged the issue.

(4) Edward Heath agreed the Treaty in 1972 and took us into the Common Market, sacrificing our fisheries behind Parliament's back. (See point 22.)

(5) During the 1975 referendum, when the British people voted to stay in the Common Market, the Labour Government sent a leaflet to every household in the land, saying: "There was a threat to employment in Britain from the movement in the Common Market towards an Economic and Monetary Union. This could have forced us to accept fixed exchange rates for the pound, restricting industrial growth and so putting jobs at risk. This threat has been removed."

(6) Radio 4 has confessed that the BBC was heavily biased in favour of a 'yes' vote before and during the 1975 campaign. The 'yes' campaign was also generously funded by the CIA. The BBC and Independent Television remain biased in favour of our EU membership today.

'The original European Common Market has been subtly changed into the European Union of today'

(7) All subsequent amendments to the Treaty have increased the power of Brussels at the expense of national sovereignty. These amendments were: the Single European Act of 1985, the Treaty on European Union – Maastricht – of 1992, and the Amsterdam Treaty of 1997, (collectively referred to as the 'Treaty of Rome'). Thus the original European Common Market has been subtly changed into the European Union of today, without the peoples' understanding or consent.

(8) Of all the Treaty changes, the Single European Act has turned out to be the most destructive, because it set up the Single Market (not to be confused with the former Common Market) and gave control of our industry, commerce and environment to majority voting in Brussels.

20 Heber Road, London NW2 6AA, UK (rhino@dial.pipex.com), 2001, 300pp, ISBN 0 948826 58 4

'Our partners do not share our international trading perspective'

(9) There are 87 'qualified majority' votes among the 15 member states. 62 votes are required to pass a law and 26 to block one. The UK has ten. This is the mechanism which has allowed so many British interests to be damaged or destroyed by Brussels' harmonising craze. We often cannot muster the extra 16 votes to form a blocking minority because our partners do not share our international trading perspective. Current examples of our damaged commercial interests are our very valuable international art market, thanks to increased VAT and a levy on the re-sale of art; and our mergers and acquisitions industry, thanks to the Takeover Directive.

(10) Other British interests which have suffered the cancerous influence of Brussels include our air space, armed forces, boat builders, bridges, cheese-makers, civil service, chocolate, condoms, dairy farmers, duty-free shopping, euro-bonds, freedom of religion, hallmarks, hedgerows, herbal medicines, legal system, the London bus, lorries, market gardeners, oak trees, paper rounds, pheasant shooting, ponies, postal service, race relations, sexual discrimination and harassment, slaughter houses, taxation, taxis, toilets, waste disposal, water, whisky, working week, etc.

(11) John Major believed he had negotiated a measure of national independence at Maastricht (1992), when the subsidiarity clause was inserted into the Treaty. He believed this meant that Brussels would only dominate when the nation states could not do something better on their own. He even claimed that 25 per cent of all EU legislation would be withdrawn under this triumph, but not one comma has been changed. The catch was in the third line. The EU agreed to allow the states to do their own thing only "in areas which do *not* fall within its exclusive competence".

(12) The question as to whether we should stay in the EU has scarcely featured in any General Election campaign since 1983.

How bad is it now?

(13) The emerging EU megastate already has its own parliament, executive, supreme court, currency, flag and anthem. It is planning its own written constitution, army, foreign policy, police force, legal and tax systems. (See points 26 & 27.)

(14) The EU is the only institution on the planet which pretends to be a democracy but whose bureaucracy, the Commission, has an almost exclusive right to propose legislation, and to conduct international affairs.

(15) The Treaty takes precedence over Acts of Parliament. So if our Government (the executive) is outvoted or agrees EU legislation in Brussels, our Parliament must put it into British law, on pain of unlimited fines in the

Luxembourg Court.

(16) The number of EU laws in force has risen from 1,947 in 1973 to more than 25,000 today. Only a handful of these were even discussed in the UK Parliament.

'Once Brussels has acquired a power from the nation states, that power is never given back'

(17) The Treaty decrees that once Brussels has acquired a power from the nation states, that power is never given back (the 'acquis communautaire', or, in plain English, the ratchet).

(18) The Treaty does not contain an exit clause, and can only be amended by unanimity among all the member states. It is therefore deceptive to suggest that we can re-negotiate the Treaty unless we are prepared to leave the EU, if our partners don't agree the changes we need (which they won't).

(19) Most of our foreign policy is now agreed in 28 EU foreign policy group meetings in Brussels.

(20) Our new Regional Development Agencies cover areas agreed in Brussels and are the blueprint for Regional Assemblies reporting directly to Brussels, thus making Westminster even more redundant.

(21) The Common Agricultural Policy is an environmental disaster, costing British taxpayers around £6 billion p.a. and hitting every person in the UK with some £250 p.a. in extra food costs. The votes to change it cannot be mustered in Brussels. With the money the CAP costs us we could look after our farmers and countryside, with billions to spare for other things.

'Millions of tonnes of fish are thrown back dead into the sea each year in the name of EU conservation'

(22) The Common Fisheries Policy is even worse. Before we joined it we owned 80 per cent of the fish in EU waters, whereas now we are allowed to land only some 25 per cent of the permitted EU catch. The policy is hopeless because the bureaucrats who designed it thought they could conserve fish by limiting the quantities landed in port. They did not realize that most fish are dead when they come up in the nets. So that is why millions of tonnes of fish are thrown back dead into the sea each year in the name of EU conservation ('discards'). The votes to change this policy cannot be mustered in Brussels. International experience (Canada, Namibia, Norway) shows that our stocks could be conserved if we controlled them, satisfied our own industry and market, and then leased any surplus to other countries.

(23) It is generally agreed that at least ten per cent of the EU's £60 billion

20 Heber Road, London NW2 6AA, UK (rhino@dial.pipex.com), 2001, 300pp, ISBN 0 948826 58 4

annual budget goes in fraud and mismanagement (probably more).

(24) The EU's £5 billion annual foreign aid budget is corrupt and misdirected. We could spend our £875 million contribution much more effectively on our own.

(25) Those who work for the EU's institutions – Commission, Council, Court and Parliament – are committed to building the EU megastate, and to marginalising national Parliaments. Every initiative is pursued, and every problem approached, with that goal in mind.

What else do they have in store for us?

(26) The next turns of the screw will be applied at another Inter-Governmental Conference in Nice in December 2000, when further amendments to the Treaty will be agreed, (to be known as the 'Treaty of Nice'). The Government has already said it may surrender our veto (ie give up our sovereignty) in more areas of transport, the environment and the workings of the Luxembourg Court. [Eds: In the event, the UK gave up its veto in 39 areas, although retaining powers to opt out in ten of these areas. See 'The 39 lost vetoes', the London Times, December 11th 2000.] In parallel with this, the Eurocrats plan:

(26a) An EU army, inspired by France's jealousy of the United States and supported by the Prime Minister. This new force is to be 'capable of autonomous action' and will therefore undermine NATO.

'An EU legal system threatens Habeas Corpus and trial by jury'

(26b) An EU legal system, 'Corpus Juris', which threatens Habeas Corpus and trial by jury.

(26c) A written EU Constitution, known as the Charter of Fundamental Rights, which is to be justiciable in the Luxembourg Court, and which will therefore take precedence over all our legislation.

(27) To make the Single Market and EMU succeed, Brussels now says that tax harmonisation is necessary (ie UK taxes up by 20 per cent). The Treaty allows us to veto this if the Commission proposes it as a tax measure (like the Withholding Tax, which threatened our huge euro-bond market). But if the Commission proposes tax harmonisation as Single Market legislation, we may well be outvoted. If we then appeal to the Luxembourg Court, we will lose.

16 common misunderstandings

(28) The Europhiles' most important claim is that the EU is essential to keep peace in Europe. However, democracies do not provoke war, whereas forced or premature conglomerations of disparate nations do (eg the Soviet Union,

Yugoslavia, and much of Africa). So the Euro-realist model of Europe's democracies retaining their identity, and trading freely together under NATO, is less likely to end in conflict than is an undemocratic EU megastate.

'Democracies do not provoke war, whereas forced or premature conglomerations of disparate nations do'

(29) The word 'Europe' has been appropriated by the Europhiles to mean both the continent of different nations and the emerging EU megastate. So when a Eurorealist is rude about Europe – referring to a product of the Treaty and Brussels he is easily cast as 'Euro-phobic', a 'little Englander', or a 'dangerous nationalist' etc. Most Euro-realists love the Europe of different nations, but hate the Treaty and the dictats from Brussels.

(30) The Luxembourg Court of Justice is not a court of law. It is the engine of the Treaty and must always find in favour of the "ever closer union of the peoples of Europe" ordained by Article 1. It can and does overturn British law.

(31a) Economic and Monetary Union (EMU) – the 'Single Currency' – is a *political* project, designed to force the creation of the megastate. Only in the UK do politicians pretend it is an economic project.

(31b) As at July 2000 the pound is not 'strong'. It is standing at a six year low against the dollar, and 60 per cent of our exports are dollar related. The euro is weak against all currencies.

(32) The Prime Minister and other Europhiles often claim that "nearly 60 per cent of our trade is with the EU". Not so. What they mean is that nearly 60 per cent of our exports of goods goes to the EU. Only some 40 per cent of our total exports goes to the EU (goods plus services plus investment income).

'Only some ten per cent of our jobs, and ten per cent of our Gross Domestic Product, are involved in trade with the EU'

But Brussels' dictats are inflicted upon the whole of our economy, so the real point is that only some ten per cent of our jobs, and ten per cent of our Gross Domestic Product, are involved in trade with the EU (declining and in deficit). Rather more than ten per cent of our GDP goes to the rest of the world (growing and in surplus). The remaining 80 per cent of our jobs and GDP depend on our domestic economy. So the mangy ten per cent tail is wagging our healthy 90 per cent dog.

(33) We do not "trade with the EU". We trade with the individual countries of the EU, and do more trade with the USA than we do with France and

20 Heber Road, London NW2 6AA, UK (rhino@dial.pipex.com), 2001, 300pp, ISBN 0 948826 58 4

Germany combined.

(34) Insignificant amounts of inward investment into the UK are attracted by our membership of the EU. Most foreign investment comes here because we have a large business-friendly economy, with light regulation, low tax and a reliable workforce; we also speak English, are free of corruption and are not in EMU.

(35) Measured by earnings, Japan has accounted for less than one per cent of inward investment into the UK. 66 per cent has come from the USA, seven per cent from France, four per cent each from Germany and Australia, and three per cent from Switzerland.

(36) It is silly to pretend that our three million or so jobs which support our trade with the Single Market would be lost if we left the EU. The trade would continue, and so would the jobs. (See point 57.)

'This makes the EU largely redundant commercially, leaving us only with its political ambitions'

(37) The World Trade Organisation has brought average international tariffs down to 3.8 per cent, and is aiming for zero. This makes the EU largely redundant commercially, leaving us only with its dangerous political ambitions.

(38) Contrary to Europhile rhetoric, we have not ceded any of our sovereignty to NATO. We could leave it at any time, and it does not interfere with our legislation or taxation.

'NAFTA relies on inter-governmental collaboration and does not employ a single bureaucrat'

(39) If the UK were to join NAFTA (the North American Free Trade Agreement between the USA, Canada and Mexico), we would *not* become the USA's 51st state, as Europhiles often claim. NAFTA is a free trade area, not a customs union like the EU. All three countries have retained their currencies, which float freely. NAFTA relies on inter-governmental collaboration and does not employ a single bureaucrat.

(40) There is no such thing as 'EU aid' to the UK. The UK pays about £11 billion annually to the EU, which is graciously pleased to give us back some £5.5 billion for projects designed to improve its own image. We could spend the whole £11 billion much better ourselves, without the superfluous, corrupt and bureaucratic filter of Brussels.

'What UK business people really support is free trade, which we would keep if we left the EU'

(41) UK business people say they support the *Single* Market because they have not understood the difference between it and the former *Common* Market. What they really support is free trade, which we would keep if we left the EU. (see point 57)

(42) Leading Conservatives say they support our membership of the EU – this is because they took us into it, and politicians are not good at public confession. That is why they say that a policy to leave the EU would 'frighten the horses'. It wouldn't frighten the voters (see point 60).

(43) It is not 'inevitable' that we must continue to sleepwalk into the emerging EU megastate. Our policy toward the EU should be like any other, and therefore subject to change by Parliament as the national interest requires.

Economics - will EMU fly?

(44) Britain's membership of the European Exchange Rate Mechanism (ERM) in the early 1990s cost one million jobs and sent 100,000 businesses bankrupt. EMU is the ERM without the escape hatch.

'The European Exchange Rate Mechanism cost one million jobs and sent 100,000 businesses bankrupt'

(45) EMU's basic flaw is that one interest rate must fit 11 different and diverging economies. Where mobility of labour is low, there is no common language and interstate transfers on the scale practised in the USA are non-existent. (To hold the US together, interstate transfers through the federal budget can reach 20 per cent of a state's GDP.)

'If EMU survives, the UK does not have a long-term opt out'

(46) If EMU survives, the UK does not have a long-term opt out, because six clauses have been left in the Treaty which commit us to run our economy in a 'communautaire' way, on pain of unlimited fines in the Luxembourg Court, (eg for 'exporting unemployment' or 'unfair tax competition'). Our adherence to the EU's Stability and Growth Pact ensnares us further.

(47) The UK's economy continues to diverge from that of the EU, while it continues to converge with that of the USA. So the pound tracks the dollar naturally, but moves away from the euro. Hence the idea that we might join a new North Atlantic Free Trade Area.

20 Heber Road, London NW2 6AA, UK (rhino@dial.pipex.com), 2001, 300pp, ISBN 0 948826 58 4

'The EU's share of world markets is declining'

(48) Thanks to its labour and social policies, the EU's share of world markets is declining (down 11 per cent over the last ten years), while that of the North American Free Trade Agreement (NAFTA) is increasing (up 21 per cent over the last ten years).

(49) The Europhile claim that interest and mortgage rates would fall if we join EMU is simplistic. We would certainly be forced to accept the *wrong* interest rate, risking inflation, unemployment and, in the longer term, higher rates than if we stay out.

'Our eventual share of our partners' unfunded pension liabilities could amount to at least £20,000 per person'

(50) If we join EMU, our eventual share of our partners' unfunded pension liabilities could amount to at least £20,000 per person, or £1.2 trillion.

(51) There won't be a referendum on EMU unless the Prime Minister is fairly sure of winning it. But the country will go on being sucked into the quicksand of the rest of the Treaty, which we cannot avoid while we stay in the EU. (see the second and third sections above.)

'Enlargement' – should the new democracies of Eastern Europe join the EU?

(52) EU membership would be very damaging to the new democracies of Eastern Europe, because their emerging economies cannot afford the EU's social and employment policies, nor the rest of the 'acquis communautaire'.

'EU membership would be very damaging to the new democracies of Eastern Europe'

(53) All that the emerging economies of Eastern Europe really need is defence through NATO and access to the Single Market, which is denied them. (But of course they like their EU subsidies while they queue to join.)

(54) Luckily, enlargement of the EU is unlikely. Existing members cannot agree to share their benefits under the Common Agricultural Policy, or the Structural Funds (£20 million per day to the so called 'Four poor' – Greece, Portugal, Spain and Ireland – who can veto any dilution). The applicant nations are also waking up to reality.

(55) The Inter-Governmental Conference at Nice in December 2000 was billed as preparing the EU for 'enlargement'. The Eurocrats in Brussels are making this the excuse to grab even more power, so that they can rule over a

larger and more disparate empire. Hence their proposals for the Charter of Fundamental Rights, an EU army and police force, and tax harmonisation (see points 24-26 above).

The way forward: A Free Trade Agreement with the EU, and then independence.

(56) The UK is a founder member of such international bodies as the UN Security Council, G7, the World Trade Organisation, the International Monetary Fund, the World Bank, the Commonwealth and NATO.

'It is absurd to fear that we would not thrive on our own'

(57) We are now the world's fourth largest economy, after the USA, Japan and Germany, having just overtaken France. It is absurd to fear that we would not thrive on our own, after negotiating a free trade agreement with the EU such as those enjoyed by Switzerland and Norway, which export more per capita to the EU than we do. The EU also has free trade arrangements with countries such as Iceland, Liechtenstein, Greenland, Turkey and the Channel Islands. Even Mexico, a NAFTA member, has just negotiated a comprehensive free trade agreement with the EU.

'They have many more jobs dependent on their trade with us than we do on our trade with them'

We have an annual £6 billion trading deficit with the EU, and a cumulative £350 billion deficit since we joined in 1973. This means that they have many more jobs dependent on their trade with us than we do on our trade with them.

The UK would therefore be able to negotiate a better free trade agreement with the EU than the agreements reached by less significant markets. We should then leave the EU, allowing our partners to build their megastate unhindered by recalcitrant Albion.

(58) Contemporarily, if we really are too frightened to stand alone (as do Japan, Switzerland and most other countries in the world), we should decide whether to join a new free trade agreement between North Atlantic countries, perhaps including other English speaking peoples.

(59) Even without negotiating a free trade agreement, the UK would be some £2 billion p.a. better off if we exported to the Single Market from outside the EU, because our contributions to the EU outweigh our tariff advantages by that amount.

(60) Consistent polls indicate that some 50 per cent of the British people

20 Heber Road, London NW2 6AA, UK (rhino@dial.pipex.com), 2001, 300pp, ISBN 0 948826 58 4

want either to leave the EU, or to reduce our relationship with it to one of free trade. At least 60 per cent are against EMU. And this is in spite of being told by all our leading politicians and media for 25 years that membership of the EU is vital to the national interest. The case for leaving the EU is much easier to understand than the complexities of EMU. If that case were properly explained, popular support for it would be clamorous.

Conclusion

It is not just that membership of the EU is wrong for the UK; the Treaty of Rome is a potential disaster for Europe. But, sadly, most of our 'partners' appear determined to achieve full political union within a failing, sclerotic, corporatist economy. Unanimity is required to amend the Treaty, which therefore will not be renegotiated as the UK wants.

'Political union within a failing, sclerotic, corporatist economy'

So, very soon, we will have to choose – in, or out. Do we want to become the subservient region of an undemocratic megastate, or do we want to stand on our own feet and take our rightful place in the world? There is surely nothing frightening, 'extreme', rightwing, or negative about leaving the EU and keeping our hard-won right to govern ourselves. It would be a liberating, positive thing to do. And we would be very much richer as well.

Preferential Approval Voting (PAV)

David Chapman

This paper puts forward a new method for electing a candidate to fill a single seat. The advantage claimed for it is that it gives candidates and parties a stronger incentive to be responsive to all sections of the electorate.

'It gives parties a stronger incentive to be responsive to all sections of the electorate'

It is put forward as an alternative to the normally used single-seat electoral systems such as Plurality (as used for the Westminster Parliament), Second Ballot (previously used in France) or Alternative Vote (used in Australia). The new system is similar in its working to Approval Voting (a system invented about 30 years ago in America), but it achieves this effect by means of *preferential* voting instead of the simple 'X' voting of the latter system. It is therefore called *Preferential Approval Voting*, or PAV for short.

Under Approval Voting, electors vote (non-preferentially) for as many candidates as they like, for one or for more than one. That candidate who gets most votes is elected. How then can PAV simulate this procedure by use of *preferential* voting (that is, voting where the elector votes by marking the candidates in order of preference, '1' for a first preference, '2' for a second preference, and so on)?

Now under Approval Voting, when voters vote for one or several candidates, they presumably vote for those whom they most prefer. Thus the voter will always vote for his first-preferred candidate. But under what conditions will he vote in addition for his next-preferred candidate, or even for several of the next-preferred candidates? It seems likely that he will do so if he expects that a candidate whom he very much less prefers has some chance of being elected, and if he thinks that voting for the next-preferred candidate or candidates will reduce this chance.

PAV simulates this voting behaviour, by use of the preference orderings provided by the voters. Thus PAV always counts the voter as voting for his first-preferred candidate. PAV counts him as voting for his next-preferred candidate *when the latter is preferred to the leading candidate, that one who so far in the counting has obtained most votes*. In other words, this leading candidate is treated as one who has some chance of being elected, and therefore voters are assumed to vote for the candidates they prefer to him.

'The vote a candidate gets for a second preference is worth just as much as one he gets for a first preference'

PAV gives candidates the incentive to be responsive to all sections of electors because the vote a candidate gets for a second preference is worth just as much as one he gets for a first preference. Although it might not be possible to get first preferences from a section of electors, it will almost certainly be possible to get second preferences from them, and thus the candidate will have the incentive to be responsive to them.

'The present single-member constituencies would be retained'

How then would PAV work out if introduced in the UK for the Westminster Parliament? The present single-member constituencies would be retained. The only difference would be that the voter would vote by putting candidates in order of preference, instead of voting for only one.

20 Heber Road, London NW2 6AA, UK (rhino@dial.pipex.com), 2001, 300pp, ISBN 0 948826 58 4

'No one party would get a majority; so that a coalition government would need to be formed'

The present system, which essentially gives a seat to the candidate with the most first preferences, discriminates strongly against the Liberal Democrats, who have the third most first preferences. However, under PAV, they would be likely to get many more seats than now, since there seems no reason why they should not get about as many second preferences as the other two major parties. Thus it seems likely that the three major parties would be more equal in their seats than they are now, and that no one party would get a majority; so that a coalition government would need to be formed, most probably by two of them.

'The Conservative Party would become responsive to strong Labour supporters; in order to compete for their second preferences'

The parties would have the incentive to change their policies to be more inclusive. For example, the Conservative Party would become responsive to strong Labour supporters (from whom it could get no votes under the present system), in order to compete with the Liberal Democrats for their second preferences. Similarly, it would become responsive to strong Liberal Democrat supporters, in order to compete for their second preferences with Labour. Thus the three major parties would tend to converge in policy, towards a policy equally responsive to each section of electors, and as a result of this convergence, a coalition government formed by any two of them is likely to be stable, and acceptable to all sections of the electorate.

PAV rules in detail

In more detail, the rules of PAV are given below. The counting of the votes proceeds in stages, as follows.

The first stage. In respect of each ballot paper, a vote is given to the candidate marked as first preference on that paper. The votes of each candidate are counted, and the leading candidate is found (that is, the candidate who has most votes).

'A vote is given to the candidate next-preferred to the candidate who last received a vote'

Any further stage. In respect of each ballot paper, a vote is given to the candidate next-preferred to the candidate who last received a vote, *provided* this next-preferred candidate is preferred to the leading candidate of the previous stage. The (possibly new) leading candidate is then found, that is, the candidate who has obtained most votes up to and including the current stage.

These 'further' stages are repeated, each one giving more votes to the candidates, until a final stage is reached at which no next-preferred candidate is preferred to the leading candidate, so that no candidate is entitled to receive another vote. At this final stage, the candidate who has most votes is elected.

How then will these rules of PAV operate in practice? Let us first consider Election 1, where the electors preferences are 'single-peaked', that is, each person has their own most-preferred point on some dimension (such as left-to-right), and prefers any other point less, the further it is from their most-preferred point.

(The notation used to describe the election is explained as follows. The first lines show the voters' preference listings of the candidates. Thus in the top line, 35 voters prefer L first, C second, and R third. The subscripts against some of the candidates in a preference listing, show in what stage votes are cast for the candidate. Thus in the third line, 16 votes are cast for C in the first stage, and 16 votes are cast for R in the second stage. After the preference listings, each line shows the total votes which have been obtained by each candidate by the specified stage. Thus by stage 2, L has obtained 35 votes, C 67, and R 49. The greatest total of votes, that of C, is shown in bold and underlined, C being the leading candidate at stage 2.)

Election 1
35 L_1C R
16 C_1L R
16 C_1R_2L
33 R_1C_2L

	L	C	R
Stage 1.	**35**	32	33
Stage 2.	35	**65**	49
Stage 3.	35	**65**	49

In stage 1, each candidate gets one vote for each first preference. L is the leading candidate, getting most votes. In stage 2, C, being the next preference of the 33 supporters of R, and being preferred by them to L, the leading candidate of the previous stage, gets 33 more votes. Similarly, R gets 16 more votes. C, having most votes, now becomes the leading candidate. In stage 3, none of the next-preferred candidates is preferred to C, the leading candidate, and so no candidate gets any more votes. Thus C, having most votes, is elected.

'This candidate is the Condorcet winner'

20 Heber Road, London NW2 6AA, UK (rhino@dial.pipex.com), 2001, 300pp, ISBN 0 948826 58 4

Thus in this situation of single-peaked preferences, PAV has elected the centre candidate in the left-to-right dimension. This candidate is also the so-called 'Condorcet winner', that is, the candidate who beats each other candidate, always being preferred to the other by a majority of voters. Note that this result is obtained despite the fact that C has fewest first preferences (which would prevent C from being elected under the Alternative Vote, that more commonly used preferential system for electing to one seat).

However, if PAV were actually in use for a series of elections, then it is unlikely that the electors' preferences would remain single-peaked. For the extreme candidates L and R would surely not accept that they were going to lose election after election, and would adjust their appeal to give themselves a better chance of winning. Thus L would appeal to the supporters of R to persuade more of them to change their preference listing to RLC instead of RCL, and R would appeal to supporters of L to change to LRC. The pattern of the electors' preferences would then no longer be single-peaked, but would tend towards what might be called a 'symmetrical' pattern, where there is about the same number of voters with each possible preference listing (that is, in this case, one-sixth LCR, one-sixth LRC, and so on). Thus a typical election might be something like the following.

Election 2
18 L_1C_4R
17 L_1R_3C
17 C_1L_4R
15 C_1R_2L
17 R_1C_2L
16 R_1L_3C

	L	C	R
Stage 1.	**35**	32	33
Stage 2.	35	**49**	48
Stage 3.	51	49	**65**
Stage 4.	**68**	67	65
Stage 5.	**68**	67	65

Thus L has succeeded in getting elected, by broadening his appeal to include the first-preference supporters of R, persuading some of them to give their second preferences to L instead of to C – thus illustrating how PAV gives the incentive to be responsive to all sections of electors.

Demarchy – small, sample electorates electing officials

Roger Knights

Summarised from a longer paper by Roger Knights entitled 'Nec Pluribus Impar' which can be read in full on the web (at www.globalideasbank.org/ demarchy.html).

I contend that if the power of electing officials were transferred to small, sample electorates, government would be more accountable to common sense.

What's wrong with current democracy is that it is too influenced by interest groups and crusading moralists. And where those two forces are in abeyance, it lacks common sense.

'The theory of democracy is that the government should be accountable to the common sense of the community'

The theory of democracy is that the government should be accountable to the common sense of the community. Now, common sense is a quality, not a quantity; it is present to the same degree in a small sample of the electorate as it is in the whole body. This system of demarchy that I propose would make democracy more real.

How would this work?

First, the micro-electorates themselves. These would usually range in size from five to 25 members. Names would be drawn at random from a ballot box containing a 50/50 (say) mixture of lots and ballots. The purpose of the lot component and the randomized drawing is to encourage the members to be independent of the majority. The purpose of the ballot component is to give the majority its due; ie to give it a way of retaining and elevating the members it prefers. Electors would serve fairly long terms (say eight to 12 years), so that at each election they'd be relatively experienced. The membership would turn over incrementally as the years went by; ie there wouldn't be a totally new group at any point. Members would be well paid, to blunt the threat of bribery.

'Names drawn at random from a box containing a 50/50 mixture of lots and ballots'

20 Heber Road, London NW2 6AA, UK (rhino@dial.pipex.com), 2001, 300pp, ISBN 0 948826 58 4

Each group of electors (hereafter called a Popular Electoral College or PEC) would meet regularly (eg monthly) in the evenings or on weekends to hear reports from officeholders, and commentary on the officeholder by spokesmen for various ancillary groups. This supervision would continue during the inter-election period, thus giving Popular Electoral Colleges a strong, ongoing influence on their representatives. Each Popular Electoral College would elect its officeholder by simple majority vote, with run-off elections being used when no candidate received a first-round majority.

Second, several kinds of ancillary groups would be associated with each PEC. These would comprise a secretariat, investigators, observers, retirees, 'shadows', editorialists, lobbyists, and petitioners.

'Each PEC would supply the candidate pool from which members of a higher level PEC would be drawn'

Third, Popular Electoral Colleges would be layered; each one would supply the candidate-pool from which members of a higher-level Popular Electoral College would be drawn. I envisage four main layers: local, county, state, and national. The ballotery selection procedure described above would be used. As part of it, each member would have multiple ballots to cast; eg in a seven-member Popular Electoral College, each member might have four or five ballots, of which he could cast no more than two for the same member, and none for himself.

'Names that are drawn thrice from the ballot box would be set aside as potential electors'

The parameters that affect a ballotery would be set so as to discourage people from campaigning to be an elector (by discarding names that get too many ballots), while at the same time elevating persons who receive an above-average number of ballots. Here's what I suggest we start out with: names that are drawn thrice from the ballot box would be set aside as potential electors. As the drawing continues, any of those names that is drawn a fourth time would be discarded.

'At the state level, Popular Electoral Colleges would elect each cabinet official'

Fourth, each Popular Electoral College would specialise on a limited topical area. Where possible, Popular Electoral Colleges would draw new members from a lower-level Popular Electoral College specialising in the same topic.

Each Popular Electoral College would supervise only one office-holder, and his office would be a specialised job – eg legislators would not belong to an all-purpose legislature. At the state level, Popular Electoral Colleges would elect each cabinet official. A higher-level supervisory legislative committee could veto or delay legislation, and would adjudicate jurisdiction when the committees under its purview came into conflict.

Advantages

(1) The most interesting justification is rather subtle and abstract: the electors in a small electorate can behave in an active rather than a reactive manner. A good parallel for a small electorate would be an executive search team, which actively selects its choice from a multitude of hopefuls. Current mass electorates can't select, they can only passively settle for one of two or three preprocessed alternatives.

'The office should seek the man, not the man the office'

Throughout the 19th century this widespread desire to keep office-seekers in a subordinate role vis-a-vis electors was expressed in the oft-repeated saying, "the office should seek the man, not the man the office". This was a sound instinct. Unfortunately, it remained only an instinct; analysis did not penetrate the problem and provide the solution: sample sovereignty. Hence the founding fathers left power as a temptation, and politics became the domain of those prepared to grab at power.

(2) There'd be fewer career politicians, because the specialised legislative bodies would handle small enough tasks to meet part-time, enabling mere citizens with other jobs to serve on them.

(3) A different type of office-holder would more often be selected – one who is less adapted to the demands of partisan conflict and more suited to the demands of the actual job. (Incidentally, few women flourish under the partisan-conflict model; the current system effectively discriminates against them. Under demarchy, a much higher percentage would be elected.)

(4) Office-holders and candidates would be able to speak to their electors in a person-to-person fashion, ie more frankly and freely.

'The power of political parties would diminish'

(5) The power of political parties would diminish, since candidates would not need a party's nomination to be viable.

(6) Money would become a non-factor in politics. This would dramatically level the playing field.

20 Heber Road, London NW2 6AA, UK (rhino@dial.pipex.com), 2001, 300pp, ISBN 0 948826 58 4

(7) The power of special interest groups would diminish, because there would be no need for their money and manpower.

(8) The power of the press would diminish, because each elector would vote in only one election, so the guidance that newspapers have provided the uninformed voter confronted by a multitude of contests would no longer be needed.

(9) There would be fewer electoral errors and fraud.

(10) It would be simple to hold run-off elections.

(11) Campaigns would be less irresponsible. The turn-around time to rebut baseless allegations would be mere hours or minutes.

(12) Electors would vote more thoughtfully and responsibly; ie with a high chance of one's vote being crucial, people would think hard about it.

(13) Electors would be more informed than current voters by a factor of 100 or so, for a number of reasons.

(14) Higher-level electorates would be abler (due to repeated ballotery selections) and more experienced (due to prior service).

'Every agency of government would be under constant electoral supervision'

The electorate would get a better grip on government, because every agency of government would be under constant electoral supervision.

(16) The power of factions would be reduced, and the consideration given to the common good would be increased. Within a Popular Electoral College, diffuse majority interests would be able to coalesce; there'd be less of an orientation to particularistic goods.

(17) Specialisation by topic would mean that the common sense would be more fully expressed. Under demarchy the majority would have the opportunity to vote in detail across the entire range of issues, because they'd be able to elect cabinet officers and special-topic legislators.

'A greater variety of policies would be pursued by legislative committees across the 50 US states'

(18) A greater variety of policies would be pursued by corresponding legislative committees across the 50 US states, which is both a benefit in itself and an opportunity to compare alternatives in practice.

(19) For all the reasons given, demarchy should provide much better performance than current democracy.

(20) For the same reasons, demarchy should be more legitimate. More interestingly, legitimacy should gain because the old classical justification for

democracy – ie that it is rule by informed public opinion in the public interest – would be reinstalled.

Implementation – government

Because this would be only an electoral change, reform could be phased in gradually. It might even be prudent to pause for a while with a partial conversion. For example, only one house of a legislature might be converted, or the heads of the departmental bureaucracies might only be overseen, not elected.

Implementation – private organisations

There are many private organisations that conduct elections that would benefit from adopting demarchic practices. The office-holders they elect include student council representatives and presidents, corporate directors, labour union leaders, charitable enterprise functionaries, fraternal association officers, political-body officials and delegates to professional organisations.

Implementation – total institutions

These are organizations that do not – and should not – elect their leaders, but where there is still a need for some form of representation of the affected populations; eg to air grievances, make suggestions, respond to managerial trial balloons and pass along managerial messages to the rest of the population. Such top-down organizations include religious bodies, armies, prisons and asylums of various sorts. Marginally, workplaces could be considered part of this category.

'These organisations have a desperate need for some bottom-up feedback'

These organisations are non-democratic because they need to have specially qualified officials making decisions and because it would be too disruptive to allow candidates to conduct public campaigns critical of them. And yet these organisations have a desperate need for some bottom-up feedback and oversight. Popular Electoral Colleges could provide those benefits without any downside, because electors would be chosen without campaigning, and because the forum they'd meet in would be private.

It's quite unfortunate that employees have no way to express themselves collectively when they feel misused or oppressed – as they so often are – by bad policies and bad bosses; most trade unions are increasingly ineffective. This is not a mere matter of social justice – the organisation's performance and profit depend on it – ie they depend on the creative destruction that internal criticism provokes.

20 Heber Road, London NW2 6AA, UK (rhino@dial.pipex.com), 2001, 300pp, ISBN 0 948826 58 4

Implementation – Second World

Consider China. It has a big problem with numerous state enterprises that are poorly run, and another big problem with rampant corruption among its lower-level officials, often operating in conjunction with the managers of the aforesaid firms. What is needed is a gigantic overlay of democratic institutions – Popular Electoral Colleges – to supervise this multitude of managers and officials and serve as an ear for complaints.

'Russia's only hope is to spread a blanket of micro-democracies across the land'

Consider Russia. It has problems similar to China's, but worse, because, for example, organised crime has its tentacles everywhere. Its only hope is to spread a broad blanket of micro-democracies all across the land. Once established, those would then begin to turn things around.

Implementation – Third World

Experts who've written about this problem-area have suggested that there are several preconditions for democracy. Among these preconditions are education, wealth, a civic culture, a free and competitive press and a common national consciousness.

'The problem is with the brand of democracy we've exported – mass democracy'

In my opinion, the problem is instead with the brand of democracy we've exported – mass democracy. Micro democracy (demarchy) either does not require such preconditions or can cope with their absence more easily.

Consider education. If only one per cent of the population is a member of the electorate, 99 per cent of the educational task would be eliminated.

Consider wealth. Running a campaign and counting ballots are expensive under current democracy; but under demarchy 99 per cent of the expense would be eliminated.

Consider civic culture. In general, it boils down to a desire to play fair, which is easier to enforce in a small forum than in an entire society.

Consider a free and competitive press. This is hard to achieve and maintain – the trend in the First World is toward one-newspaper towns. But with Popular Electoral Colleges, a wide variety of information and opinion could be acquired from various sources. The secretariat would have a library (probably a mobile one), as well as a collection of videotapes and a (member-only) Intranet site. Editorialists, lobbyists, shadows, retirees, and petitioners would supply opinions.

I will conclude with a quotation from John Burnheim (*Is Democracy Possible?*, pp. 93 & 114):

'We will accept the decision of a group of people who are statistically representative of us as a group'

"On most of the issues that affect us most of us have no strong opinions ... There cannot be anything like Rousseau's general will ... There can only be conventions to accept certain results or decision procedures for the sake of getting things done ... Let the convention for deciding what is our common will be that we will accept the decision of a group of people who are well informed about the question, well-motivated to find as good a solution as possible, and representative of our range of interests simply because they are statistically representative of us as a group."

Summary

To sum up:

(1) The deliberative public opinion of the community – their common sense, to use a shorthand term – should rule.

'The potential for common sense can be found in every segment of the community'

(2) Because the potential for common sense can be found in every segment of the community, it is allowable for a small segment of it to replace the larger body in political functions. For example, the lottery was widely used in ancient Greece to select small political bodies.

'Only a small body can function as a political insider'

(3) It is preferable for a small segment to replace the whole community, because only a small body can function as a political insider. Only an insider can be on top of things and be in charge. An outsider is inherently out of touch.

(4) If common sense is to be truly on top of things, it must operate through a multitude of small electorates, because a single body would be overwhelmed by the number and complexity of the political issues that must be dealt with.

(5) The natural way to organise this multitude of micro-electorates – which I call Popular Electoral Colleges – is into a pyramid structure composed of (a) horizontal layers of increasing territorial scope (eg town, county, state and nation) and (b) vertical topics of specialisation corresponding (where possi-

20 Heber Road, London NW2 6AA, UK (rhino@dial.pipex.com), 2001, 300pp, ISBN 0 948826 58 4

ble) to the specialised legislative committees that already exist at the state and national layers (for example for education, justice, the environment, etc).

'Members should evaluate one another so their votes will tend to elevate the most common-sensical of their number'

(6) Electors serving in a given layer should be drawn from the next-lower layer; electors serving in the lowest layer should be drawn from the populace as a whole. The box from which names are drawn should contain not just lots but also ballots. Popular Electoral College members should evaluate one another so their votes will tend to elevate the most common-sensical of their number.

(7) Legislative offices should be rearranged so as to match up with this pyramid structure – ie there would be no more multi-topic, general-purpose legislatures, but only special-topic legislative committees, each of whose members will have a Popular Electoral College dedicated to overseeing him or her.

(8) Each executive officer at the cabinet level will be individually elected by a Popular Electoral College. This means common sense will have the chance to express itself more exactly on the make-up of the leadership team. Similarly, common sense will be able to express itself more exactly on the details of policy preferences through the election of special-topic legislators.

(9) A variety of ancillary groups would be associated with each Popular Electoral College to assist its operations clerically, to investigate on its behalf, and to supply advice.

'The decline of professional politicians, political parties, interest groups and factions'

Besides the advantages already mentioned (eg electoral knowledgeability and control), the benefits of this new political arrangement include: the selection rather than the settling for of office-holders; the rise of a less partisan, more common-sensical office-holder; and the decline of the following: professional politicians, political parties, interest groups and factions, the need for money for campaigns, the power of the press, electoral errors and fraud, the frequency of irresponsible charges, the frequency of irresponsible voting and political illegitimacy.

• *Roger Knights, 5446 45 AV SW, Seattle, WA 98136-1108, USA (tel Int.+1 206 932 9323).*

Lowering the voting age to give the young more say

Summarised from an article by Jeevan Vasagar, entitled 'Votes at 16 would curb poll apathy' in the Guardian (June 27th 2001).

Reducing the voting age to 16 and permitting 18-year-olds to stand as MP's could combat voter apathy amongst the young and increase their engagement in mainstream politics. A report commissioned by the Carnegie UK trust indicated that almost three quarters of all 16-24 year-olds wanted a greater say in the decisions which affected them, while a large proportion felt they were not taken seriously because of their age. The Carnegie UK trust also recommended introducing lessons in citizenship to primary schools and for young people to be installed on the governing bodies of schools.

'The lack of representation may well engender an apathy towards mainstream politics'

Considering that most public sector decisions influence the young more overwhelmingly than any other age group, including those concerning transport, schooling and leisure, their lack of significant representation may well engender apathy towards mainstream politics – an apathy that has made itself evident in recent elections. The survey indicates that the young may be more disillusioned by their apparent political impotence than with politics itself, and their growing involvement with single issue activism would seem to support this.

The UK Youth Parliament

Summarised from information supplied to the Institute by the UK Youth Parliament's Project Co-ordinator, Kate Parish.

The UK Youth Parliament (UKYP) sat for the first time in February 2001, with over 200 elected young people coming together to discuss and debate a range of issues of concern to them. The UKYP is intended to give the young people of the UK between the ages of 11 and 18 a voice which will be listened to by local and national government and by organisations who have an interest in the views and needs of young people. It is an apolitical organisation, and its predominant concern is involving the youth of the UK in democracy at a national level, whilst also empowering young people to take positive action on a more local level. With this in mind, the first sitting of the UKYP resulted in the establishment of a Youth Manifesto, detailing the UKYP's views on issues

20 Heber Road, London NW2 6AA, UK (rhino@dial.pipex.com), 2001, 300pp, ISBN 0 948826 58 4

ranging from bullying to the NATO rapid reaction force.

'Youth Parliament Select Committees will provide direct links to government departments'

The Manifesto has since been presented to the government and the opposition parties, and members of the Youth Parliament (MYPs) have been discussing how to take some of the outlined proposals forward. The UKYP may now set up its own Select Committees to provide direct links to government departments and to give them advice on particular topics. In this way, it is hoped, members of the UKYP can be involved in the democratic process on behalf of young people in the country on a regular basis.

On a regional basis, the MYPs have continued to meet up, and have taken part in meetings with Regional Development Agencies, headteachers, police chiefs and other leading figures in the community. Indeed, this participation in local democracy has led to several local authorities allocating budgets to their MYPs to allow them to cover any expenses involved in attending a variety of meetings in the area. It may be that it is at a local level where the UKYP will have most impact, with opportunities for social change at a local level being easier to achieve. By raising awareness of issues such as youth councils, drop-in centres, community gardens and the like, MYP's could have a very real impact on local issues.

And the work continues, with elections every autumn and a sitting planned for Easter each year – young people have a voice, now they just have to use it.

• *For more information on the UK Youth Parliament, contact Kate Parish, UKYP co-ordinator, 7 Mildmay Terrace, Hartley Wintney, Hook, Hampshire RG27 8PN, UK (tel Int.+44 [0]1252 844241; e-mail kparish1@aol.com). For the Institute for Social Inventions' vision of what a youth parliament could be, see www.globalideasbank.org/BOV/BV-23.HTML*

The International Youth Parliament

Summarised from information sent to the Institute by Fred Clark, the Media Officer of the International Youth Parliament.

The first ever International Youth Parliament (IYP) was held in Sydney in October 2000, with delegates from 161 different countries being represented. Its intention is to unite and energise the youth of the world to tackle issues of poverty, conflict and culture. Its aim is not simply to meet and discuss, but to develop strategies that can effect positive social change at local, national and international levels. With that in mind, delegates were encouraged to concentrate on taking back what they had learned and being a force for positive change in their own communities. The outcomes of the discussions in Sydney have also helped to form a basis for other forthcoming youth initiatives, including the 2001 Youth employment Summit and the UN World Youth Forum 2001.

- *For more information on the International Youth Parliament, see their website at www.caa.org.au/parliament or e-mail fredc@sydney.caaa.org.au*

Online voting – more accurate, efficient and error-free

Summarised from an article by Lisa Hoffmen, entitled 'Internet advocates say online voting could help US election system', in the Seattle Post-Intelligencer (24th November 2000). Additional information from articles in Computer World by Ann Harrison, Lee Copeland and Dan Verton, entitled 'Online voting moves closer to acceptance' and 'Arizona, California pilot voting over the Internet' (October 30th and November 27th 2000). All articles monitored for the Global Ideas Bank by Roger Knights.

After the voting fiasco in Florida in the US election, proponents of online voting have come to the fore. They maintain that online balloting would be more efficient, more error-free and more accurate, as well as allowing easy absentee voting and instantaneous recounts. An Internet voting system would also eliminate any premature declarations or long waits for results.

There are things that would have to be in place for an online system to work, and the implementation of these would be of paramount importance. Firstly, there would have to be ways of guaranteeing each voter's genuine identity. Secondly, hackers would have to be prevented from interfering with the vote in any way. Thirdly, the voter's choices would have to be ensured to remain anonymous and confidential. Finally, there would have to be equal access for all, including those without computers. But the technology for these already exists – authentication systems that use fingerprints or eye scans, sophisticated encryption systems, and multiple backups and protections to ensure security. VoteHere.net, a start-up company specialising in online voting systems, runs a system which encrypts each electronic ballot, but the key for decrypting the ballots is shared among election officials so no one person can view the ballot alone. Others propose the use of digital signatures alongside encryption systems, or of some sort of smart card system.

'The voting records were burned on to CD, rather than being kept as piles of paper files'

Counties in Arizona and California have already conducted trials, as have the US military and several businesses, and with no little success. As well as

20 Heber Road, London NW2 6AA, UK (rhino@dial.pipex.com), 2001, 300pp, ISBN 0 948826 58 4

improved efficiency and accuracy, the voting records were able to be burned on to CD, rather than being kept as piles of paper files. Now it is thought that some sort of online voting could be used in as many as 37 states by 2002.

Like postal voting, though, an online voting system would bring its own problems. Coercion of individuals would be more possible if the ballot is being done from home rather than secretly in a polling station. There is also the potential for fraud if the security and identity systems are not completely watertight. And some also argue that it would tilt the system towards the haves and away from the have-nots. Jim Adler, the founder of VoteHere.net, unsurprisingly disagrees, although he is well aware of how long it will be before the public will trust new technology for such an important civic role. Therefore, he envisions a system that would introduce online voting gradually: at first, voters would go to polling stations in grocery stores, schools or shopping malls, then go through a normal address and name check with officials before voting using a computer. With time, however, online voting could revolutionize the electoral system with home voting a common occurrence. For now, though, Adler and his colleagues are preaching caution, saying, "This is voting, after all, and we don't want to be responsible for unravelling the free world here. We [just] want to take some extra steps."

A proposal to allow citizens to make laws directly

Summarised from information on the Philadelphia II / Direct Democracy website (http://p2dd.org), monitored for the Global Ideas Bank by Tom Atlee of the Co-Intelligence Institute (www.co-intelligence.org).

Mike Gravel, a former senator in the US has put forward a proposal which would allow American citizens to make laws directly, independent of their elected and appointed representatives.

Under the title 'The National Initiative for Direct Democracy', the detailed proposal includes a Direct Democracy Constitutional Amendment and a Direct Democracy Act. The former asserts the right of the American people to make laws using ballot initiatives, while the latter proposes a federal law to establish legislative procedures and an Electoral Trust to administer such law-creating initiatives.

Collectively, this would be known as the 'Legislature of the People', a supplement to the present representative government. In essence, this would allow American citizens to put direct democracy into action, and to introduce legislation in a deliberate and clear manner.

The process would be as follows:

• An initiative is put forward for election either by referral from the legislature, citizen petition or public opinion poll.

'All corporations, unions, and political organisations are banned from contributing to campaign funding'

• All corporations, unions, political action committees and organisations are banned from contributing to campaign funding for or against an initiative; all campaign contributions will be fully disclosed and available as public records.

• The initiative cannot be modified or blocked before being voted on, either by the legislature, the judiciary or the executive, although they can advise on a law's constitutionality and suitability.

• There will be a deliberative process of public hearings, public information, and findings from a randomly selected Deliberative Committee, to allow a full debate of a new initiative.

• The proposed law is voted on in a national election; then if the majority vote for the new law, it is enacted.

This direct democracy is particularly sophisticated because of the safeguards it includes against exploitation by wealthy, corporate interests, against undue influence from lobbyists and against citizen's lack of understanding. All possible options are considered, and there is a clear process along which each new initiative must pass.

The first initiative to be voted on is the idea itself, though, and Philadelphia II, Mike Gravel's non-profit organisation, intends to hold a private national election to allow this to happen.

• *For a flow chart demonstrating how the new legislative process would work, see http://p2dd.org/graphics/process.gif*

Fax your MP for free, and be directly involved in democracy

Summarised from information on the Fax Your MP website (www.FaxYourMP.com).

The number of people who actually have any direct contact with their constituency MP tends to be made up of lobbyists, pressure groups and those who can get time off work, but a new online innovation could change that for good. The website Fax Your MP.com uses a customised 'web to fax gateway' to enable you to fax your questions or concerns direct to your own MP. At the

20 Heber Road, London NW2 6AA, UK (rhino@dial.pipex.com), 2001, 300pp, ISBN 0 948826 58 4

website, the process is a simple one: type in your postcode to discover the name of your MP, put in your own details and write your letter, and then simply click to send the fax.

If that seems like a system open to misuse, then the designers are one step ahead. Before the fax is sent, the site sends an e-mail to the person writing the letter, requiring them to respond by clicking on a web link. Once that confirmation has been given, the fax is sent to the MP's Westminster office. And while this opportunity for mass faxing might attract pressure groups, the knowledge that the MP will probably ignore such rote letters on one issue should allow individual concerns to get priority.

> 'The website's aim is simply to allow
> constituents to make direct contact with the MP
> who is duty bound to represent them'

The website is run by a not-for-profit group of individuals who claim that they "belong to no lobbying groups, no political parties and will happily declare any of our interests if asked." Their aim is simply to allow constituents to make direct contact with the MP who is duty bound to represent them. It is an aim in keeping with the Internet's supposed rationale of broadening access and making contact easier and quicker, and the site is an example of technological democracy in action.

• *For frequently asked questions and answers about the website, see www.FaxYourMP.com/q_a.php3*

SPIRITUALITY

Neighbours committing to visit one other faith per year

Richard Thompson

Summarised from a submission to the Global Ideas Bank.

Religion at the national and international level is perceived as a source of strife. At the local level, however, there are countless acts of good neighbourliness and helpfulness. This project aims to extend the contact of ordinary families with each other across the faith communities in a modest and very simple way.

Initially six voluntary co-ordinators, each from a different faith community, recruit ten members or families from their own community. The members commit themselves to accept one invitation for a cup of tea or a small snack from a member of another faith community and follow it up with a return visit, once a year, or as a meeting of co-ordinators decides.

It is the co-ordinators who meet in pairs to match the members of their communities, to communicate the telephone numbers and give support in the form of a little guide and possibly an evaluation.

One organiser in each town finds the six co-ordinators. They are crucial. If there is sufficient interest in my area of the UK, I would apply for a grant to recruit volunteer organisers, (for travel expenses etc) For example the six co-ordinators may come from the major communities of their town, eg Anglican, RC, Quaker/Free Churches, Black Christians, Muslim, Hindu,

  • *Richard Thompson (richardthompson@clara.co.uk).*

Follow another religion for one day

Dr K.R.S. Murthy

Summarised from a submission to the Global Ideas Bank.

There are many beliefs, faiths, and religions around the world based on diverse ways of interpreting the tenets based on the foundation of human, social and spiritual values. Apparently, similar tenets of the different religions have also separated the people and the respective leaders. Instead, they should be unifying the people of religions.

I have some ideas to bring the people of different religions together little at a time to ultimately create harmony among diversity. The religions have created distance between each other for many centuries. It will take many small steps to bring the people back closer.

This idea requires a host family for the religion, a host organization and a host place of worship. The host would contact the willing participant from any religion and explain ahead of time what to expect on the day. The host would provide all the necessary support. This may include books to read, tapes to hear, videos to watch, religious costumes to wear and information on diet. The participant is given complete freedom to choose the parts they consider acceptable and those they consider are not acceptable. Simple yet important reasons for something being 'not acceptable' might include diet. A Muslim or Jew may not like to eat pork. A Hindu or Buddhist may want to restrict to vegetarian food. For example, the Jain religion requires strict vegetarianism. Additionally, a Jain does not eat any vegetable grown underground. This includes vegetables like potatoes, onions and garlic. It is very important to be

20 Heber Road, London NW2 6AA, UK (rhino@dial.pipex.com), 2001, 300pp, ISBN 0 948826 58 4

sensitive to the religious practices of the participant. In fact, it indirectly creates awareness of some aspects of the participant's religion in the host, host family and organization. Most importantly, proper preparation eliminates any unnecessary surprises.

The participant may stay over with the host family the night before the day so that participation could truly start bright and early. Many religions have religious activity the moment one opens their eyes waking up from sleep. The host family carefully and delicately explains any activities, with a demonstration, so that it is very clear to the participant. The host may also have to do research on the history and foundations of their religion, in order that they can answer the participant's questions on that subject.

'The key is not necessarily practice, but awareness'

Please note that the participant may also choose only to observe, and not decide to practice, any one or all of the aspects of the host religion. The key is not necessarily practice, but awareness.

The participant goes through every aspect of the host religion for the whole day, to include breakfast, lunch and dinner, as well as any snacks and drinks. Respecting the participant's diet choices and restrictions makes way for reciprocal understanding. It would be wise to discuss the items, contents and cooking processes long before the day itself occurs.

'The chosen day could be one with particular religious significance'

The participant might also make notes of the activities of the day. It may be a good idea to take photographs and videos of the day, for later discussions. Another use of the photos and videos would be for another participant to learn before taking participation on another day. It is a good idea to choose special religious days so that the participant gets to see the colourful aspects which could not be experienced on other days.

It is also extremely important that the participant and the host try to exchange their roles on a subsequent day, so that there is true mutual awareness between the two people. One can choose to visit a place of worship that may take up part of the day instead of a full day.

There are a lot of cultural practices embedded in religious practices and aspects. So, this interaction between the host and the participant would also create mutual understanding of the cultural aspects also.

• *Dr K. R. S. Murthy, CEO, Virtual Think Tank, Silicon Valley, California, USA (tel Int.+1 408 219 2236; e-mail: geniuspoet@hotvoice.com; web: http://members.fortunecity.com/geniuspoet/genius/index.html).*

Swadhyaya – a movement for interrelation and selflessness

Summarised from an article by Pramila Jayapul, entitled 'India's silent but singing revolution', in YES! magazine (Winter 2001 issue; www.yesmagazine.org). This item was monitored for the Institute by Tom Atlee of the Co-Intelligence Institute (www.co-intelligence.org).

Swadhyaya, a spiritually-based community movement in India founded in the 1960s by Padnurang Shastri Athavale (known to his followers as Dada) is sweeping across India and revitalising society wherever it goes – it has spread to about 100,000 villages and has affected the lives of perhaps 20 million people. Swadhyaya's central tenet is that a person's responsibility is "to do one's duty to the best of one's capability for God and without attachment to the fruits of labour". Projects are undertaken to help people achieve this and to change the way they view the world. Further, the movement emphasises the fact that all humans are related by virtue of their creation by God – and it is this interconnectedness which is at the heart of their work. Dada, who is the movement's leader, advises that this is an equalising creed: there is no discrimination because of gender or caste amongst Swadhyayees – individuals are simply viewed as creations of a higher power.

'The Swadhyayees visit villagers, often of a lower caste, on a regular and long-term basis'

One of the primary methods by which Swadhyaya is changing society is through its devotional visits, or *bhakti pheris*. These involve the followers (Swadhyayees), who are often from the cities, visiting villagers (often of a lower caste) on a regular, long-term basis, in order to befriend and to re-establish connections with them: talking and getting to know them without trying to convert them or having an ulterior motive. The process of change begins to occur when the people being visited accept that the visits are entirely selfless, and that the Swadhyayees are asking nothing except friendship – this helps to rebuild a basic trust in humanity.

'Each day a different person from each village is assigned to work on the land'

Swadhyayees also work in a more literal way as well, with one project having turned a wasteland into fertile farmland, just through villagers working together to build wells for water. Elsewhere, land sharing takes place under the aegis of the movement. A *Shri Darshanam* is a piece of land that is purchased

20 Heber Road, London NW2 6AA, UK (rhino@dial.pipex.com), 2001, 300pp, ISBN 0 948826 58 4

by the Swadhyaya trust for it to be cared for by a cluster of 20 villages. It is only acquired if at least 90 per cent of the villagers are Swadhyayees and make the request. Each day a different person from each village is assigned to work on the land.

'The fields are worked for eight hours a day. Intellectuals and businessmen also come to work'

In this way, 20 people are always working the land, providing their own tools, labour and seeds. Produce is sold to Swadhyayees at market prices (demand is high, as it is considered to be *prasad* or holy food) with any profits from extra sales going to the foundation to purchase more land or help more people. Each month an expert meets with a group from the villages to talk about issues arising and about new ideas for farming such as worming composts. The fields are worked for eight hours a day. Intellectuals and businessmen also come to work. In the evening hours, all are free to contribute to the discussions. It is projects of this nature which expand notions of community, allowing individuals to give their time and effort with no thought of reward or gain.

The ethos of Swadhyaya is Hindu, and some Muslims have taken offence at the worship of idols, while Buddhists reject the acceptance of God as a central figure. Nevertheless, people from all religions are gradually accepting the movement for its social, rather than religious, ideals. This is not a movement for conversion, but a movement that aims to spread a message of the innate good of humans. And in an increasingly dysfunctional, isolated world, it is reconnecting people irrespective of their differences.

International Ultimate High Day, 24 June 2001

Adapted from web material from the authors of the book In search of the ultimate high *(published by Rider, 2000; www.ultimatehigh.org.uk).*

We propose June 24th each year as a good day for people to set aside for reaching their ultimate high.

'What makes you feel like you want to burst with joy, transcendence and wonder?'

What makes you feel like you want to burst with joy, transcendence and wonder? Have you ever had a moment where you've felt beyond yourself?

How would your dreams come true? Perhaps you would spend the whole day with your lover in bed, look at the world from a mountaintop, have a community celebration, sing hymns lustily in church or trance dance your heart out.

'Look at the world from a mountaintop, have a community celebration, sing hymns lustily in church'

Or would you prefer to go inward and take the time to meditate, to seek spiritual oneness or to experience nature. Have you got favourite ways that help you?

If you're planning a group event and need to recruit others, please place a free ad under your city on www.DoBe.org in the Spirituality section. Others can then sign up or write messages and comments. If you're happy to share your account with the world, write to us with your plans and your past experiences of the Ultimate High: e-mail ultimatehigh@ndirect.co.uk or place them as messages on the site.

The most interesting correspondence will be published to inspire others – for instance by posting it on the www.DoBe.org website and on the ultimate high website (www.ultimatehigh.org.uk), and the best three descriptions of personal experiences of the ultimate high will be sent a copy of the book *In Search of the Ultimate High – Spiritual experiences through psychoactives.* These should include a description of your personal experience of the ultimate high in no more than 500 words, and should include the title, circumstances and how you were feeling before, during and after. Say if you would like your name or e-mail address or other contact details left out when your item is published.

Here are some ideas for publicising International Ultimate High Day in your locality, just to get you thinking:

• A discussion evening on the theme of the 'ultimate high' in a local meeting room.

• A local exhibition on the theme of the 'ultimate high' with pictures, quotes or installations.

• Put a free ad about International Ultimate High Day in a local events magazine referring people to the www.DoBe.org and www.ultimatehigh.org.uk websites for more details.

20 Heber Road, London NW2 6AA, UK (rhino@dial.pipex.com), 2001, 300pp, ISBN 0 948826 58 4

OLD AGE

A community work centre makes the elderly feel less redundant

Summarised from the book 'Radford Care Group' (published by Plowright Press, 2000).

This recent publication extols the virtues of those who set up the Radford Care Group, a pioneering community group for the elderly in Nottingham. Initially founded in 1968 to try to get the housebound elderly out of their homes, the group have now been helping the elderly to help themselves for over 30 years. In 1978, they started their work centre which ran up until March 1997, and have more recently been involved in new special day care units.

The work centre provided work for a few hours and good company for those taking part, and a small nominal wage per hour. It was strictly non-profit-making, with the emphasis on the camaraderie of the workers and on the feeling of 'doing something', rather than being isolated at home. The first job for the elderly 'workers' was to sort bicycle parts from the nearby Raleigh factory, but in later years work also included postal distribution, button-sewing, packing knitwear and even inspecting string vests for holes. This work, alongside the other work of the care group, gave elderly people a continuing and dignified place in their local community. This was not a case of exploitation or of a patronising attitude, just an escape route for elderly people from being labelled as redundant to society.

'The history of the community is inextricable from its elderly members, who bring with them memories and stories of the locality'

As Alan Simpson, the MP for the area, writes in the introduction to the book, "The Radford Care Group always stood for something larger and more defiant than just another community activity." He points out that the history of the community is inextricable from its elderly members, who bring with them memories and stories of the locality. If this is borne in mind, the actions of such a pioneering group can be seen to be as important to the community as those people whom they help directly. It is perhaps more important today than ever, in this age of globalisation, that people stand up for the local, community priorities, and this includes the wisdom and experience of elderly people. In this field, the Radford Care Group is an example of what can be done when a few determined people on a shoestring budget set out to help those who society has wrongly put a sell-by date on.

• *The book 'Radford Care Group' can be ordered from Plowright Press for £6.50 (+£1 towards p&p in the UK) at Plowright Press, PO Box 66, Warwick CV34 4XE, UK. The Plowright Press is a not-for-profit publisher of community history, whose aim is to make sure aspects of community history do not go unrecorded.*

Young@Heart, political theatre from the over 65s

Summarised from programme notes by Bob Cilman for the London Lyric Theatre production of 'Road to Heaven', November 2000.

The Young@Heart began as a lark. It was a way to break up the tedium at a low-income meal site for the elderly in Northampton, Massachusetts. The food, typical government issue, was not great, but there was a stage with a piano and a woman who wanted to accompany a chorus. It seemed like the right thing to do. As the director of the meal site, my artistic resumé was shaky at best, I was in a short-lived cover band called the 'Self-Righteous Brothers' with a small, yet, fanatical following. For theatre experience I had spent a year as an actor, stage manager and general manager for a theatre that had managed to alienate just about every artist in town (before I worked with them).

I found a woman to direct this new elderly chorus, but she only lasted three months because her choice of music was too condescending for the elders. I decided to take over the directing because I loved the excitement of the people in the group and they seemed very willing to try anything.

After less than a year we decided to stage a production at the meal site where they ate and rehearsed. Roy Faudree, from No Theater, was intrigued by the project and agreed to work with us. That was a thrill for me, because Roy created the most wonderful and inventive art in our community.

'The first production was more memorable for the sensation and buzz it created than for any great artistic merit'

That first production was more memorable for the sensation and buzz it created in town, than for any great artistic merit. The show sold out four times and brought in a broad cross-section of younger and older people from the community. The star attraction in that show was an 85-year-old woman, Anna Main, who developed into a stand-up comic with plenty of filthy jokes that only she could get away with. We knew from the beginning, if the songs

20 Heber Road, London NW2 6AA, UK (rhino@dial.pipex.com), 2001, 300pp, ISBN 0 948826 58 4

weren't going over, we could give them Anna and she would keep it entertaining. Right from the start the chorus had the reputation of being different from most elderly groups and a bit outrageous. In the second year, things became even more outrageous, when two female impersonators, Ralph lntorcio and Warren Clark showed up along with Eileen Hall, a Brit with unique vaudeville routines.

I've always been asked about the significance of this work with old people. To explain what it is, I first have to make clear what it isn't. The Chorus was never intended to be a social service to aid the elderly. I am sure there are benefits derived by the people involved and that this all adds years to their lives. If so, great, but it has never been the reason for doing the work. There has always been a very strong political element to the art. Northampton, Massachusetts, like most New England towns, is divided between the people who have lived there all of their lives and the newer people, who have moved to town in the past 25 years. The Young@Heart has helped bridge that gap with the theater we've been performing for the past 17 years.

'The breakdancers created routines to songs that the older people liked to sing'

Some examples: in 1984, we created Boola Boola Bimini Bop which combined the Young@Heart with a group of young breakdancers from one of the housing projects in town. The breakdancers created routines to songs the older people liked to sing. It was the first in a long line of shows that featured a clash of cultures. The benefits to that production went well beyond the performance. There is a bus route in town that goes to all the public housing throughout the city. Both groups were based in housing projects and had often seen each other on the bus. Before the show they were wary of each other; after the show they were sitting together on the bus.

In 1988, the show 'Oh No, A Condo' examined the rampant gentrification in town. The seniors, displaced from their housing project by a condominium developer, meet up with Cambodians in the local park, who have been recently displaced from their country, and with some punks who rule the park. By the end of the production the seniors are singing traditional Cambodian folk songs, the Cambodians are singing "Let Me Call You Sweetheart" and the punks are dancing to lrving Berlin.

In 1991, the Chorus had two major productions 'The Devil in Ms. Main' and 'Louis Lou I'. The first combined the chorus with young Puerto Rican dancers and an African American gospel choir. The highlight was Anna Main's (95 at that time) unique version of Madonna's 'Vogue. In 'Louis Lou I', the chorus was reunited with Roy Faudree. The production, a re-telling of the French Revolution told through the songs of Sinatra, was a departure from the traditional Y@H narrative. The show was a stunning visual piece that was a revolution for the chorus in that it changed our thinking on how we could present ourselves on stage.

'Old cowboy songs were combined with disco, and the old people and the gay people in the audience were screaming together in appreciation'

In 1994, the Chorus created 'Flaming Saddles', a big campy production with the Pioneer Valley Gay Men's Chorus. Old cowboy songs were combined with disco and the old people and the gay people in the audience were screaming together in appreciation.

When we were invited to the R Festival in Rotterdam 1997, we created 'Road to Heaven', a compilation of some of the best work from all of these shows. We dedicated the work to Anna Main and Warren Clark and all the other chorus members who had died. The performance in London in 2000 was the sixth time in the past three years we've been to Europe with this production. Chorus members have discovered that there is something interesting about the music they begged their kids to turn off. For those of us who were brought up with the music, it's amazing how much it becomes transformed when it's sung by older people.

Throughout most of our 18 years, the Y@H has presented concerts in public schools for students of all ages. These programs have followed the concert format as described above. Currently we are touring a show called 'From Radio Days to Rap ... and Back' which is a musical tour of the songs and styles that were popular from 1930 until now. We have performed this show in over 100 schools throughout Western Massachusetts. The show is fun and very interactive with students performing with the Chorus. Some of the students performances are spontaneous and some are planned in advance between our director and the school's music teacher. What makes the performances truly unique is that the students are joined in the audience by senior citizens from their own community. Typically, the seniors are invited to attend school concerts (during school hours) through local Councils on Aging, as well as by the students themselves.

- *Young@Heart can be contacted by e-mail at rcilman@hotmail.com or on the web at www.youngatheartchorus.com*

20 Heber Road, London NW2 6AA, UK (rhino@dial.pipex.com), 2001, 300pp, ISBN 0 948826 58 4

SOCIAL INVENTIONS

Cultural Creatives – 50 million people changing the world

Summarised from a submission by Tom Atlee to the Global Ideas Bank.
There are 50 million adult Americans who believe in:
* personal authenticity, development and spirituality,
* holistic healing,
* ecological sustainability,
* social justice,
* feminism and
* caring about what happens personally, locally and globally.

Most of them are quite mainstream, and don't identify themselves as either liberal or conservative. They come from all classes, geographic locations, ethnicities, and ages. They are 26% of the population of the United States – and they think there are only a few other people like them around.

These remarkable people have been dubbed 'Cultural Creatives' by the researcher who discovered them – Dr. Paul Ray. He and Dr. Sherry Anderson have written a book about these folks; a subculture which includes many of the people whose innovative work goes unnoticed by most of the world. Their book is entitled *The Cultural Creatives: How 50 Million People Are Changing the World.*

'They are creating cultural and social innovations all over the country'

Why 'cultural creatives'? Because they are creating cultural and social innovations all over the country – indeed, all over the planet. Paul Ray estimates that there are 80-90 million more of them in Europe. There are probably millions more, unresearched, on every continent. And the key is that they are crossing categories and boundaries all the time – the old lines drawn between left and right politics, and between charity and business are no longer valid. People are turning their grass roots projects and ideas into new institutions for the future, be they not-for-profit, ethical investors or passionate believers in equality and sustainability. It is authenticity that is at the core of everything they do.

Is this for real? Paul Ray has polled 100,000 Americans through his market research firm, American LIVES, Inc., including polls for the US. Environmental Protection Agency, the President's Council on Sustainable Development, and the Institute of Noetic Sciences. He's sponsored hundreds of focus groups related to these surveys. (He's also had numerous other clients, from General Motors to Hewlett-Packard, from the government of Canada to the City of Detroit...) In addition to being a therapist, Zen teacher and Paul's wife, Dr. Sherry Ruth Anderson chaired psychological research at the Clarke Institute of Psychiatry in Canada and co-authored *The Feminine Face of God*. What they found in their research is pretty clear, and is documented in this book. But the book isn't just dry statistics. They interviewed sixty people whose lives embody these values; they turn the statistics into people you know.

'Find out if you're a Cultural Creative and meet other like-minded people'

As their book was getting off the ground, they were working diligently with two groups – New Stories and Big Mind Media in Washington State – to create a website by, for and about Cultural Creatives. There are resources and information there, including a questionnaire to find out if you're a Cultural Creative, and the beginnings of a major online meeting-ground where you can meet like-minded people. At a sister website, the New Stories site, they're trying to pull together a way for people to share the Cultural Creative Assets in their local region, with each community having a page dedicated to them online.

Depending on what we all do with this information, it could be a breakthrough – a pulling together of enough people to 'get the job done'. If Paul Ray's figures are correct, these people could radically alter and affect the way life is run in every country. Imagine if 55 million people all went out to vote for a Green candidate in America, for example, or if alliances amongst them could begin to be formed. I suspect it will only work that way, however, if we use it to reach out to everyone else, as well as to each other. But then, that's what it's all about, isn't it?!

- *Tom Atlee runs the Co-Intelligence Institute (www.co-intelligence.org).*
- *See www.culturalcreatives.org for more information.*
- *See also www.newstories.org for further links to culturally creative resources.*

Integral Institute
Ken Wilber

Adapted from a web page entitled 'Announcing the Formation of Integral Institute' at http://wilber.shambhala.com

Integral Institute (I-I) is a nonprofit organisation dedicated to the integration of body, mind, soul, and spirit in self, culture, and nature. This integral

20 Heber Road, London NW2 6AA, UK (rhino@dial.pipex.com), 2001, 300pp, ISBN 0 948826 58 4

vision attempts to honour and integrate the largest amount of research from the greatest number of disciplines – including the natural sciences (physics, chemistry, biology, neurology, ecology), art, ethics, religion, psychology, politics, business, sociology, and spirituality.

'The integration of body, mind, soul, and spirit in self, culture, and nature'

I-I is dedicated to the proposition that piecemeal approaches to the world's problems – war, hunger, disease, famine, over-population, housing, technology, education – not only no longer help but often compound the problem, and they need to be replaced by approaches that are more comprehensive, systematic, encompassing – and integral.

I-I functions as a network of many of the most highly influential integral theorists now working, an international information clearing house, a source of funding for integral research, and a co-ordinating center for thousands of integral researchers from around the world.

All Quadrant, All-Level

The guiding vision of Integral Institute is best summarised by the phrase 'all-quadrant, all-level' (AQAL). Although this phrase is taken specifically from the work of Ken Wilber, the idea itself is very general. It is basically a union of perhaps the two most widely shared cross-cultural views about reality: the Great Chain of Being; and first-, second-, and third-person dimensions.

The Great Chain maintains that reality consists of increasingly inclusive spheres of being and knowing, stretching from body to mind to soul to spirit. Each senior sphere 'transcends but includes' its juniors, much as a cell transcends but includes molecules, which transcend but include atoms. Thus, spirit transcends but includes soul, which transcends but includes mind, which transcends but includes body – a series of concentric spheres reaching from dust to Deity.

'Each senior enfolds, includes, and embraces its juniors – it's really the Great Nest of Being'

The Great Chain is thus something of a misnomer. These levels are not linked in a linear fashion, like a chain; rather, each senior enfolds, includes, and embraces its juniors – it's really the Great Nest of Being. Although some cultural relativists have spent much of their time trying to deny the existence of anything universal (except for their own pronouncements), scholars of the world's wisdom traditions point out that virtually all of the great spiritual systems recognise at least these four realms of reality. (See, for example,

Huston Smith's *Forgotten truth* or Roger Walsh's *Essential spirituality*.) Thus, the 'all-level' part of 'all-quadrant, all-level' refers to the Great Nest of Being in any of its legitimate versions.

The 'all-quadrant' part refers to the fact that every major human language possesses first-, second-, and third-person pronouns--'I', 'we', and 'it' – which refer to subjective, intersubjective, and objective dimensions of reality (eg, art, morals, and science; the Beautiful, the Good, and the True; Buddha, Sangha, and Dharma; self, culture, and nature, and so on). The reason that every language contains these three pronouns is that language evolved in response to these very real dimensions, and these real dimensions are universally reflected in the structure of language itself.

'Any integral view would want to make room for art, morals, and science'

Although scientific materialism spends much of its time trying to deny reality to the 'I' and 'we' dimensions and reduce the entire Kosmos to third-person 'it' language, the effort is ultimately futile, as the structure of any existing language tells us. The point is that any integral view would want to honour and include the 'I', 'we' and 'it' dimensions – would want to make room for art, morals, and science; the Beautiful, the Good, and the True; self, culture, and nature. (The 'it' domain can be subdivided into singular and plural – it and its – and thus these four dimensions are also referred to as 'the four quadrants'.)

These two major realities (the Great Nest and the three dimensions), which are recognised by every major culture the world over, actually fit together quite specifically. Basically, each and every level of reality (body to mind to soul to spirit) has these four dimensions or four quadrants, so that we want to include body, mind, soul, and spirit as they manifest in self, culture, and nature.

Thus, any truly integral view would be, at the very least, 'all-quadrant, all-level'. The only requirement for associates of I-I is that they are comfortable with an AQAL view, since that is the general vision that guides the Institute itself. This is, after all, nothing but a combination the two basic realities recognised by every major culture the world over.

The Structure of Integral Institute

Integral Institute itself has three general tiers or spheres: its board, its associates, and its members. The board of I-I includes Ken Wilber, Roger Walsh, Frances Vaughan, Jack Crittenden, Tony Schwartz, Sam Bercholz, and Mike Murphy. New board personnel can be added by a majority vote.

The associates of I-I include all of those who are actively participating in the

20 Heber Road, London NW2 6AA, UK (rhino@dial.pipex.com), 2001, 300pp, ISBN 0 948826 58 4

various branches of I-I (see below). These associates are individuals who have made outstanding and widely recognised contributions to integral psychology, politics, medicine, business, education, art, spirituality, and so forth.

The members of I-I include all those who share the vision of the Institute and have joined by subscribing to its newsletter, journal, conferences, and so on.

The affiliates of I-I include outside advisors, other recipients of funding, and friends and associates of the Institute itself.

The easiest way to think of I-I is as a type of wagon wheel, with a hub, numerous spokes reaching out from that hub, and the surrounding wheel itself.

The hub is the center of I-I, whose functions include an information clearing house and a co-ordinating center for the various branches of I-I.

Reaching out from the hub are numerous spokes or branches of I-I, populated by the associates. As of this moment, these branches include the Institutes of Integral Psychology, Integral Politics, Integral Business, Integral Medicine, Integral Spirituality, Integral Art, and Integral Education, with branches of Integral Ecology, Law, Diplomacy, and Media in the planning.

Around those are the members, affiliates, and friends of Integral Institute.

'Any person who is an associate of one branch is automatically an associate of all of them.'

Any person who is an associate of one branch of I-I is automatically an associate of all of them. The whole point of an integral approach, of course, is that you can't really separate politics, psychology, business, spirituality, and so on, because all are an interwoven part of reality. But, generally speaking, associates start by joining the branch of Integral Institute for which they are best known (eg, psychology, business, politics, etc). As things continue to unfold, associates can attend any of the other branch meetings that they wish.

The Dynamics of Integral Institute

Given that structure of Integral Institute, the dynamics of it include the following:

The funding made available to Integral Institute goes into the hub, and from there is distributed to the various branches (as outlined below). This money will help fund both the research and dissemination of integral knowledge. Here the dynamic flows from the hub outward to the various spokes (associates and members).

Any research findings generated by the various associates, members, or affiliates will flow back into the hub (and its computers, as part of the information clearing house), and from there it will be disseminated outward to the other branches and affiliates (and the public at large).

For example, Mike Murphy and several of his colleagues (George Leonard, Ken Pelletier, Fred Luskin) are now involved in research with Stanford Medical School on the effects of Integral Transformative Practice (ITP). The results of this research will be fed into the hub of I-I, and from there to its branches. For instance, several members of the Institute of Integral Business are involved in 'integral leadership training', which help business leaders learn the art of integral business management and transformational leadership. Results from the ITP research will have direct relevance for these members and their clients, and this information will be shared directly with them. In turn, the results of their experience with integral transformative practices in the business world would go into the hub, and from there back to the other branches (and made available to the public at large in a series of White Paper reports; see below).

'A multi-dimensional feedback dynamism where each of the branches is giving and receiving research from all of the others'

The result is a multi-dimensional feedback dynamism where each of the branches is giving – and receiving – research from all of the others. The findings of integral psychology will have direct relevance to integral business, politics, education, and medicine, and these reciprocally will have direct relevance to psychology – and so on around the wheel with all of its spokes and affiliates. The result is a creative synergy between the hub, spokes, and surrounds, furthering the integral meshwork--in both its theory and its applications--that is the core of Integral Institute.

Pragmatic Steps for the Institute's branches

Each associate of the various branches of I-I is asked to do the following:

'Assume you have unlimited funding. Make a list of the items that you would most like to see funded'

Assume you have unlimited funding. Make a list of the items that you would most like to see funded. This can include research projects, books, publications, foundations, individuals – anything, really – for both yourself and others. These are the items that you think will not only contribute to advancing a particular field, but also can most contribute to changing the world in a positive fashion. For each of those items, write a short (from one paragraph to one page, but no longer) outline of the project, one item to a

20 Heber Road, London NW2 6AA, UK (rhino@dial.pipex.com), 2001, 300pp, ISBN 0 948826 58 4

page. If you have five items, this would be five pages you will submit. You can do literally any number of items that you wish.

We take those pages and file them. We also make copies of them and give them to all the other associates of the various branches. The immediate benefit is that each associate has the advantage of seeing what the other experts in various fields think are the most world-changing projects that need funding. This exchange of information helps individuals clarify their own ideas about what they believe to be the most important ways to further an integral vision at large and contribute the most to changing the world in a positive and beneficial fashion.

As funding becomes available, all of the associates of the various branches of Integral Institute look at all of the pages submitted, and basically vote on those items they believe to be most worth supporting. The final decisions will be made by the board.

'All opinions are taken into account - a living example of the integral meshwork being promoted'

This does not rule out some associates' votes being given more weight. For example, when it comes to research designed specifically with integral transformative practice in mind, the opinions of associates of the Institute of Integral Psychology could certainly be given more weight. At the same time, how associates of the other branches view the relative importance of this research could be most illuminating. The idea is simply that the opinions of all of the associates of the various branches of I-I will be taken into account in arriving at final decisions, a living example of the integral meshwork that we are attempting to promote.

Examples of Funding

There are literally hundreds of different types of funding that Integral Institute intends to support. Here is a small sampling.

A Theory of Everything – a PBS series, in six parts, about the integral vision, based on 'all-quadrant, all-level' and highlighting integral medicine, politics, business, art, science, and spirituality. This would be a major production and would act to define and promote the field for the coming decades.

Longitudinal research on transformation. There exist dozens of widely respected tests of development and transformation – cognitive development, moral development, values, self sense, altruism, creativity, and so on. Take any purported means of transformation – meditation, ITP, shamanic voyaging, hatha yoga, psychotherapy, and so on – and give a large battery of these tests before, during, and after the practice.

'Consistent meditation practice over a several-year period increases self-development substantially'

As only one example of the types of results that might be expected: less than 2 per cent of the adult population scores at Jane Loevinger's highest two stages of self development (autonomous and integrated). No practice (including psychotherapy, holotropic breathwork, or NLP) has been shown to substantially increase that percentage . With one exception: studies have shown that consistent meditation practice over a several-year period increases that percentage from 2 per cent to an astonishing 38 per cent (see *The Eye of Spirit*, second edition). Replicating these types of longitudinal studies could have a profound impact on our understanding of how to actually help individuals transform (research that would have immediate application in the Institutes of Integral Education, Business, Politics, and so on).

Integral awards and grants. We intend to start an annual Integral Award for the person or institution that most promotes the integration of body, mind, soul, and spirit in self, culture, and nature. This is meant to complement the Templeton Award, which focuses specifically on religion.

Integral grants, on the other hand, will be similar to the MacArthur Grants. Where Awards will be given for past performance, Grants will be given for specific proposals.

Advertising existing works. In addition to funding future research, we would like to promote and advertise existing work of outstanding merit – books, for example. This would consist of taking a particular topic and selecting a half-dozen exemplary books in that area, then doing a national advertising campaign around them – in newspapers, magazines, and other appropriate media. For example, we might select the topic of integral psychology, and include books such as Murphy and Leonard, *The Life We Are Given*, Ken Wilber's *Integral Psychology* and many others.

'Take out full-page ads in newspapers and magazines across the country'

We would then take out full-page ads in newspapers and magazines across the country. We would do the same with integral business, medicine, art, and so on. There are literally hundreds of good books that have not received the attention they deserve, and we would like to rectify this.

Endowing university chairs. Although this a tricky endeavour, we would eventually like to endow several chairs in integral and transformative disci-

20 Heber Road, London NW2 6AA, UK (rhino@dial.pipex.com), 2001, 300pp, ISBN 0 948826 58 4

plines.

Stipends for teaching integral topics. We would like to offer stipends to any qualified professor who teaches a course in integral psychology, integral business, integral medicine, and so on. We would also like to offer scholarships to qualified students to attend such classes.

University students outreach. The tendency of the 'knowledge workers' today is to 'divide and conquer'. Specialisation and over-specialisation rule the day and this fragmented state of affairs often contributes to as many problems as it solves. I-I has already started a sophisticated outreach program to promising university students who recognise the need for more integrative thinking. Since professors have often made up their minds and settled into their specialised ruts, we seek students who are open to all the new and exciting integral possibilities.

Conferences. Each branch of I-I meets several times a year. At least once each year, all of the branches of I-I come together for a 'mega-conference', which represents the largest gathering of integral thinkers ever assembled. The results of both the regular conferences and the mega-conferences will be published in various forms, from books to websites.

Specific items. Although we wish particularly to fund items that are oriented to more integral approaches, this does not prevent us from supporting specific projects that have exceptional merit in themselves. An example is the project to fund female education in Third-World countries – a move that has been shown to have the single greatest impact on liberal social transformation. The number of these types of projects is virtually unlimited.

White Paper reports. At some point, each branch of Integral Institute will be asked to draw up a series of general tenets with which most of its associates can agree. For example, can the associates of the Institute of Integral Psychology come up with a series of very general conclusions as to the overall stages of psychological development? Many liberal political theorists have a great deal of trouble accepting 'stages' of anything, since they imagine that stages are always marginalising, oppressive, etc. If I-I could issue a summary statement on this topic – backed by the widely respected stature of the Institute itself – this would have an important impact on politics. These types of summary reports from each of the branches of I-I could have a significant impact on culture at large.

Web presence. We intend to create the definitive web site for integral studies – in psychology, spirituality, art, business, politics, medicine, law, diplomacy, and education.

All-Quadrant, All-Level. The gold standard of research involves those projects that are 'all-quadrant, all-level'. An example of this would be the Integral Transformative Practice introduced by Mike Murphy and George Leonard. Another example would be stipends for teachers using AQAL textbooks (eg, 'all-quadrant, all-level' medicine, business, education). Nonetheless, there are a great number of worthy projects that, although less than all-quadrant, all-level, are deserving of support, since they provide important pieces of the integral puzzle, and we intend to strongly support those worthy projects.

'Integral Institute will become a profound source of positive, compassionate, transformative social change'

Our legacy

Integral Institute seems to represent a rather extraordinary confluence of factors which comes along once in a lifetime. If we handle this opportunity wisely, Integral Institute will become a profound source of positive, compassionate, transformative social change, and an Institute that lasts decades, even centuries. I believe we can all work together to make this a landmark occasion.
• *Note: At this time, Integral Institute is not accepting new associates or members. However, in the near future, we will be accepting new associates and we will be opening up membership to any who would like to join us. Please stay tuned to http://wilber.shambhala.com for further news.*

Developments

Developments within the Integral Institute are outlined in several interviews that Ken Wilber has given. In one dated April 16th 2001 with Jordan Gruber of www.enlightenment.com, Ken Wilber refers to the dot com and stock market crash:

'We lost one hundred million dollars in pledges'

There are many ways to talk about the immediate impact [this crash] has had on Integral Institute. One of them is basically that we lost one hundred million dollars in pledges in about an eight month period. [Laughter.] It's not every day you lose one hundred million dollars. It left me feeling a little cranky and testy.

In terms of what it's actually done, the scope of Integral Institute hasn't changed. The money itself, well, we still have several other pledges lined up for frankly comparable amounts and we'll know how these unfold over the next year. The economic situation, of course, could not be worse. It is just a crying shame that the bubble burst during this period. A lot of companies that should have gone out of business went out of business, but it took down a lot of work that was really top-notch and didn't deserve to go out in that ignoble a fashion ...

20 Heber Road, London NW2 6AA, UK (rhino@dial.pipex.com), 2001, 300pp, ISBN 0 948826 58 4

The biggest change in our orientation happened not because of the market, but quite independent of that, a change we would have made whether the market went up or down. And that is, we went from being a kind of community of some 400 founding members to focusing more on producing what we call 'integral product', actual books, texts, academic material in each of the ten branches. So we're working on books in, for example, What is Integral Politics? What is Integral Business? Integral Medicine? Integral Law? We found that there were no really strong statements about an integral approach to any of these fields.

'Give him this 400 page textbook, and here's three hundred references'

... Once we have this kind of book on, let's say, integral anthropology, and a student calls up and says "I'm going to Arizona State," for example, "and I would like to take an all-quadrant all-level all-line approach to anthropological research. My professor thinks I'm nuts. What should I do?" And we say, "Give him this 400 page textbook, and here's three hundred references, and here are the supporting documents."

• *For the full interview see www.enlightenment.com*

Human Change Process and Skilful Means

Adapted from Shambhala's very long interview with Ken Wilber (for the full interview see http://wilber.shambhala.com):

In the Institute of Integral Psychology, we have a core team called 'Human Change Process'. This is a massive literature review of all the known techniques of human transformation. What are the actual ways that human beings can grow, develop, change, transform? What evidence is there that any of these techniques actually transform people? It seems that almost everybody wants a coming transformation, but we are all clueless as to what actually, truly, really works to transform humans.

'This core team is creating the first encyclopedia of the ways that people grow – an *Encyclopedia of Human Transformation*'

So this core team is creating the first encyclopedia of the ways that people grow – an *Encyclopedia of Human Transformation*, which it will then publish. This Encyclopedia will be updated every decade or so, to create the definite overview of human transformation. This team is headed by Allan Combs (*The Radiance of Being*) and Dick Mann, editor of the transpersonal series at SUNY, and includes senior advisors Mike Mahoney (whose brilliant book,

Human Change Process, set the tone of this team) and Susanne Cook-Greuter, who is Jane Loevinger's foremost student and the editor of numerous superb texts (such as *Transcendence and mature thought in adulthood*). Plus around five or six 'integral kids' who are doing much of the intense literature review.

'How can we skilfully present the results of Human Change Process in a way that it can be heard by those who could use it?'

A second core team in the Institute of Integral Psychology is called 'Skilful Means'. Given that virtually all forms of genuine transformation involve some sort of levels, stages, or waves of unfolding—some sense of higher states and lower states, or more compassionate states and less compassionate, etc – and given that 25 per cent of the population, or some 50 million green memes [Eds: similar to people labelled as 'Cultural Creatives', see earlier item], are very uncomfortable with any sort of hierarchy, then how can we skilfully present the results of Human Change Process in a way that it can be heard by those who could use it? Obviously, polemic is not the way to proceed in this case ([laughing], so, um, I'm not on that team). Robert Kegan of Harvard, probably the world's most respected developmental psychologist, is heading up this team. We also have teams on integral pedagogy (what would a truly integral education look like?) and integral diagnostics (can we come up with a fairly simple series of diagnostics that are 'all quadrants, all levels, all lines' and would help therapists diagnose their clients in a more integral, inclusive, compassionate way?)

• *For more on the background to Ken Wilber's thinking about the need for an Integral Institute see his* A Theory of Everything *(published by Shambhala Publications, 2000, ISBN 157062 724 X).*

UnLTD – £100m endowment fund for social entrepreneurs

From a press release entitled 'The Millennium Awards Legacy Competition – Preferred bidder announced', dated December 14th 2000 and put out by the Millennium Commission (on the web at: http://www.millennium.gov.uk/ latest_news/newsroom/recent/14-12-00.htm).

The Millennium Commission have announced the preferred candidate to take over and manage a £100 million Endowment to ensure the Commission's Millennium Awards Scheme, which gives small lottery grants to individuals, will carry on in perpetuity.

20 Heber Road, London NW2 6AA, UK (rhino@dial.pipex.com), 2001, 300pp, ISBN 0 948826 58 4

The successful bid was put together by unLTD, The Foundation for Social Entrepreneurs – a new partnership of seven leading non-profit organisations: Ashoka (UK) Trust, Changemakers, Comic Relief, Community Action Network (CAN), Scarman Trust, School for Social Entrepreneurs and Social Entrepreneurs Network Scotland.

The proposal put forward by unLTD will use the Endowment in an innovative scheme of 'staircase' funding for individuals consisting of three main levels of support:

'To give as many people as possible the chance to do something for their community'

• Level one is designed to give as many people as possible the chance to do something for their community in the form of cash, training, advice and mentoring; grants of up to £2,500 will be awarded.

• Level two will provide funding for projects or ideas that require the full time involvement of the individual. These include project ideas capable of further development from level one or which have been funded under one of the Commission's existing Awards schemes, as well as new ideas. Grants will average £15,000.

• Level three will be funded outside of the Millennium Awards Endowment from a Social Venture Fund that unLTD are establishing. This will be for more substantial funding to support projects at an early stage of development where funding is currently hard to come by.

The existing Millennium Awards Fellowship will also be developed to include mentoring of new Award winners, support, training and a general sharing of skills and expertise.

As well as the Social Venture Fund, which will aim to act as a broker between investors and social entrepreneurs, an Institute will be established dedicated to exploring more effective ways of investing in individuals to create change in their communities raising the profile of these social entrepreneurs.

'The potential of individuals to create change in their communities is limited only by their ideas and their energy'

Michael Norton, Executive Chairman of Changemakers, one of the seven partners in unLTD said "We believe that the potential of individuals to create change in their communities is limited only by their ideas and their energy. But that the benefit they can bring to their communities and to society at large is unlimited. We want to seek out and invest in such individuals, whoever they are, wherever they are and whatever they want to do that is of public or community benefit. We want to build on the success of the Millennium Awards launched by the Commission to celebrate the millennium and establish these on a continuing basis for the future."

Prior to confirmation of the grant the Commission will work with the preferred candidate, unLTD, over the next few months to ensure the delivery of this important legacy will be achieved. After confirmation of the grant unLTD will be required to report to the Commission or its successor body on a regular basis.

Michael Norton adds:
• The first grants will be made in early Spring 2002.
• Regional awards panels will be set up to decide awards in each of nine regions of England, with a staff to promote the scheme, invite applications and interview applicants, as well as to provide support to those who are successful in getting an award.
• In Scotland, a devolved structure is being put in place, under a new charity to be called 'Scotland unLTD', and the arrangements for Wales and Northern Ireland are under discussion.
• *For details of the unLTD website and contact details, please get in touch with Bert Leslie on Int.+44 [0]20 7401 5478.*

Michael Young – what made him a social inventor?

Michael Young – Social entrepreneur, *by Asa Briggs, published by Pegasus (Houndmills, Basingstoke, Hampshire RG21 6XS, UK, tel Int.+44 [0]1256 329242; fax Int.+44 [0]1256 479476; web: www.palgrave.com; ISBN 0 333 75023 3, 413 pages, hardback, £50). Reviewed by Nicholas Albery.*

Michael Young, also known as Lord Young of Dartington, is the UK's unsurpassed social inventor. He helped draft the Labour Party's radical 1945 manifesto and he has since helped start a large number of imaginative and unusual projects, ranging from the Open University and the University of the Third Age to *Which?* magazine and the Mutual Aid Centre.

'Lessons to be learnt as to how to encourage the development of more social inventors in future'

But my interest in this new book about him is not its dissection of his achievements but rather the opportunity it provides to see what makes him tick, what helped make him into a social inventor, in case there might be

20 Heber Road, London NW2 6AA, UK (rhino@dial.pipex.com), 2001, 300pp, ISBN 0 948826 58 4

lessons to be learnt as to how to encourage the development of more social inventors in future – lessons which in turn could be incorporated into one of his latest creations, his institute for creating future social inventors, the School for Social Entrepreneurs.

The following are the factors I isolate from this book:

'A permanent and necessary sympathy for the underdog'

• One essential ingredient, I believe, was the moderate suffering and cruelty he experienced as a child, sufficient to enrage him without breaking his spirit. For instance there were the teachers at his elementary and preparatory schools who beat the children ("the ... master ... flogged wrongdoers, who had to strip naked in front of fellow pupils. Their letters home were censored. ... Michael vowed at the age of eight to murder this tyrant if he ever met him again"). Such incidents perhaps helped give Michael a permanent and necessary sympathy for the underdog.

• Since childhood, Michael has had a handicap – "crippling asthma" – which is no handicap at all when it comes to feeling sympathy for those who are ill at ease with the way things are; and no handicap for Michael later in life when he came to set up the College of Health as a patient-power organisation.

• There were insecurities and anxieties for Michael in his family background – his parents parted; at one point Michael "was afraid he might be disposed of altogether by his parents"; his father died when Michael was still a young man ("Michael was so shocked ... that he would not speak of him for over a year"). This lack of stability may have helped create Michael's lifelong urge to promote the institutions of the family, the extended family and the supportive community.

'See beyond the social norms and transform sociology into a creative art'

• The liberal and artistic outlooks of his parents – his mother mixing in Bohemian circles and having affairs, his father a musician – may have brewed up that particular Michael who could see beyond the social norms, transform sociology into a creative art and become a Renaissance man – poet, painter, writer, social architect.

• As a teenager Michael was sent to a progressive school, Dartington in Devon. It proved to be a superb training for entrepreneurial activism. "Its central idea," wrote W. B. Curry, the headmaster who arrived during Michael's time there, "is that the new world will be created not by politicians, but by men and women of goodwill, in large and small groups throughout the world, undertaking the task of creation, wherever their influence extends."

Institute for Social Inventions, £15 subs, £17 from abroad by credit card, tel London 020 8208 2853

At one stage, however, politics was the focus. Michael, aged 14, and his class were asked to imagine themselves as politicians running the country: "In the last fortnight or so of term," the teacher writes, "the group responsible for all the work done with me (History, English, Social Studies, Philosophy) formed a cabinet with Michael as Prime Minister, planned the work, and took the classes themselves, only referring to me when special help was needed."

'A little world in itself, like the village community of earlier times, which was in many respects self-sufficing'

Founded by the Elmhirsts, a rich American couple, Dartington school was designed to be, they said, "a little world in itself ... like the village community of earlier times, which was in many respects self-sufficing ... [it had] to engage in many practical enterprises. {The classrooms of the school were to be] "a farm, a garden, workshops, playgrounds, woods and freedom". The school set out to respond to the children's interests, with learning through doing.

Michael founded and ran several businesses whilst at the school: one was Darfowls Ltd, which sold eggs to the Totnes market and to the school, with Michael cleaning the hen houses, wringing the chickens' necks when necessary and doing the double-entry book keeping. The other business (until halted by Curry as new headmaster) was the buying and selling of motorcycles. Michael enjoyed "revving his Triumph on the Devonshire hills – it had cost him 30 shillings – and trying to clip seconds off his own time record on the private roads of Dartington".

• Somewhere along the line, perhaps thanks to the attentions of a good teacher (although this book doesn't dwell on this aspect), Michael began to learn to write well. He himself values this skill highly when selecting colleagues – he once specified that "in choosing new staff, it should be realised that the only essential qualifications are (1) drafting ability, (2) intelligence". And most of his projects would be given a boost at their launch by a subtle and penetrating article by him in the Guardian newspaper.

'Rich and well-connected mentors who loved and cherished and supported him in all his endeavours'

• Most vitally of all, Michael had rich and well-connected mentors who loved and cherished and supported him in all his endeavours. Leonard and Dorothy Elmhirst came to treat him as a child of their own. He would write to Dorothy with stories as to how he was getting on out in the wider world, she would visit him, and he became a trustee for half a century of their

20 Heber Road, London NW2 6AA, UK (rhino@dial.pipex.com), 2001, 300pp, ISBN 0 948826 58 4

Dartington Hall. Michael's first and most important break as a young man was securing a job – thanks to the Dartington network – writing papers for the research organisation Political and Economic Planning (PEP). When he set up the Institute for Community Studies and numerous other projects, the first seed money often came from the Elmhirsts or from the Dartington Hall Trust.

The Elmhirst also introduced him to society's movers and shakers. As a teenager, for instance, he stayed at the White House and talked with President Roosevelt and dined with his cabinet – and even gave Roosevelt advice on Cuba; and on an ocean liner crossing the Atlantic with Leonard Elmhirst, Michael listened to Leonard questioning Henry Ford.

'A modern version of the village squire, a sort of benevolent Robert Owen figure'

Thanks to the Elmhirsts and to Dartington, Michael became in effect a modern version of the village squire, a sort of benevolent Robert Owen figure, introducing innovations not only to help the local workers and residents (he helped set up the Dartington Glass factory) but also projects with a global perspective (Open Universities for South Africa and elsewhere).

So, what lessons could society and more particularly the School for Social Entrepreneurs (SSE) learn from Michael's life story? I suggest the following:

'SSE needs to open a branch that would take on younger teenage pupils'

• At present SSE takes on adult pupils and is based in Bethnal Green. It needs to open a branch at Dartington or elsewhere that would take on younger teenage pupils. Social inventors are more likely to be formed then rather than in adulthood.

'Encourage pupils to set up businesses supplying real needs'

• This junior SSE – and indeed all secondary schools – should encourage pupils to start businesses supplying real needs, should have youth parliaments and cabinets, should lay great stress on encouraging writing ability and allowing the children to practise the various arts. The teachers should act mainly as mentors, with the school's facilities treated as a resource to enable children to learn what really interests and motivates them, with a great deal of learning through doing and a great deal of freedom to experiment.

• The junior SSE – and all schools – should serve the needs of their local communities and be integrated into them and should help run farms, allotments and workshops.

Institute for Social Inventions, £15 subs, £17 from abroad by credit card, tel London 020 8208 2853

• SSE should get would-be pupils to write their life stories and should select pupils based on these stories and on interviews – pupils who have handicaps, who come from broken homes, who show evidence of sympathy for the underdog, who show evidence of having an outsider's perspective on society and who have artistic ability and writing skills. Applicants should be asked to describe several imaginative and unusual changes big or small that they would like to see introduced in society.

'SSE should establish a substantial fund to provide current and ex-pupils with seed money for their projects'

• SSE should establish a substantial fund to provide current and ex-pupils with seed money for their projects, but this money should be channelled through mentors, who would have a personal and long-term relationship with their particular pupil. The pupil would thus apply for the money to the mentor not the school and would report back to this person. At the outset of their courses, the pupils would each make an in-depth presentation to the audience; and potential mentors in the audience would subsequently tell the school their preferred choices of who they would like to mentor, leading to a meeting and a mutual vetting – this partnership being more likely to last and to work well if based on a genuine sympathy between both parties. The mentors should themselves be social entrepreneurs with good track records; and if the mentors can be rich and powerful and well-connected, so much the better.

• Everything should be kept small and human-scale, with the feel of a village community.

All this might be worth a try. Michael was never very confident about the likely success of his new projects ("I have never been set back much by failures because I've almost expected them to fail"). All these measures might fail too. It could well turn out that Michael is an unreproducable one-off.

Johnny Dolphin – social inventor

Adapted from the website at www.synergeticpress.com/dolphinpr.html that out- lines the extraordinarily socially innovative life of Johnny Dolphin, the pen name of John Allen, co-founder of the Institute of Ecotechnics and the Biosphere 2 project, and also a writer, poet and playwright.

Johnny Dolphin – poet, playwright, scientist, and savant – in 1963 abandoned his New York international project development career to make a two and a half year journey around the planet, living with the avant-garde and Berbers in Tangiers, Morocco; then as an Arab across North Africa; then living

20 Heber Road, London NW2 6AA, UK (rhino@dial.pipex.com), 2001, 300pp, ISBN 0 948826 58 4

with tribal chiefs and shaman from Malakal, before journeying on south through the Sudan, continuing east to India, Nepal, Vietnam and Japan – all the while studying the art, science, and literature of civilisations on this planet. He emerged as a writer from the Tangier school at age 34. Since then he has chronicled a personal and social history of the essence of the places he has been through poetry, short stories and plays.

'Inventor and co-founder of the Biosphere 2 project – the world's largest laboratory for global ecology'

Johnny Dolphin is the nom de plume of John Allen, inventor and co-founder of the Biosphere 2 project – the world's largest laboratory for global ecology. Biosphere 2 set a number of world records in closed life system work including, among others, degree of sealing tightness, 100 per cent waste recycle and water recycle, and duration of human residence within a closed system (eight people for two years – see www.biospherics.org). Allen began the first manned Biosphere Test Module experiment in September, 1988, residing in the almost fully recyclable closed ecological system environment for three days and setting a world record at that time.

As the vice-president of Biospheric Development for the project, Allen was responsible for overseeing the research that created the materially closed life system, as well as the development of spin-off technologies. He is currently the Chairman of Global Ecotechnics Corporation, an international project development and management company with a Biospheres Division engaged in designing and preparing to build the second generation of advanced materially closed biospheric systems and ecologically enriched biomic systems (www.biospheres.com); and its EcoFrontiers Division which owns and operates ecological projects of which he was the chief designer in France, Australia, Puerto Rico and England (www.ecotechnics.edu).

'Planetary Coral Reef Foundation, devoted to studying the health and vitality of coral reefs'

He is also co-founder and Chairman of Planetary Coral Reef Foundation, a non-profit corporation devoted to studying the health and vitality of coral reefs, both at its base in the Yucatan and aboard the Heraclitus, a research vessel now sailing in the Indian Ocean (www.pcrf.org).

In the early sixties, John Allen worked on regional development projects with David Lillienthal's Development Resources Corporation in the US, Iran, and Ivory Coast. Before that he headed a special metals team at Allegheny-Ludium Steel Corporation which developed over 30 alloys to product status.

He has led expeditions studying ecology, particularly the ecology of early civilizations: Nigeria, Iraq, Iran, Afghanistan, Uzbekistan, Tibet, Turkey, India, and the Altiplano.

Dolphin has over two dozen publications to his credit, about half of them scientific, the rest in poetry, drama, prose, and film. A Fellow of the Linnean Society, Allen holds a degree in Metallurgical-Mining Engineering with honours from the Colorado School of Mines, an MBA from the Harvard Business School where he graduated with distinction as a Baker Scholar, and an Engineering Physiology Certificate from the University of Michigan. Before engineering, he studied anthropology, classics, writing, and history at Northwestern, Stanford, and Oklahoma universities and served in the US Army's Engineering Corps.

As Johnny Dolphin he has read his poetry and prose in many places around the world including George Whitman's Shakespeare & Co. in Paris, the Green Street Cafe in New York – where Ornette Coleman accompanied him on the saxophone – The October Gallery in London and the Caravan of Dreams in Fort Worth, Texas. His plays have been performed in many countries on seven continents, from the ICA in London and Theatre du Soleil in Paris. to villages on the Amazon and streets in California, from Wroclaw to Oshogbo. As an acting teacher, he has taught over 200 actors and set up 10 studios. He now performs several times a year with four musicians as Johnny & The Dolphins.

'The key role of space biospheres in the future'

As a scientist, John is an accomplished speaker. He has spoken at a variety of international forums on the emerging science of biospherics, the implications of Biosphere 2 for health, environment, science, and culture, and the key role of space biospheres in the future, and the place and role of humanity in the biosphere.

• *Johnny Dolphin's books (available from Synergetic Press, PO Box 2510, Novato, CA 94948, USA tel Int.+1 415 883 3530; e-mail: biospheres@compuserve.com; web: www.synergeticpress.com) include:* 39 blows on a gone trumpet *(novel, $5.95);* Journey around an extraordinary planet *(novel, $5.95);* My many kisses *(short stories, $14.95);* Off the road *(poetry, $14.95);* Wild *(poems, aphorisms and short stories, $7.95). Under his John Allen name, he has a non-fiction book published by Viking/Penguin books:* Biosphere 2 – The human experiment *(out of print, but available through websites for second-hand books such as www.bibliofind.com for approx. $24).*

20 Heber Road, London NW2 6AA, UK (rhino@dial.pipex.com), 2001, 300pp, ISBN 0 948826 58 4

Applying sociology

Applying sociology – Making a better world, *edited by William du Bois and R. Dean Wright, published by Allyn & Bacon (www.abacon.com, ISBN 0 205 30616 0, 272 pages). Reviewed by Nicholas Albery.*

All sociologists should be like William du Bois, the co-editor of this superb book, an artist of life who realises that the purpose of his profession is to help make a better world, to design programmes, to imagine a new society, to invent new social forms and to produce social inventors and social architects.

'To help make a better world, to imagine a new society, to invent new social forms'

Graduate schools may encourage students "to stuff the library with meaningless trivia disguised as PhD dissertations and masters' theses. Can you imagine what would happen if instead we were encouraging these people to create new projects in the community. ... The final product of an applied sociology is [not the research paper but] the invention itself: the day-care centre, the homeless youth shelter, the new rule or policy, the new organisation. Theories, papers and insights are means, not goals."

'Tables for one to four people need to be 30 inches across for comfortable communication'

He's been involved in some wonderful projects himself. Called in to redesign a nightclub, he raised club sales from $1,500 a week to $10,000 by simply prompting positive interaction and community so that people met each other more, stayed longer, returned more often and told their friends. No detail was too small for him to pay attention to it. For instance if a cocktail serviette has a cartoon on it, he found that it encouraged the customer to share the joke with someone seated nearby. Tables for one to four people need to be 30 inches across for comfortable communication, even for lovers face-to-face. A couple of inches more and people feel remote from each other, a couple of inches less and people feel that their space is intruded on. If the table is round, the ideal size is 42 inches.

'Designed to provide excuses to enter territory, to engage in the mating dance'

Everything needs to be designed to provide excuses to enter territory, to homestead close by, to engage in the mating dance – the 'go away a little closer' ritual. Booths and hang-out nooks and drink shelves to attract people to the perimeters of the space. Three jukeboxes linked together, with a thousand songs on open display, so that people can get together and converse as they choose songs. A DJ stand with a plush chair-height step built around it, to encourage people to come up and give their requests to the DJ.

In another chapter of the book, William du Bois describes how he was employed by the local Chamber of Commerce to revitalise the small town of Bloomfield in Iowa. Up until his time, ideas for change coming up at their meetings tended to be shot down. From now on, he proposed, they would carry out almost all the ideas suggested. "If an idea isn't terribly illegal, terribly immoral or terribly fattening (or terribly expensive) we do it." Although he is canny enough to add an undemocratic footnote: "Actually, we did every idea except for one that I 'forgot' to write down on the newsprint on the wall. Retaining the pen at a community planning session also allows one to rephrase and reframe suggestions to avoid pitfalls."

'He suggested horse-drawn tours of the Christmas lights'

In the end, the ideas that worked best were his own. He suggested horse-drawn tours of the Christmas lights. By advertising the route, almost all the house owners on the route decorated their houses ("lights were sold out of every store in a 30-mile radius"). More than 10,000 people rode the tour of lights each year, some coming from more than 60 miles away. Again, there was the attention to detail, for instance he provided a box of donated gloves, mittens, caps and scarves for riders to wear who weren't adequately dressed, even extra blankets that people could share, and laid on hot chocolate and coffee at a special warming house.

'$20 to anyone caught in the act of doing good or who personified the Christmas spirit'

To draw shoppers into Bloomfield, du Bois invented the Secret Elf, who gave away $20 in 'Elf money' (redeemable at participating stores up to Christmas) to anyone "caught in the act of doing good or who personified the Christmas spirit". At least four elves a day, 10 or more at weekends, gave away a total of $5,000. A non-secret Elf, in costume, also appeared on TV and ran raffles, with crows following the elf from store to store.

Bloomfield proceeded to bloom, the only county-seat town of its size in Iowa to have an actual increase in the number of firms in the county during a five year period. Du Bois concludes that "Bloomfield – an area where once 20 per cent of the people had wanted to flee and had put their homes up for sale – voiced faith in the future. Attitudes had changed."

20 Heber Road, London NW2 6AA, UK (rhino@dial.pipex.com), 2001, 300pp, ISBN 0 948826 58 4

'Social inventing is the creation of social arrangements that encourage synergy'

For DuBois and his colleagues, social inventing is the creation of social arrangements, social forms and social contexts that encourage synergy. In effective social arrangements, society is arranged so that the communal good and the individual good are identical. The same act accomplishes both the individual good and the communal good. Realistic self-fulfilment demands a context of community, supportive social resources and supportive others.

Synergy also implies win-win solutions. Whether in neighbourhood or family disputes, or in business or international relations, win-win solutions are the only ones that produce a lasting peace. A social inventor must align the interests of the individual and the organisation. Otherwise, the organisation pays the price in absenteeism, employee theft and sagging morale.

Social inventors need to design ways whereby when people come together the meeting is more than the sum of the parts. The zero-sum approach assumes a pie of a fixed size. But the social inventor strives to create a synergistic process in which the size of the pie actually grows, so that although someone's individual proportion may shrink, the individual pieces are actually larger.

'To believe in your own thought, to believe that what is true for you in your private heart is true for all men: that is genius'

The social inventor asks, "what social resources would be helpful to people experiencing the same problems that I am experiencing?" Du Bois quotes Ralph Waldo Emerson: "To believe in your own thought, to believe that what is true for you in your private heart is true for all men, that is genius." Sociologists need to invent resources that people can use in their individual struggles.

'Try to achieve maximum individuality with maximum community'

DuBois also quotes Ernest Becker, who noted that the ideal for overcoming alienation is to : "try to achieve maximum individuality with maximum community". This formula, DuBois adds, is nothing other than synergy: "It should be how we evaluate social inventions."

"Research methods," he writes, "too often hover between being quantitative or being qualitative. There is a third force in sociology. It is action sociology. Applying research findings and theoretical insights, sociology could become the major incubator for new projects – an inventors' fair. ... What would we invent? We know of one university that gets grants for millions of dollars a year to study rural mental health in the region. For that kind of money, we could *fix* the rural mental health of the region. Imagine the resources that could be generated from that kind of money with creative applications of sociology! Universities are intent on creating researchers. We would encourage artists."

A new innovatory idea e-mailed to you every day

Summarised from information on the 'Idea-a-day' website, at www.idea-a-day.com

A website set up in the year 2000 sends people an idea every day, with the hope that it can fire people's imaginations and foster creative and innovative thinking.

Once someone has subscribed to idea-a-day.com, they receive an e-mail direct to their computer containing that day's idea. The service is free, and the founders of the site stress that it is not in any way a money-making scheme, just a fun one.

'Each idea is there to be read, enjoyed, used or abused'

Subscribers and visitors to the site are encouraged to respond to the author of a particular idea, as well as being invited to submit their own original ones. Each idea, as the website puts it, is "there to be read, enjoyed, used or abused." As this statement might imply, none of the ideas themselves are copyrighted in any way (only the way they are phrased on the site is), which is intended to foster the propagation and dispersal of new ideas wherever their e-mails land.

There is also an archive of every idea the website has featured, of which there are now hundreds. Recent ideas have included a suggestion for parking space sensors to be introduced in multi-storey car-parks, which would then allow each driver (via a ticket system) to pinpoint the closest free space before they actually enter the car park. Another suggested giving voters the chance to vote against a party with their one vote, rather than forcing disillusioned people to vote for one side or the other. Looking through the ideas can be a little like sifting for gold, but that contributes to the site's interest and it makes coming across a genuinely thought-provoking and radical innovation all the more pleasurable.

20 Heber Road, London NW2 6AA, UK (rhino@dial.pipex.com), 2001, 300pp, ISBN 0 948826 58 4

International Social Innovations Day

The Institute for Social Inventions and www.DoBe.org are jointly sponsoring International Social Innovations Day for the first Tuesday in November each year.

'Get together in the evening and have a brainstorm about socially innovatory and imaginative ways to improve your locality'

The proposal is that on this day you get together in the evening with people in your area and have a brainstorm about socially innovatory and imaginative ways to improve your locality, and either meet in a local restaurant or in a local meeting place (in which case each person can bring food and drink to share for a potluck meal afterwards).

Those wanting to help get this going should invite their friends, advertise locally and sign up as interested on www.DoBe.org (under 'Social Innovation' in the city of their choice – DoBe already covers cities in the UK and USA and should soon cover many of the major cities in the world). Then people can get together through e-mail or other means and plan a venue, again posting the details on www.DoBe.org

Subscribers to the Institute for Social Inventions can ask to be put in touch with other members locally by e-mailing rhino@dial.pipex.com; and the Institute publications will provoke many ideas for the brainstorms (subscriptions cost £15 in the UK, £17 overseas, from www.globalideasbank.org/bookorder.html – see also the sample ideas below). The event is however open to everyone without charge.

'A club that travelling social entrepreneurs can make contact with'

The hope is that the International Social Innovations Day will bring social entrepreneurs together from a variety of organisations and professions to form informal local clubs that meet regularly for brainstorms and debates – a club that travelling social entrepreneurs can make contact with via www.DoBe.org so that it becomes a freemasonry for social innovators, a way to support each other.

• *To contact one of the Day's co-ordinators, phone them on Int+44 [0]20 8208 2853 or e-mail rhino@dial.pipex.com*

Institute for Social Inventions, £15 subs, £17 from abroad by credit card, tel London 020 8208 2853

The World's Greatest Ideas Party

To celebrate International Social Innovations Day, the Institute for Social Inventions is holding a World's Greatest Ideas Party at its HQ at 20 Heber Road, London NW2 on November 6th 2001 from 7.30pm (prompt) to 10.30pm.

'World's Greatest Ideas Party in London NW2 on November 6th 2001 from 7.30pm'

Everyone is invited as long as they register either on DoBe.org (at: www.dobe.org/events/880.html) or by sending an e-mail to rhino@dial.pipex.com or by phoning London 020 8208 2853. The space is limited. First booked, first placed. No tickets are issued but you will be told if there is no place left. There is no charge, but please bring food and drink to share for the potluck meal afterwards.

The 2001 Award Winners for the World's Best and Most Socially Innovatory Ideas will receive their certificates and the £1,000 prize money on this day. The Award Winners will talk about their schemes and answer questions. There will then be a brainstorming session on ways to improve London – see below for some ideas to get you thinking.

Ten ways to improve London

Here are some of the imaginative schemes that came up the last time www.DoBe.org and the Institute for Social Inventions were involved in provoking ideas for improving London life. These ideas could be adapted to work in most cities of the world.

'A paving stone in memory of someone who has died, with a poem engraved on it'

• Friends and relatives could be allowed to donate a carved paving stone in London in memory of someone who has died, with a poem or extract from a poem engraved on it. Having been passed by an approval committee (who would prevent racist, blasphemous and other such epitaphs), the paving stone would then be placed in a location desired by the relatives. In due course, thousands of poems on the pavements would provide an attraction for tourists and natives alike.

'Artwork could replace some ads on the underground (with sponsors to make the scheme financially viable)'

20 Heber Road, London NW2 6AA, UK (rhino@dial.pipex.com), 2001, 300pp, ISBN 0 948826 58 4

- Artwork could replace some ads on the underground, in a similar manner to the successful poetry on the underground scheme. Sponsors could put up a small advertising message alongside the artwork, thus making the scheme financially viable. Artists could submit the artwork to the London Transport website, where it could be shown in advance. The pieces of artwork that are voted as the best on the site would then be used on the underground, with the chosen artists possibly being paid a fee.
- A bicycle route should be instigated that goes right through the green Royal Parks of the city, from Holland Park to Kensington Gardens and on to Hyde Park, Green Park, St James' Park until ending at Trafalgar Square or Westminster.
- Shoeshine machines could be reintroduced at railway stations and other public places.
- The parks should be used more for entertainment and relaxation. There could be giant chess sets near cafés, open-mic poetry and music from the bandstands.

'A Poetry Corner could be instituted in a London park, similar to Speakers' Corner'

- A Poetry Corner could be instituted in a London park, similar to Speakers' Corner in Hyde Park. Anyone who brought a stepladder with them could then declaim their poetry to the world. Donations could either be collected for the poet reciter, or for a chosen charity.
- Horse-drawn buses could be brought back on certain central London tourist routes.
- An announcement could be given that once every ten years the pavements on appropriate London streets will be widened by one metre. Gradually, this will reduce in the reduction of traffic and the prioritisation of cyclists and pedestrians.
- The Millennium Bridge should have its wobble increased not muted. With adequate safety precautions, it could then become a tourist attraction, the London equivalent of the Leaning Tower of Pisa: the Wobbling Bridge of London.

'Racks of bunks could be provided at airports and stations where people have to wait around'

- Racks of bunks could be provided at airports, stations and other places where people have to wait around for long periods of time. They could be booked in half-hourly slots, and be equipped with alarm clocks, curtains and earplugs. Attendants could look after any luggage you have so that you could lie back and rest completely stress-free.

Institute for Social Inventions, £15 subs, £17 from abroad by credit card, tel London 020 8208 2853

50 tips for social inventors

Nicholas Albery

The following tips have been taken from a talk given by Nicholas Albery to the School for Social Entrepreneurs in January 2001. The talk was intended to give tips to those wishing to start their own socially innovatory not-for-profit organisation, possibly one involving publications and websites. The advice covers everything from photocopiers to trustees, and from standing orders to surrealism.

Financial

- Simple accounts to be done every 6 months
- Get alternative funds for the future within lifetime of present grant
- Do multiple grant applications for maximum possible funding of ventures
- Gradually introduce charges for e-mails and information that used to be free
- Get an online payment facility
- Pay fundraisers a percentage only, to get them to hand in applications
- Charge for your website by changing URLs – so word doesn't spread about information locations
- Scatter shot fundraising does work
- Always fund raise for a new project, not an old one
- Standing orders for "Friends Of" your not-for-profit help give regular income

Structural

- Have a flexible 'uncle' body that can launch any charitable project initially
- Keep overheads low (work at home, do own typesetting etc)

'Keep things small and human-scale'

- Keep things small and human-scale
- Let people take initiatives, run committees etc.
- Have two friends to do it with: move mountains
- Get impressive names for your organisation's notepaper
- Keep in touch with your projects – don't let them escape you
- Choose your trustees carefully depending on what you want from them

Work environment

- Get a good photocopier that does double-sided leaflets reliably
- Mature, responsive co-workers; try the Guardian and the ApprenticeMaster Alliance (www.apprentice.org.uk)

20 Heber Road, London NW2 6AA, UK (rhino@dial.pipex.com), 2001, 300pp, ISBN 0 948826 58 4

- Make work fun and surreal – eg poetry recitals over lunch
- Have a few things kept back, use things more slowly, to allow for periods of doldrums
- Involvement in every part of the process for you and co-workers

Personal Health / Staying Sane

- Do exercise you enjoy; maintenance of physical health
- Know your own work patterns (eg 11.30 am, work time alone)
- Don't take yourself too seriously – be willing to play the fool
- Don't get isolated from your tribe
- Imagine life as a target

Idea Generation

- Brainstorm to overcome worthy-but-dull ideas
- Take the wildest idea and bring it down to earth
- Look for synergy, win win win, ... solving lots of problems at once.
- Ask how can I solve the problem in such a way?
- Gather other people's ideas and reward them in order to get them (see Global Ideas Bank)

'Be flexible with your vision'

- Be flexible with your vision
- Try the most ambitious ideas first
- Humour and imagination are more than a match for bureaucracy (see the article on Frestonia in the 'International' section)
- Try and make your living from amongst your 20 main pleasures

Outreach / Publicity

- Wait 50 years, be patient for results
- Make a book, a publication, or organise an event for each project
- Keep a full log and record all details of events and happenings in the organisation
- Keep all books in print, on the web
- Find a niche that is also an interest and exploit it
- Collect details of journalists – put together an e-mail list of journalists
- Maximum coverage from minimum effort where possible
- Send information (press releases etc.) to every publication at once
- Make web site interactive (ratings lead to best coming to surface), interesting etc
- E-mail or fax TV contacts who are always looking for features
- Make sure journalists give prices and phone number in articles

- Invite people on a personal basis to events
- Posh DTP (desktop publishing) and design goes a long way

• *To see how Nicholas Albery put these tips into practice, see his other ideas in this book and the websites of all the organisations he set up and the publications he produced. The websites, with links to the publications, are listed on page 297.*

LETTERS
Praise for the Global Ideas Bank

The Global Ideas Bank has this year been nominated for a number of awards including the **OmPlace Conscious Living Award**. Susan Parker of www.omplace.com writes: 'Congratulations! We have reviewed your website, and it certainly qualifies for our OmPlace Award. Good job! Excellent and extensive content!'

The New Statesman Online (www.newstatesman.co.uk) was also enthusiastic, nominating the Global Ideas Bank for a **New Statesman and BT New Media Award**.

The Internet Mole (www.molemag.net) an independent newsletter which alerts subscribers to new and topical sites, also praised the site highly: 'This British site is an unexpected find, and hard to categorise, but it is a fascinating browse. It also demonstrates the power of the Internet as a cheap global publishing tool'. Meanwhile, a Heads Up! online report on the subject of creativity cited the GIB as 'one of the best resources on the Web for creativity applied to social problems'.

Re-discover your tribal connections
Elizabeth Anne Jones

From an e-mail to the Institute for Social Inventions
Just read an excerpt from your Utne Reader article Jan-Feb 2001. It appeared in The Real Paper in Pensacola, Florida. I used to live in a very close and supportive community in Swansea, Wales. In 1987 I moved to Pensacola and consequently suffered great tribal losses. I scored very low on the quiz due to living here, but I would have scored very high had I still been living in Wales.

20 Heber Road, London NW2 6AA, UK (rhino@dial.pipex.com), 2001, 300pp, ISBN 0 948826 58 4

No wonder I feel so insane a lot of the time: there is a sad lack of neighbourly interaction in my community. I always try to acknowledge people on the street, but as far as popping in to a friend's for a cup of tea and a chat, forget that unless it is prearranged at least a few days ahead. It's like everyone is trying to be too "civilised" and socially correct. Anyway, I just wanted to thank you for reminding me that I need to find a way to rediscover my tribal connection, or give up the ghost and go home to my roots.

• *Elizabeth Anne Jones (e-mail: nyrsanne@juno.com).*

A great admirer

Vivian Wright

From an e-mail to the Global Ideas Bank.

I have just discovered your website through the sad occasion of reading Nicholas Albery's death in the Guardian. I was a great admirer of his – although I did not realise half of what he did until I read the obituary. I loved *Poem for the Day* and his work around natural funerals and I have always meant to do the Poetry Challenge. Well, this year, I hope. I think the website is great and especially the walks. I hope I shall be able to come along to one soon.

The need for a Nicholas

Harold Ne'Work

From an e-mail to the Global Ideas Bank.

Nicholas was one of the very few people to have new social ideas and to put them into practice. He was not afraid of thinking differently. He was a strong believer of people in local communities organising themselves. He is irreplaceable, I hope in today's and future generations there are people of his calibre, we certainly need them.

A force to be reckoned with

Lynne Franks

From an e-mail to the Global Ideas Bank.

Exciting, creative, more ideas in one week than most people have in a lifetime; supportive, loving husband, father, friend; stimulating, original, innovative, compassionate; one who got things done, light, blessed, influential, modern, dynamic, modest, energetic – it just goes on and on – haven't seen you for a while but will certainly miss your presence in this world – see you in the next.

A self-created life

Lindesay Levine

From an e-mail to the Global Ideas Bank.

I don't think I have ever met anybody as dedicated to making use of his every waking hour as Nicholas. I remember his complete bewilderment when a colleague admitted to reading trashy magazines to unwind. 'Why?' Nicholas wanted to know. 'I don't understand the point of it'.

I worked for Nicholas for a year-and-a-half at the crammed family home which also served as headquarters for his myriad projects. Nicholas' days began relatively late, because he liked to beaver away in the uninterrupted solitude of the small hours. I will never forget the sound of his morning routine: the sounds of the chorusing Hare Krishnas providing the backdrop for his patent poetry-learning dance, before he came downstairs and proceeded to bury himself in work for three or four hours before allowing himself to eat breakfast.

'It would be very hard to identify the dividing line between his work and his pleasure'

My impressions of him as a compulsive worker, driving himself to create positive projects as an antidote to a naturally somewhat melancholy disposition, seemed to carry on into the rest of his life. (It's symptomatic that it would be very hard to identify the dividing line between his work and leisure).

His was a decisive, principled and admirably self-created life – there were few aspects of it that he had not tailored to his own beliefs – and a huge number of different campaigners will miss his energy and commitment.

Carrying on the work of transforming the world

Caroline Hutton

From an e-mail to the Global Ideas Bank.

Nicholas came to talk to our group at the School for Social Entrepreneurs. His delightful English eccentricity charmed us all as he shared what he'd

20 Heber Road, London NW2 6AA, UK (rhino@dial.pipex.com), 2001, 300pp, ISBN 0 948826 58 4

learned. I was off to La Gomera shortly afterwards and we enjoyed his guide as a companion to our visit. Let's remember him as we carry on our work to transform the world.

A tribute to Nicholas' enthusiasm

Pat Hartridge

From a letter to The Guardian.

In 1986, Nicholas Albery awarded me the Social Invention Institute's Ecology Prize – £50 in coins, presented in a red velvet drawstring bag – for an idea for wildlife gardens around hospitals wards, which had come to me after spending time in an isolation unit with legionnaire's disease.

He bombarded me with lists of useful organisations, and telephoned cheerful encouragement when my limited energy flagged. His support (although he did not know me), and the prize, indirectly resulted in a national campaign. The wildlife gardens at the Churchill Hospital, Oxford, which I still maintain, are a tribute to his enthusiasm

• *Pat Hartridge, 49 Old Road, Wheatley, Oxford, OX9 1NX, UK.*

Envisaging the larger picture

Yvonne Malik

From a letter to the Guardian.

Many of us hope that the work and ideas which Nicholas Albery did so much to encourage will develop and flourish. He was a generous spirit with an ability to envisage the larger picture. His energy was amazing – as was his handwriting – and letters were usually answered the same day: I don't know how he managed it. One of Nicholas' ideas which I hope to develop and encourage is a spiritual experience advisory service, a form of loose network to help the individual build on his or her own style of spirituality.

• *Yvonne Malik, Sweet Briar, Wray, Nr Lancaster, 2AZ 8QN, UK.*

Great mind and loving heart

Gordon Carrick

From an e-mail to the Global Ideas Bank.

I never met him, but I first encountered Nicholas through the *Time Out*

Book of Country Walks, which radiates enthusiasm and energy and at the same time is exemplary in the clarity of its instructions. I remember reading the introduction one lunchtime while on one of the walks and realising that this was no ordinary guidebook, but a genuine tool for positive social change. And then I discovered the websites, and was amazed at the range and depth of his ideas and the wisdom and compassion that underpinned them. The world cannot afford to lose people like him – a possessor of a great mind and a loving heart.

A Remembrance from California

Gregory Wright

From an e-mail to the Global Ideas Bank. Gregory Wright's idea of a Global Suggestions Box was one of the main inspirations for the Global Ideas Bank.

I live in Los Angeles, and my relationship with Nicholas was almost completely at a distance – from 1986, as a contributor by post to the Institute's publications and books, and later, from 1995, as a contributor over the 'Net to the Global Ideas Bank.

'Possibly my favourite day in the previous decade was Nicholas telling me I'd won that year's International Social Inventions Award'

Possibly my favourite day in the previous decade was June 3rd, 1992 – the day I received, to my delighted astonishment, a long-distance telephone call in San Francisco at a temporary (just three days!) phone number, from London: Nicholas telling me I'd won that year's International Social Inventions Award, for the idea of the Global Suggestion Box, one of the conceptual tributaries of what we all know is one of the best destinations on the World Wide Web!

(Later that afternoon, I was walking in San Francisco's Chinatown, and saw in a shop window a Chinese astrological calendar that informed me that for Taureans like myself early June of that year was to be a time of effort rewarded -- a prediction that had come true an hour before, making of me a believer! What an irony that the same date nine years later was to be such an opposite kind of day.)

I visited London in August 1999, and the Institute and Nicholas and Stephanie and the social-inventions crew on a drizzly day of that month, having come over to the UK to see the Solar Eclipse. I was at the house in Cricklewood scarcely two hours, and wished it could have been at least a

20 Heber Road, London NW2 6AA, UK (rhino@dial.pipex.com), 2001, 300pp, ISBN 0 948826 58 4

couple of days, there was so much ideation and information that could have crossed between us. (And I was annoyed at myself that I had just missed by a day one of the Countryside Brainstorm [Brainwave] Walks. I consoled myself that I would make sure I joined Nicholas and fellow brainwavers on a countryside walk on my next visit to England; and now I realize that that probably will not be – unless this great tradition is continued!)

One of the numerous ideas of mine the GIB has been good enough to share with the world is a proposal for 'Networking Funerals'. Whether planned as such or not, I'll bet Nicholas's memorial occasion was one such!

I plan to remain a contributor to, and part of, the Global Ideas Bank and the Institute for Social Inventions. Please carry on Nicholas's (and our) work.

A lifeline to the sanity of the race

Rowland Morgan

From an e-mail to the Global Ideas Bank.

When he signed in 1999 my treasured copy of the library edition of his Directory of Alternatives, published in 1973, the well of ideas Nicholas had tended for 26 years seemed to stretch into eternity. Through him, as with his fellow visionaries, men like Aldous Huxley and Alan Watts, I felt in touch with the sanity of the race, and it was great solace. I believe he had many books to write, much leadership to offer in the future he worked for, much recognition to come, and it is a sad loss.

The loss of a very fine man

Richard Sinnott

From an e-mail sent to the Global Ideas Bank.

I was very saddened to hear of Nicholas Albery's sudden death in a car crash. I never had the privilege of meeting him but would like to pass on to his family my admiration of his vision and selfless achievements.

In 1994 he published one of my ideas and when, flushed with success, I sent him a second – and utterly barmy – concept, he not only took the trouble to turn it down with a hand-written note but did so with a kind and light-hearted encouragement.

> 'Where he found the energy to be so hands-on, heaven knows'

Institute for Social Inventions, £15 subs, £17 from abroad by credit card, tel London 020 8208 2853

Likewise, when I recently tried again he personally contacted me within the hour – despite it being gone two in the morning – and was equally as diligent in updating the links on my page. Where he found the energy, let alone the time, to be so hands-on, heaven knows, but if this was typical of his response to the many thousands of people who have contacted him then the world, as well as his family, has lost a very fine man.

A Blakean double vision

Roger Knights

Roger Knights is the Assistant Editor of the Institute for Social Inventions in the US.

I didn't know Nicholas personally. I spoke to him about a dozen times on the phone. I also received about a dozen notes a year in response to clippings I submitted to the Institute for the Global Ideas Bank. But from those, plus his writing in Institute publications, I felt I knew him. His comments to me were always generous. He could become quite enthusiastic when he found clippings that hit the spot.

Nicholas wasn't just warm and friendly; he had many objectively admirable qualities. Energy, idealism, dedication, creativity, conviviality, breadth, nerve, initiative, love of nature, sense of humour, editorial skills, quickness to grasp a point, openness, frankness, etc. The only negative quality I can think of was his bad handwriting.

What was most notable about him wasn't his single qualities, but the way he balanced qualities that aren't normally found together. He was 'high-minded but hard-headed', principled but flexible, broad but particularistic (eg, in favouring local autonomy), crisp but tolerant of ambiguity, and edgy but common-sensical. He had Blake's double vision — What the World Needs. I feel as though I've lost my best friend.

[*Roger adds:* Nicholas often encouraged me to send more clippings, and stated that he wished he had more correspondents like me. Now that he is gone, we who remain must take up part of the workload. Attention Institute subscribers: you should make a habit of collecting clippings on innovative (or just interesting) social practices, filing them in a folder, and sending the bunch to the Institute at the end of the year. Keep your eyes open when reading books, magazines, and the Internet for methods of doing things differently. Keep in mind the wide range of items that have run in the annual compendiums before. Function as a feeder to the Institute and the Global Ideas Bank, and help them prosper.]

20 Heber Road, London NW2 6AA, UK (rhino@dial.pipex.com), 2001, 300pp, ISBN 0 948826 58 4

Nicholas Albery
July 28th 1948 – June 3rd 2001

The co-editor of this ideas compendium, Nicholas Albery, died in a car accident on June 3rd 2001, shortly before its completion. Nicholas was the founder and chairman of the Institute for Social Inventions, the charitable project which collates socially innovatory ideas from around the world and aims to help put the best of them into practice. This book contains the best of those ideas from the past year, as judged by Nicholas and the rest of the editorial team.

His belief in the power of ideas to change society led Nicholas to start projects as various as the ApprenticeMaster Alliance, the Global Ideas Bank, the Natural Death Centre, the Poetry Challenge and www.DoBe.org (the website for listing participatory events in every city in the world). Some projects arose from ideas sent in to the Institute and others came from Nicholas' own fertile imagination. Indeed, many of his own ideas are included in this compendium, and they are an enduring testament to his vision and creativity.

'Nicholas never doubted that a small group of committed people could change the world'

He never doubted that a small group of committed people could change the world, and he proved this most effectively with his involvement in the

Republic of Frestonia, in which a small group of West London residents declared their independence from Britain (see page 204), and successfully saved their residential area from destruction. He was also ahead of the game on green issues, suing the petrol companies in 1979 for his child's health being adversely affected by the lead in their petrol.. Not many years later, it was the same petrol companies who began marketing lead-free petrol back to us: a belated victory of sorts. Before the Institute for Social Inventions came into existence in 1985, Nicholas had also stood for parliament, travelled around Wales in a horse-drawn caravan, and written his memoirs (sadly only up until 1977).

'The huge resource of inspiring and inspired ideas that he helped to collate over the years'

In recent years, Nicholas had overseen the rise of the Global Ideas Bank from a sketched-out idea to a website receiving over three million accesses a year. People from Australia to Zimbabwe have been using the huge resource of inspiring and inspired ideas that he and others have collated over the years, and they are increasingly submitting their own ideas to the site. It stands now as an online memorial to Nicholas' vision, energy and belief in the power of imaginative solutions.

As a prolific social inventor, writer, publisher and activist, Nicholas Albery touched the lives of thousands of people. The evidence is all around us: schoolchildren are learning poetry for charity, woodland funerals are being organised, apprentices are being taken on, city people are walking and talking together through the countryside, and millions are using and contributing to the Global Ideas Bank every year.

What he achieved will never be forgotten, and his work will be continued by the people he inspired.

• *For examples of Nicholas' work, and the myriad of projects he has been involved in, see the following websites:*
  • *www.globalideasbank.org*
  • *www.DoBe.org*
  • *www.apprentice.org.uk*
  • *www.naturaldeath.org.uk*
  • *www.walkingclub.org.uk*
  • *www.poetrychallenge.org.uk*
  • *www.gomera.org.uk*

There is also a memory board online with links to the obituaries in all the major UK papers at www.globalideasbank.org/nicholas/wwwboard

20 Heber Road, London NW2 6AA, UK (rhino@dial.pipex.com), 2001, 300pp, ISBN 0 948826 58 4

Publications available

Orders can be placed by cheque or (using Visa or Mastercard) by phone, fax, letter, e-mail or securely online (at www.globalideasbank.org/bookorder.html).

• **I wish to be sent the following <u>ticked</u> PUBLICATIONS** – (UK p&p included. Add 9% for European p&p, 32% for airmail p&p for the rest of the world. 10% off for Institute subscribers, except for those books marked [*])

[*] **'The New Natural Death Handbook'**, 120+ woodland burial grounds, cardboard and regular coffins, best buy funeral directors, legalities of funerals, caring for the dying at home. £13.50 first class.

[*] **'How to Organise a Woodland or Inexpensive Funeral'**. For a credit card phone or web donation of £6.99, this summary (less detailed than the handbook above) can be e-mailed to those with e-mail and web access who are in urgent need. It is only available as an e-mail.

[*] **'Living Will & set of forms'**. Living Will, Life Values Statement, Death Plan and Advance Funeral Wishes form. Set of forms for a donation of £5 or more.

[*] **'Ways to Go - Naturally'**, greener approaches to death and improving the 'quality of dying', £6.20 first class.

NEW! [*] **'Progressive Endings'**, complements the New Natural Death Handbook, with more in-depth articles and items on death and dying, £6.20 first class.

[*] **'Poem for the Day – 366 Poems, Old and New, Worth Learning By Heart'**, with foreword by Wendy Cope. 400 page book with a poem for each day of the year. £11.97 (incl. p&p.).

NEW! [*] **'Seize the Day'**, a calendar of tips for living, a hardback companion to 'Poem for the Day'. £13.99 (incl. p&p.).

[*] **'Time Out Book of Country Walks'** by Nicholas Albery. The new blue cover revised 416-page calendar of walks easily reached by train as day outings from London, with a pub lunch and a tea place afterwards. £11.99 (incl. update sheets, train times for Saturday Walkers' Club, p&p.).

• **'Alternative Gomera – Guide to a fortnight's walking round Gomera Island near Tenerife'** by Nicholas Albery, 6th edition. £9.99 incl. first class p&p. Map £5.85 extra.

• **'Future Workshops - How to Create Desirable Futures'**, by Robert Jungk, used by groups throughout Europe as a manual. £8.99.

• **'The Forest Garden'** by Robert Hart, How to establish a food-growing permaculture Forest Garden, in town or country. £3.50. 4th edition.

• **'Book of Inspirations – a directory of social inventions'**, preface by Brian Eno, £15 incl. p&p.

• **'Social Dreams & Technological Nightmares – a global ideas bank compendium'**, predicting the next 500 years, £14.85 incl. p&p.

• 'DIY Futures – people's ideas and projects for a better world', 250 new social incentives and schemes. £14.85 incl. p&p.

• 'Creative Speculations – a compendium of social innovations', 'An amazing book, ambitious and successful' (Stewart Brand). £14.85 incl. p&p.

[*] 'Social Dreams', 'DIY Futures' and 'Creative Speculations' (all £14.85) – these three books for £34 incl. p&p (if ordered by a new Institute subscriber): a saving of over £10.

• '1,001 Health Tips – from recent medical research'. **FREE!** to new Institute subscribers. Get well and stay well.

• 'How to Feel Reborn? Varieties of Rebirthing Experiences' an investigation of primal and rebirthing therapies by Nicholas Albery. The 1985 edition is now available only in a non-paper, digital version which can be downloaded and printed out. 260 pages, £9.99. Go to www.globalideasbank.org/rebirthing.html for free chapter and ordering details.

• 'The Neal's Yard Story', full of useful ideas for urban renewal. £3.95.

• 'Community Counselling Circles' by John Southgate, for improving the atmosphere in groups. £6.95.

• 'The Solution for South Africa', an influential cantonisation scheme. £6.95.

• 'Social Invention Workshops – a manual for use in schools', as used by the Institute in its school workshops. £2.50.

• 'The Problem Solving Pocketbook', an overview of the main ways to solve problems, plus some wilder alternatives. £2.95.

• 'Being True to Yourself', by Margaret Chisman, insight exercises for groups. £4.95.

• 'Auction of Promises – how to raise £16,000 in one evening', for church, school and community groups. £1.95.

• The original Institute **journals** from the 1980s. £10 for a random selection of five issues.

Institute subscriptions

• Enclosed is £15 for an Institute **subscription**. (Outside UK £17 by credit card.) Members and subscribers receive at least one large book per annum in August or September - *state if you want this year's or next year's* - plus 10% off most Institute publications, except those with [*]. Those supplying an e-mail address may be sent occasional interesting mailings. Subscribers can also join in Social Invention events via the Institute's www.DoBe.org website.)

[The cheapest way to pay from outside the UK is by credit card securely online at www.globalideasbank.org/bookorder.html, or by credit card through phone or fax.]

20 Heber Road, London NW2 6AA, UK (rhino@dial.pipex.com), 2001, 300pp, ISBN 0 948826 58 4

NAME (caps) ....

ADDRESS...

....

....

TEL. No...

E-MAIL ....

Please photocopy and return this form with cheques payable to: **'Institute for Social Inventions'**, 20 Heber Road, London NW2 6AA, UK (tel 020 8208 2853; fax 020 8452 6434; e-mail: rhino@dial.pipex.com; web: www.global ideasbank.org/bookorder.html).

— —

UK STANDING ORDER FORM – please fill in and return to Institute for Social Inventions, 20 Heber Road, London NW2 6AA. USE CAPITALS.

MY BANK...

BANKADDRESS ....

....

MY ACCOUNT NO. ....

Please pay to the Institute for Social Inventions £........**annually**, starting on

the ...... day of ....20....... (or as soon after this date as possible).

Their account is bank number 60 13 34, account number 38843803, bank

address: National Westminster Bank, 298 Elgin Avenue, London W9, UK.

NAME (caps) ....

ADDRESS...

....

TEL. No...

SIGNATURE..

DATE...

THE GALLANT
PIONEERS

150TH ANNIVERSARY EDITION

THE GALLANT
PIONEERS

150TH ANNIVERSARY EDITION

GARY RALSTON

DEDICATIONS

Gary: To Lewis and Jennifer and my wee mum, Marion.

Gordon: To Pam and Alfie – Pam, for her help and time with the tours, presentations and grave hunting.

Iain: For my late parents Emma and Archie and my two grandsons, George and Lewis.

In memory of Walter Smith, 1948-2021.